Guiding Teachers into Bilingual Education

A Bridge Between Theory and Practice

Edited by
Valérie Fialais and Reseda Streb

CALEC – TBR Books
New York – Paris

Copyright © 2025 by Valérie Fialais and Reseda Streb

All rights reserved. No part of this publication may be reproduced, distributed, or transmitted in any form or by any means without prior written permission.

TBR Books is a program of the Center for the Advancement of Languages, Education, and Communities. We publish researchers and practitioners who seek to engage diverse communities in education, languages, cultural history, and social initiatives.

CALEC – TBR Books
750 Lexington Avenue, 9th floor
New York, NY 10022
USA
www.calec.org | contact@calec.org

Cover illustration © Sibylle Knapp
Cover design © Toscane Landréa

ISBN 978-1-63607-361-3 (Paperback)
ISBN 978-1-63607-470-2 (eBook)

Library of Congress Control Number: 2025939483

Table of Contents

1. ABOUT THE BOOK

1.1. Preface
Fabrice Jaumont 1

1.2. Why This Book?
Valérie Fialais and Reseda Streb 3

1.3. Introduction
Christine Hélot 7

2. THEORY

2.1. From Two Solitudes to Crosslinguistic Translanguaging: Evolution of Theoretical Concepts in the Education of Plurilingual Learners
Jim Cummins 25

2.2. From Teaching Languages to Teaching Students: How Teachers of Bilingual Students Take Up Translanguaging Theory in Practice
Kate Seltzer and Ricardo Otheguy..39

2.3. On Biliteracy and Theory(ies). A Bilingual Teacher's Journey
Cecilia M. Espinosa 51

2.4. Equitable Assessment Practices for Emergent Bilingual Students
Marcela Ossa Parra..75

2.5. The Linguistic Repertoire from the Perspective of Lived Experience
Brigitta Busch 89

2.6. Transculturality and Plurilingualism
Jürgen Erfurt 105

2.7. Language and Education Policy: Power, Prestige, and Bilingualism
Anne-Marie de Mejía 123

3. PRACTICE

3.1. Making Space for Teachers' Voices to Research Together on Teaching and Learning Issues in an English Immersion School Setting
Aurore Isambert, Damien Céné, Delphine Jeandel, Véronique Lemoine-Bresson, Anne Choffat-Dürr, Valérie Fialais, and Latisha Mary 135

3.2. "Difference is Always There, of Course; the Question is How You Deal With It." Experiences from a German-Italian Primary School Project in Frankfurt am Main, Germany
Gabriele Budach and Ulrike Dreher 153

3.3. Building Up Bilingual Practice in Rural India: Current Efforts of Language and Learning Foundation
Cynthia Groff and Dhir Jhingran 161

3.4. The Role of Key Actors and an Innovative Biliteracy Program in Bringing National Languages into Primary Education in Senegal
Erina Iwasaki and Carol Benson 179

3.5. The Parity School in Ladinia: How a Language Minority Preserves its Own Language(s) as Well as Italian and German
Stephanie Risse 197

3.6. Pomeranian-Portuguese Literacy in Brazil: Experiences from the Genesis of a Multilingual Project
Peter Rosenberg, Mônica Savedra and Reseda Streb 211

3.7. Bilingual Co-teaching of Writing Genres in Quebec
Joël Thibeault and Marie-Hélène Forget 236

4. FINAL CONSIDERATIONS

4.1. Afterword. G(l)iding Through the Inter-Lived Bilingual Experience: Beyond Guiding and Bridging as Afterword
Ofelia García 251

4.2. Acknowledgments
Valérie Fialais and Reseda Streb 261

5. REFERENCES 263

About the Authors 293
About TBR Books 305
About CALEC 309

1. About the Book

1.1. Preface
Fabrice Jaumont

It is with great enthusiasm that I present this landmark volume, *Guiding Teachers into Bilingual Education: A Bridge Between Theory and Practice*. This book represents a timely and essential exploration of the dynamic intersection between academic research and classroom practice, offering invaluable insights for educators, researchers, and policymakers. Bilingual education emerges here not just as a pedagogical approach but as a transformative force for cultural preservation, social equity, and personal empowerment. Through a thoughtfully curated collection of contributions, this volume illuminates these dimensions with depth and innovation.

Guiding Teachers into Bilingual Education: A Bridge Between Theory and Practice exemplifies the mission of the Center for the Advancement of Languages, Education, and Communities: to champion multilingualism, preserve cultural heritage, and empower communities through education. By bridging the gap between theory and practice, the volume not only offers a roadmap for educators and policymakers but also articulates a bold vision for a more inclusive and equitable global future. The collaborative spirit, adaptability, and shared commitment reflected in these pages are a testament to the enduring value of linguistic diversity as a foundation of both education and society.

I am deeply grateful to the contributors for their illuminating insights, to the editors for their visionary leadership, and to everyone who supported this project. Together, we advance a shared vision of vibrant multilingual communities grounded in equity, understanding, and innovation.

1.2. Why This Book?
Valérie Fialais and Reseda Streb

Guiding Teachers into Bilingual Education is a project that is especially close to our hearts as editors. Its conception and development were shaped by numerous factors, which we briefly acknowledge here due to their significance and diversity, although space constraints prevent a more detailed discussion. Both of us have researched bilingual teaching and learning in Brazil, Germany, France, and the United States and have extensive experience in teacher education. In addition, Valérie Fialais brings nearly 30 years of bilingual teaching experience in Alsace, France.

One fundamental realization in connection with the school projects is the urgent need for better communication and closer exchange between universities and schools, or more precisely, between researchers and the school community. This closer collaboration between theory and practice, as referred to in the title of the volume, is to be understood as a mutually necessary and beneficial complement of perspectives. Among teachers and school administrators, there is a strong demand for training and ongoing professional development. However, training materials and opportunities are often inadequate or poorly disseminated. This involves not only being familiar with academic theories and evaluating their classroom applications but also being prepared to defend bilingual teaching when it is viewed as problematic or impractical.

On the academic side, it is essential to gain a deeper insight into practice, to understand how theoretical approaches can be applied in practice, and where improvements at the theoretical level are necessary. Similarly, the practical environment serves as a source of inspiration for developing innovative ideas, new terminologies, and concepts that would not be possible without immersion in the field. For the collaboration between theory and practice, it is necessary to improve mutual appreciation and recognize that both sides need each other and that maximum knowledge construction can only arise through mutual exchange.

The idea of this volume is to promote exchange between the two sides. Contributions from both theory and practice are presented. While the academic contributions aim to explain their practical benefits, project contributions provide critical insights into the implementation of theoretical approaches. Initially, we intended for each theoretical concept to have a specific project as its practical counterpart, demonstrating its implementation. However, it quickly became apparent that practical implementation involves diverse concepts, and focusing on a single approach is not only impossible but also limiting.

Another goal of this volume is to serve as a foundation for further training. For this reason, we have sought to gather contributions that cover as wide a range as possible, both theoretically and practically. Nonetheless, it must be acknowledged that the volume does not claim to be exhaustive, not only because of the multitude of theoretical approaches and projects but also due to their continual evolution and shifting status.

For academic contributions, we invited renowned researchers in the field, including several who have played a key role in developing foundational concepts in bilingual teaching and learning. Their prompt agreement to contribute underscores the significance of this endeavor. We are grateful to the authors for adapting their concepts for this audience in line with the aims we proposed. The selection of project contributions was made to include as many different regional and linguistic contexts as possible. It was also important to us that projects in their preliminary stages be given a voice alongside those with decades of experience. The continuum of project existence, spanning different phases and contexts, predictably presents distinct challenges and solutions. These initiatives are designed to support teachers and the school planning sector in their implementation, demonstrating that they are not the only ones facing challenges and, ideally, leading to networking among various stakeholders.

The multilingual nature of the original submissions—spanning German, French, and English—reflects the linguistic diversity at the heart of this volume. This diversity also speaks to our ongoing interest in plurilingual practice and in supporting teacher training across a range of linguistic and regional contexts.

In conceptualizing the volume, we also made a deliberate decision to focus primarily on bilingual teaching and learning. This thematic focus was necessary to ensure a more cohesive and manageable selection of contributions.

At the same time, we invite researchers and educators to contribute to a future volume by sharing the concepts and learning contexts they have explored. In doing so, you take an active and responsible role in fostering the exchange between theory and practice in the field of continuing education.

Please see this call as an invitation—and an encouragement—to share your knowledge with the broader bi-/plurilingual community.

1.3. Introduction
Christine Hélot

Guiding Teachers into Bilingual Education: A Bridge Between Theory and Practice stands out as a notable contribution to the field of bilingual education. Editors Valérie Fialais and Reseda Streb draw on deep expertise as bilingual teachers and researchers in diverse international classrooms. They bring a rich understanding of the challenges and needs faced by educators entering bilingual programs. Both have been involved in the implementation of new bilingual programs in France and Germany and have authored doctoral theses grounded in extensive classroom observations across these and other contexts. They also share a strong commitment to co-constructing research with—and for—the teachers they collaborate with. Their dual roles have enriched their professional identities and strengthened their pedagogical expertise. They also believe, as expressed by Jim Cummins, that "theory and practice are infused within each other" (this volume, page 25), which is why their research has enabled them to experiment with new pedagogical approaches. Their broad professional background has informed and enriched the theoretical concepts developed in this core field over the past fifty years.

In this volume, Valérie Fialais and Reseda Streb share the insights they have gained through their years of immersion in both the theory and practice of bilingual education. Their goal is to "guide" new bilingual teachers to understand the reciprocal relationship between research and practice—how theories inform pedagogy, how a grounded understanding of classroom realities enriches research, the daily questions teachers face, and what it means for children to learn academic subjects through two (or more) languages. Moreover, because they have researched bilingual education in various socio-political and sociolinguistic contexts, they are aware of the role of language policies, the different symbolic statuses of languages, linguistic discrimination affecting language-minoritized speakers, and the challenges of bilingual teacher education. With these concerns in mind, they invited 24 researchers to contribute to the volume, addressing key theoretical questions in Part One and exploring their practical implications in Part Two. The authors come from diverse contexts across South and North America, Asia, Africa, and Europe. Together, they offer compelling evidence that bilingual education can be successfully implemented in a wide range of settings, with any combination of languages, whether minoritized or official, and most importantly, for all learners. They all reassert a positive stance towards bi-/plurilingualism as a learning resource rather than a problem, and each, in their context, demonstrates how the field of bi-/plurilingual education has undergone a radical shift in the past twenty years.

The first chapter, by Jim Cummins, entitled *From Two Solitudes to Crosslinguistic Translanguaging,* is a telling example of a significant shift in the conceptualization of bilingual education. Cummins uses the metaphor of 'two solitudes' to describe models of bilingual education that emphasize a strict separation of languages and promote the belief that learners should avoid mixing them, allowing each language to develop independently. Researchers used terms such as code-mixing, code-switching, and interference to describe instances where learners incorporated items from one language while expressing themselves in another. Teachers feared that allowing such mixing of both languages would slow down bilingual acquisition (parents did as well). It took quite some time for both teachers and researchers to understand that it was an issue of ideology, that a compelling ideology of monolingualism influenced our thinking about language learning, bilingualism in the home and at school, and bi-/plurilingual pedagogy. In a sense, challenging the dominant ideology of monolingualism in the classroom, for example, remains somewhat of an issue today for teachers and parents who often do not understand teachers' new pedagogical approaches. Many teachers were also aware that keeping two languages strictly separated in a bilingual classroom was unrealistic, silencing learners and making teachers feel guilty when they did not adhere to the two-solitude model as they thought they should.

We have known for a while now that a bilingual person is not equivalent to two monolinguals. Indeed, when researchers observed children engaged in learning activities simultaneously in two or more languages, they saw the transfer of knowledge and skills across languages, as well as the positive effects on the acquisition of both languages. For Cummins, who has been one of the most influential advocates for the education of students from immigrant backgrounds, this meant that these students' home or family languages should be supported in school to a high academic level for bilingual education to demonstrate cognitive advantages. It also meant that minoritized students were not receiving an education responsive to their needs due to the societal context in which they lived. Thus, the question for Cummins was whether and how schools could challenge the negative impact of societal factors. This led him to question issues of power and to utilize the notion of empowerment to convince teachers that they have agency in their classrooms, enabling them to transition from coercive to collaborative relations of power. He then proposed the concept of identity texts, also known as dual identity texts, where children are encouraged to utilize their full linguistic repertoires and various other semiotic resources to produce bilingual texts. When children are allowed to use their complete linguistic and semiotic resources in class, they engage in a process that has been termed "translanguaging" by many researchers; indeed, this concept underlies all the chapters in this book. Thus, one can say that a translanguaging turn marks 21st-century research on bi-/plurilingualism, and researchers have been able to observe how this new stance has maximized the learning engagement of bi-/plurilingual learners, has helped them to affirm their identities and connect what they learn in school with their lives, their cultures, and their communities.

The shift of perspective proposed by Cummins is well illustrated by Kate Seltzer and Ricardo Otheguy's chapter title, *"From Teaching Languages to Teaching Students,"* as well as Brigitta Bush's concept of the *"lived experience of plurilingualism."* In both chapters, the authors (like Cummins in the previous chapter) are primarily concerned with the fair education of minoritized bi-/multilingual children and the languaging at the center of their lives in schools, classrooms, and their everyday lives. The critical point here is the use of the term 'languaging' as opposed to 'languages,' the verb expressing what speakers do with their languages, how they make meaning in learning situations and elsewhere, and how their bi-/multilingualism gives them affordances when they are encouraged to function across and beyond named languages. Therefore, the focus has shifted from linguistic objectives in two named languages to be achieved following a fixed curriculum to understanding what learners can do and can learn thanks to their lived experiences of languages in the plural and how they can express themselves with far more fluency if they are not obliged to censor themselves in class and use only one part of their plurilingual resources.

Moving away from teaching one or two 'named' languages, for example, French and German in Alsace or English and Spanish in the United States, is not easy for bilingual teachers constrained by curricula based on linguistic objectives in two discrete languages. But Seltzer and Otheguy's very clearly written chapter helps to understand recent research that has argued for a unitary conception of the linguistic cognition of bi-/multilinguals. This means seeing bilingual individuals from the inside, not just from a social vantage point or outside perspective. This has had a direct and significant impact on pedagogical approaches based on the concept of translanguaging, i.e., acknowledging how bilingual communities use language and how this understanding can be applied to the pedagogical space of the classroom. Therefore, Seltzer and Otheguy ask a most relevant question: "What would teachers do differently once they understood translanguaging"? After explaining the various stages in the elaboration of translanguaging pedagogy (the notions of stance, design, and shifts), the reader is invited into three different classrooms in the United States where we see teachers adopting a more humanizing and equitable conception of the education of bilingual students and reimagining their classrooms and their practices through putting the needs of bilingual learners first. The three classroom vignettes also illustrate theory being put into practice, and perhaps more importantly, that in three vastly different contexts, we witness these teachers being well able to manage curriculum constraints and rigid language and assessment structures.

The next chapter, by Cecilia M. Espinosa, takes us on a bilingual journey through the theories of biliteracies developed by an immigrant bilingual teacher. It explores how her studies and the professional dialogues she engaged in with colleagues informed her reflections, as well as the impact this learning journey had on her practice. At the heart of Espinosa's claims for literacy education in the 21st century lie four principles: authenticity, social relevance, purpose, and equity. She adopts, like all the authors in this book, a critical stance towards bilingual education, which should allow learners to capitalize on their languaging practices and experiences. She also questions the long-standing marginalization of minoritized language groups and the dominant deficit perspective towards racial or specific social groups. As in the previous chapter, her theoretical starting point is based on the bilingual person having one linguistic repertoire comprising multiple linguistic and semiotic resources. Therefore, biliteracy learning, as expressed by García and Kleifgen (2019), should enable learners "to liberate their full potential to construct meaning."

Cecilia M. Espinosa does not hesitate to state that "biliteracy, after all, is a political right" because power structures impact biliteracy practices. She then illustrates the role of experiences continuously reshaping a teacher's theories on biliteracy teaching with the journey of a Bolivian teacher learning English in secondary school, in a context where bilingualism was highly valued because it involved English, however, when she moved to the United States, she was confronted with a new language experience where her Spanish was devalued. Her English was not considered proficient. Upon studying to become an early and elementary bilingual teacher, she encountered numerous theoretical readings regarding new conceptualizations of reading, including the understanding of the power of reading in and out of school, as well as the use of children's literature to transform children's reading experiences.

The final part of the chapter examines various research studies that demonstrate the transformative and even transgressive role of a translanguaging pedagogy, where the languaging practices of bilingual learners are legitimized and leveraged as resources, potentially leading to the transformation of the curriculum. As a result, literacy teaching is not limited to being multilingual. It is also purposeful, expansive, and multimodal. Teacher educators, bilingual or not, will find Espinosa's chapter especially useful in understanding that theories cannot be imposed or consumed by teachers; they need to be nurtured in daily practice, and they evolve with teachers' ongoing experiences in a dialogic space where they feel safe to discuss their questions and practices.

Chapter 4 follows with the topic of assessing bilingual and multilingual students. This issue has been a subject of research for a long time.[1] Though many dimensions of inequality remain poorly understood by education policymakers, the chapter describes how multilingual, holistic, and equitable assessment practices can be implemented in oral, reading, and writing activities. Marcela Ossa Parra advocates for equitable evaluation practices based on culturally and linguistically appropriate assessments of bilingual and multilingual students. As in previous chapters, her theoretical stance is informed by the need to take into account the entire linguistic repertoire of learners to gain a comprehensive understanding of what they know and can do. And she answers a persistent question from teachers working in classrooms where learners speak a multiplicity of languages that teachers do not know. She recommends asking for the help of interpreters, parents, or community members, not just for support but also because it will help make the many diverse cultures more accessible. The author also reminds the reader of the way ideologies shape our representations of race and language and how linguistically diverse learners are so often still perceived negatively and assessed inequitably. She emphasizes the importance of contextualized tasks, asking learners to create a product or perform an action that leverages their existing knowledge and skills. However, she does not eschew the recurring problem of disentangling content knowledge from language, and she proposes conducting conceptual scoring that distinguishes between the two. Most importantly, ethical assessment should be based on a strength-based perspective that focuses on what children know rather than what they do not know.

Chapter 5, by Brigitta Busch, examines the feelings of belonging, difference, power, and exclusion as they are linked to linguistic diversity in a highly diverse world, where many children, upon

---

[1] See Shohamy, 2016.

entering school, experience being in the wrong place with the wrong language. This is what she describes as lived experiences of language when children perceive themselves through the eyes of others as they interact using language. Teachers need to understand that such language experiences are not neutral but are linked to emotional experiences, which determine whether children feel comfortable with a language and can use it effectively. Since 1990, Bush's work has primarily contributed to linguistic biographical research, which focuses on activities that make speakers aware not only of their subjective experiences of language but also of linguistic and ideological evaluations by others and how these are reflected in one's linguistic repertoire. The author examines several dimensions of experience that are often made invisible in research, explaining that the linguistic repertoire, for instance, is embodied or inherently connected to a bodily subject. Such conceptualization implies that emotions play a significant role in learners' ability to utilize their linguistic resources. This biographical dimension is also intertwined with the historical and political context in which language is used. She then exemplifies how the language portrait can be a representation of the linguistic repertoire of a speaking subject at a given time in their life and that the linguistic repertoire should not be conceived just as a toolbox but as "a heteroglossic realm of possibilities" and that in Bakhtin's[2] compelling words "language is dialogical because it moves on the border between oneself and the other."

Let's suppose one adopts Bakhtin's perspective on the dialogical nature of language. In that case, one is also confronted with the dialogical nature of culture in a world of intense mobility and migration, as well as cultural contacts and interdependencies. This is the subject of the next chapter by Jürgen Erfurt, who is interested in analyzing transcultural processes, differences, inequality, conflict, and transformations. He explains why the perspective of transculturality is more productive than the previous concept of interculturality, which he thus considers outdated in light of recent social and cultural developments. Even if the concept of

---

[2] 1981: 293.

transculturality is related to bi-/plurilingualism and interculturality, it differs from these concepts in that it is used to scientifically describe social and cultural processes rather than aiming at pedagogical negotiation or the management of cultural conflicts. Transculturality is deeply anchored in the conditions of globalization and late capitalism, where borders between people and cultures are being eroded.

In contrast, the nation-state was the frame of reference for the concept of interculturality. Erfurt, like several other researchers in this volume, proposes a shift in perspective: from viewing cultures as properties of communities to focusing on individuals, their cultural practices—what they do with culture—and the processes of exchange between speakers who constantly move across space, time, and societal orders. Of course, language is part of these processes; therefore, subjects restructure their linguistic repertoires and their plurilingualism as they encounter numerous challenges in the context of migration, for example. Thus, transcultural processes alter the perception of language as a normative standard, separating systems, and this paradigm shift explains the success of the concept of translanguaging as a process that expands a subject's capacity to act.

The concluding chapter in Part 1, written by Anne-Marie de Mejía, examines language and education policies in bilingual education for diverse learners, including minoritized speakers in indigenous or immigrant communities, as well as those learning international languages. She advocates for policies of inclusion, an ecological approach to linguistic diversity in schools, and the support of hybrid and multiple identities. She also reminds the reader of well-known 20th-century research that emphasized the role of the first language in bilingual pedagogy and the importance of intercultural sensitivity for teachers encountering cultural differences and inequalities. Based in Colombia, the author makes references to the deep disparities between bilingual programs in various Latin American contexts, where English is the dominant choice, and therefore, bilingual education often serves the elite. In contrast, bi-/multilingual programs in Indigenous and immigrant communities usually render invisible learners' existing bi-/multilingualism due to the minoritized status of languages developed outside the school context. And unfortunately, well into the 21st century, De Mejía reminds us that this situation has not improved. However, quoting Menken and García (2010), she argues that teachers are at the epicenter of language policy in education and that they can function as agents of change if they understand that it is possible to negotiate their policies within a social justice agenda and therefore empower their students to become confident bi-/multilingual individuals. That said, an additional point must be emphasized regarding bottom-up language education policies: they should not rely solely on individual teachers. For such policies to be sustainable, they must be implemented at the whole-school level, as convincingly demonstrated by Little and Kirwan (2019) in their study of a multilingual school in Ireland.

The second part of the book, entitled *Practice,* takes us on a fascinating world journey of bilingual education in highly multilingual countries on four continents where the language ecologies seem at first sight too complex to give proper educational space to minoritized languages, yet, in all these contexts we are given evidence-based examples that bilingual education works because it answers the learning needs of children who are at last given the opportunity to learn in languages they understand. Whether in Senegal, where 14 languages are now recognized as national languages, or India, where the linguistic survey has documented 780 languages and made 22 of them official, or South Tyrol in Italy, where three school systems cohabit based on the declared languages of students, or Brazil which counts 274 languages of which 180 are Indigenous and where the languages of immigrants from Germany and Italy have survived over time, we are discovering how bilingual education has been developed and implemented despite many challenges at the level of policy, practice, the production of teaching materials or the education of teachers.

The seven chapters in this second part make for very compelling reading because we are given the opportunity to hear from many teachers from diverse contexts recounting their experiences with and implementation of bilingual or multilingual education. We listen to their voices through dialogues and interviews with researchers and read about their subjective experiences in texts that are the product of collaborative research between researchers and teachers. Thus, the reader can witness how the process of teachers and researchers reflecting together on theoretical and practical issues leads to a novel approach to producing academic knowledge, including the process of teachers and researchers writing together. This process of co-authorship is best described in the chapter by Isambert, Céné, Jeandel, Lemoine Bresson, Choffat-Dürr, Fialais, and Mary, who analyze the complexities of implementing a bilingual English French program in France with plurilingual learners speaking many diverse home languages.

Similarly, the dialogue between Gabriele Budach and the experienced primary teacher Ulrike Dreher enables us to gain insight into the perspective of a teacher involved in bilingual education in Italian and German at a Frankfurt school in Germany. Dreher chooses to orient the discussion around the notion of difference, which she insists is present in all classrooms, whether they are monolingual or bilingual. Thus, from her point of view, bilingual education poses the same challenges as monolingual education if one is focused on children's learning needs. Her extensive experience as a monolingual teacher has given her the confidence she needed to conceptualize her bilingual pedagogical approach. Therefore, she can negotiate the linguistic and cultural differences between Italian and German as pedagogical resources. In other words, bilingual education benefits her students, whom she teaches from the outset, by allowing them to compare the two instructional languages and engage in metalinguistic reflection.

In the case of the dialogue between Cynthia Groff and Dhir Jhingran, who explains the support of Language and Learning Foundation to develop bilingual education in Hindi and Wagdi in 30 public schools in Rajasthan, India, we are exposed to the history, the development, and the achievements of the bilingual project through the very words of its principal author, Dhir Jhingran. In a country where 60% of children receive education in a language other than their home language and where many face severe learning disadvantages, Dhir Jhingran's testimony stresses the crucial importance of developing bilingual education in a language the children understand as well as in the state's official language, Hindi.

Indeed, he makes us aware of the many institutional constraints and ideological resistance to bilingual education, which implies that specific strategies must be developed for the program to be sustainable. In the case of Rajasthan, it was a matter of "starting small" to obtain state approval later on. As for ideological resistance, it centered on the issue of assessment being conducted exclusively in Hindi and on the expectation that children in the bilingual program perform at least as well as those in the monolingual program. Therefore, for the bilingual model to be implemented in many more schools, a classroom monitoring instrument had to be developed, and an external evaluator (requiring additional funding) had to be identified so that the project's positive results could influence language education policy for the entire state of Rajasthan.

The role of key actors in advocating bilingual education in national languages in Senegal is the focus of the chapter by Erina Iwasaki and Carol Benson, who examine the impact on policy and practice of an innovative bilingual education approach in a country where the language of instruction is a colonial language, French, the first language of less than 1% of the population. Similar to India, an NGO implemented a bilingual program in 101 schools in collaboration with the National Ministry of Education—the two authors of the chapter report on the external evaluation they conducted. Wolof, with an estimated five million speakers, and Pulaar, with 3.5 million speakers, were the two national languages chosen to be taught simultaneously with French; literacy was also introduced in the two languages from the very first day of school. Again, the goal of the program was to demonstrate that students attending the bilingual program would achieve higher learning outcomes than those enrolled in monolingual programs, which they did, for example, in the primary school leaving examination. While such research is necessary for the broader implementation of bilingual programs, this chapter addresses another key issue in bilingual education: who advocates for the defense and promotion of national languages in Senegal—and why? The 36 people interviewed by Erina Iwasaki all report on the negative impact of their lived experiences of being educated through French only, not to mention corporal punishment when they spoke their home languages. The testimonies are most striking. For example, one person says the children did not have the vocabulary to play in French, and another says that she thought that poetry existed only in French. In this post-colonial context, bilingual education in national languages has clear political aims, such as self-determination and sovereignty, aimed at moving away from inherited patterns of colonial education. It is promising to read that, in 2021, a national bilingual education policy was adopted, and the Ministry of Education plans to implement bilingual education in nine regions in Senegal for the 2023/2024 academic year.

The context of South Tyrol, also known as Alto Adige or the Autonomous Province of Bolzano, presents a striking contrast to that of Senegal, primarily because it is a small border region (with approximately 500,000 inhabitants) situated in northeastern Italy, bordering Austria, and Switzerland. Yet this micro-European territory boasts an overly complex legal structure, three distinct school systems, and three language groups, hence the country's three names. Among these languages, Ladin, a Bavarian variety of German spoken differently in the two main valleys of Ladinia, is a minority language spoken by less than 5% of the population. Still, it is used as a language of instruction in Ladin schools, just as German and Italian are in the respective schools. Readers will discover the fascinating historical, political, and legal dispositions that were established for the multilingual population of South Tyrol to live together peacefully, as well as the role of the three languages in the organization of educational matters.

Stephanie Risse's chapter examines the development of multilingual education, particularly in Ladin schools, where children learn through the use of two Ladin varieties, as well as German and Italian (and later, English as a foreign language). Whereas in German and Italian schools, each non-L1 language is taught as a second language, and competence in the other language of young Germans and Italians has declined, in Ladin schools, a parity model of bilingual education is in place in all schools, with an equal amount of time devoted to German and Italian and since 2003 both Ladin varieties are also being used throughout elementary school. There is a particularly compelling dimension to the success of this educational approach, which is available to all learners in Ladinia. As argued by the author, the population has managed to maintain a collective Ladin identity over many years despite the language's weak political status. In other words, the South Tyrol case exemplifies that when multilingualism is highly valued in society and when dominant languages, such as German and Italian (in this case), are not perceived as a threat, multilingual education becomes a sine qua non.

A no less fascinating context of bilingual education is presented by Peter Rosenberg, Mônica Savedra, and Reseda Streb, who describe a multiliteracy project in Brazil that incorporates four languages: Pomeranian, Portuguese, German, and English. As in previous chapters, we encounter a captivating sociolinguistic situation in which minority languages have endured over time after being introduced to a new country through migration and are gradually being recognized under new language policy measures. In the case of Pomeranian, which is the language discussed in this chapter, it has become co-official with Portuguese in 8 Brazilian municipalities since 2007, even though the language is mainly spoken and is in the early stage of standardization. However, this legal recognition, which occurs at the municipal level, is crucial because it enables Pomeranian to become a language of instruction alongside Portuguese. The structure of the plurilingual project being described is worth paying attention to because, as in Senegal or India, it is not easy to include a non-standardized or recently standardized minority language into a bilingual program. The policy chosen in this case is the use of Pomeranian and Portuguese during the first two years of elementary school. When German is introduced in the third year, Pomeranian is used as a bridge language, and again when English is offered in the fifth grade.

Therefore, plurilingual education is implemented following the didactic model of intercomprehension. As in previous chapters, it enables Pomeranian-speaking children to be educated in a language they understand while also witnessing their language acquire a higher societal status through its legitimation at school. However, the danger is that standardization may alter the character of the language. This said, as in all the contexts described in the book, many practical challenges remain. A positive aspect, however, lies in the fact that many stakeholders participated in the development of the model, including mayors, administrators, principals, teachers, and families. This point is worth emphasizing: For bilingual or plurilingual education to be effective, teachers require the support of multiple stakeholders, including families and the local community. The more actors understand what it means to learn in several languages, the more confident teachers will feel—for example, in using translanguaging as a pedagogical approach in their classrooms. It is also essential to acknowledge the insecurity of teachers who have to implement a bi/multilingual project without pedagogical materials, as is often the case in minority languages, even if teachers in the French project reported on by Isambert et al. also felt they did not have enough pedagogical resources to teach bilingually in French and English.

While the above chapters are all concerned with minoritized, colonial, or minority languages, the chapter by Joël Thibeault and Marie-Hélène Forget addresses the issue of integrating English into a bilingual program in an elementary school in Quebec. They describe a biliteracy project in which two teachers co-teach a unit on writing genres, with one teacher using French and the other using English, allowing learners to use either language or both. Again, readers are given the opportunity to discover the lived experience of the two teachers who discuss the materials they designed together, the choice of language to use first for writing tasks, their observations of students' motivation, and the better impact of language transfer from French to English rather than the reverse. Perhaps the most important result of the co-teaching approach was that the students understood that the two languages of instruction in a bilingual program do not have to be separate because they witnessed both teachers translanguaging. For the teachers, the co-teaching experience helped them overcome their linguistic insecurity (in French, in one case) and conceptualize the integration of the two languages more effectively in their didactic design for teaching writing genres simultaneously in two languages. Unfortunately, co-teaching in bilingual education is not often part of bilingual curricula. Still, another example is featured in the chapter by Budach and Dreher, where the German and Italian teachers discuss what they call "tandem (or team) teaching," stating again that it provided significant support to the Italian teachers who had limited experience in bilingual teaching. Tandem teaching also increased the opportunities for children to use both languages to accomplish tasks without having to think about which language they were using at the time.

To conclude, Valérie Fialais and Reseda Streb's purpose in coordinating the volume *Guiding Teachers into Bilingual Education: A Bridge between Theory and Practice* is to offer teachers and researchers a unique insight into many diverse bilingual settings. These are contexts where educators grapple with a vast sweep of theoretical and practical issues—such as how and why to integrate two languages, whether to translanguage or not, how to develop teaching resources in minority languages undergoing standardization, how to involve families and communities, how to negotiate institutional language policies, and how to advocate for schools to transform their monolingual, often colonial, habitus so that children are no longer forced to learn in languages they do not understand. The impressive range of geographical and political contexts described in this volume, the evidence-based research demonstrating that bilingual education works in all the classrooms we are invited to visit, the remarkable engagement of the teachers we witness becoming agents of change, and the variety of innovative pedagogical approaches described— without forgetting the convincing theoretical arguments advanced in the first part of the volume—all combine to give readers—whether beginner or experienced teachers, monolingual, bi- or multilingual, researchers, or policymakers—a powerful incentive to rethink language education.

Hence, children are no longer in the wrong place with the wrong language (Busch, p. 90), and the many barriers to implementing a socially just education—one where learners *and* teachers feel linguistically secure, creative, and emancipated—can begin to be crossed.

2. Theory

2.1. From Two Solitudes to Crosslinguistic Translanguaging: Evolution of Theoretical Concepts in the Education of Plurilingual Learners
Jim Cummins

When Valérie Fialais and Reseda Streb invited me to contribute to this volume, I was extremely enthusiastic about the opportunity to make connections between theoretical concepts relating to the education of multilingual students and the instructional practice of teachers who were teaching these students on a daily basis in their classrooms. In the early autumn of 2021, I had just published a book entitled *Rethinking the Education of Multilingual Learners: A Critical Analysis of Theoretical Concepts*, which set out to explore the two-way interactions between classroom instruction and the development of theoretical concepts relating to language learning and multilingualism. In that book, I expressed my perspective on the intersections between theory and instructional practice as follows: "*theory and practice are infused within each other*. Practice generates theory, which, in turn, acts as a catalyst for new directions in practice, which then inform theory, and so on."[3] A major theme running through the book is that *teachers are knowledge generators*—the instructional initiatives that teachers implement in their classrooms position them as co-creators of theory rather than simply as recipients of pre-packaged instructional strategies that have been proposed by university researchers and/or mandated by educational policymakers.

After my initial enthusiasm, I was faced with the challenge of how to express coherently in just 10 pages ideas that had spread themselves over more than 400 pages in the book. I decided that the easiest way to communicate the two-way intersections between theoretical ideas and classroom practice in relation to multilingual learners was to step away from the idea of 'writing a book chapter'

---

[3] See Cummins, 2021: xxxiii.

and instead imagine myself having a friendly conversation with the editors of this volume, Valérie and Reseda, about how to enable multilingual learners to extend their awareness of what they can do with language and to use their entire multilingual repertoires in carrying out academic tasks and activities.

In 2015, I spent some time in Strasbourg and had the privilege to spend a morning observing Valérie teaching her bilingual French-German Kindergarten class, in which children from many different language backgrounds were developing awareness not only of connections between French and German but also a sense of pride in their own plurilingual abilities and their home language cultures. Valérie's inspirational instruction illustrated well the idea of *teachers as knowledge generators*. She was pushing the boundaries of what educational authorities in France considered 'appropriate' or 'normal' instructional practice. As I observed Valérie's teaching, it was clear to me that her instruction was clearly consistent with research showing strong positive relationships between the development of students' home language (L1) and their progress in learning the school language(s). However, Valérie's teaching went far beyond what was implied by existing research. Not only was Valérie the creator of her own instructional practice, but she was also creating knowledge as she observed and documented plurilingual students' engagement in learning, their emerging insights about language and literacy, and the expansion of their identities as they collectively brought multiple languages into productive contact.

Valérie's instructional practice illustrates a growing trend that has emerged in many countries in Europe and North America over the past two decades. Teachers, often collaborating with university researchers, have begun to explore and document instructional innovations that extend our knowledge and insight (i.e., theory) about what constitutes effective teaching in multilingual contexts.[4] A common element in these instructional innovations is that they enable plurilingual students to bring their languages into productive contact in carrying out academic tasks and activities.

---

[4] See, for example, Cummins, 2021; Mary & Young, 2021; Prasad, 2016; Velasco & Fialais, 2016.

The term *pedagogical translanguaging* is increasingly being used to refer to this orientation to teaching plurilingual students. The emergence of pedagogical translanguaging represents a radical departure from the perspective, common throughout the 20th century, that students will perform better in learning additional languages if their languages are kept separate and develop in isolation from each other. The rationale for this *two solitudes* orientation was to prevent interference from students' L1 as they learn additional languages.

In order to maintain a conversational tone, I have taken the liberty of imagining questions that Valérie and Reseda might ask about the research I have carried out, and theoretical ideas I have proposed over the past 45 years, and how this research and theory have intersected with classroom practice. I have minimized explicit citation of scholarly articles in the 'conversation' but have included a reference list at the end where the details of the relevant research and theory can be consulted.

Valérie and Reseda: Can you briefly outline some of the major theoretical ideas that you suggested in your early work during the 1970s and 1980s?

Jim: The research that I carried out during the 1970s and early 1980s gave rise to several findings and theoretical ideas that are still relevant today. I'll describe each of these ideas below.

Additive forms of bilingualism are associated with cognitive and linguistic benefits.
My 1974 Ph.D. dissertation research, carried out at the University of Alberta in Edmonton, Canada, replicated some previous studies in reporting that bilingual students who continued to develop literacy in both languages during the elementary school years experienced some cognitive and linguistic benefits compared to students who were developing literacy in just one language. I found similar results in Irish-English bilingual programs when I returned to Ireland between 1974 and 1976, specifically with respect to students' awareness of language and how it works—what researchers call *metalinguistic awareness*. When I returned to Canada in 1976, I found the same pattern of results among students in Ukrainian-English bilingual programs, which had recently been initiated in Edmonton.

Since that time, a large number of research studies have reinforced the general conclusion that *bilingualism has positive effects on children's linguistic and educational development when the school supports students in developing literacy in both languages.* Unfortunately, until recently, the experience of many immigrant-background students has been very different in countries around the world. Students were frequently punished for speaking their home languages in the school, and some teachers and school psychologists advised parents that they should not speak their home language to their children. Wallace Lambert, who evaluated the initial French immersion program in the Montreal area during the 1960s and 1970s, introduced the distinction between *subtractive* and *additive bilingualism* in order to contrast educational programs that attempted to 'subtract' or eradicate children's bilingualism with those that attempted to add a second language to children's home language by promoting literacy in both languages. The cognitive benefits of bilingualism will be realized only in additive contexts where the school and/or parents and caregivers, strongly support the development of both L1 and L2.

There are significant differences in the ways we use language in everyday face-to-face conversation and the ways we use language in school contexts and other formal settings. These differences have major implications for the education of immigrant-background students who are learning the language of instruction in school.

This distinction emerged initially from an analysis of more than 400 psychological assessments administered to primary school immigrant-background students in a western Canadian city. Teachers were concerned that many students who seemed to be making good progress in learning everyday conversational English were quite far behind their peers and below grade expectations in English reading and writing skills. They referred these students for psychoeducational assessment to establish whether or not they had special educational needs, such as a learning disability, that might require additional support and intervention. The assessment typically measured students' verbal academic abilities (e.g., vocabulary knowledge) and non-verbal abilities (e.g., spatial intelligence). The analysis showed that immigrant-background students were performing much closer to grade norms in non-verbal abilities than in verbal academic abilities despite the fact that their conversational abilities in English were very similar in most cases to those of native English-speaking students. In other words, there appeared to be a clear difference in how quickly immigrant-background students acquired functional interpersonal conversational skills in English compared to the length of time required to catch up in English literacy and other academic language skills.

Shortly after completing this study, I moved to Toronto (in 1978), and I was able to carry out a reanalysis of data from the Toronto Board of Education showing that at least five years' length of residence was required for immigrant students from non-English speaking home backgrounds to catch up to grade expectations in English verbal academic skills, despite the fact that most students developed English conversational fluency much more rapidly (typically 1–2 years length of residence).

The distinction between conversational fluency and academic language proficiency carries major implications for classroom instruction and assessment of students' educational progress. Specifically, educational tests and examinations, as well as psychological assessment of immigrant-background students, are likely to underestimate their academic progress and potential for at least five years after they have started learning the school language. Additionally, the extended catch-up trajectory in literacy and other academic content highlights the need for *all* teachers to modify their instruction to make academic content comprehensible for students who are still learning the school language. In order to accelerate students' progress in the school language, teachers also need to reinforce their awareness of how academic language works in science, mathematics, and other subject matter across the curriculum.

There are strong positive crosslinguistic relationships between the development of academic skills in bilingual students' two (or more) languages. First- and second-language literacy and academic language skills are interdependent, and manifestations of a common underlying proficiency.

The consistent finding of strong crosslinguistic relationships in the development of bilingual students' L1 and L2 literacy skills, observed among students from both 'majority' and 'minority' language backgrounds, is reflected in the following realities:

- Children who are encouraged to develop language and literacy skills in two or more languages in their preschool and primary school years transfer knowledge and skills across languages, resulting in consistently positive correlations among their languages as they progress beyond the primary school grades. This implies that educators should strongly support parents and other caregivers to support the development of their children's home language abilities (e.g., by interacting actively with their children in the home language and by reading home-language books to children on a regular basis). In the absence of this explicit and sustained support for L1 development in both the home and school, many immigrant-background students will experience language erosion and will not extend their L1 fluency into reading and writing skills.
- Teachers can promote the development of multilingual children's language awareness and accelerate their knowledge of the school language by encouraging students to bring their languages into productive contact and to use their L1 to carry out academic tasks (e.g., writing dual language books and/or carrying out projects in both L1 and L2).

The research supporting pedagogical translanguaging that has been reported over the past 20 years represents a radical departure from traditional beliefs about second language learning and bilingual education. For many years, teachers and researchers focused on students' L1 as an impediment to learning L2, and consequently, instruction that used the target language almost exclusively was considered 'best practice.' Similarly, in bilingual education and second language immersion programs, the 'two solitudes' assumption dominated instructional practice. Lambert (1984) expressed this assumption in the context of Canadian French immersion programs as follows:

> No bilingual skills are required of the teacher, who plays the role of a monolingual in the target language ... and who never switches languages, reviews materials in the other

language, or otherwise uses the child's native language in teacher-pupil interactions. In immersion programs, therefore, bilingualism is developed through two separate monolingual instructional routes. (p. 13)

These instructional assumptions are strongly rejected by researchers who endorse pedagogical translanguaging, which involves teaching for crosslinguistic transfer and explicitly attempting to bring students' languages into productive contact.

Valérie and Reseda: In addition to these psycholinguistic ideas, you also highlighted the centrality of societal power relations in determining educational outcomes for immigrant-background and minoritized students. Can you explain how these power relations operate in school contexts?

Jim: From the time I started to propose psychoeducational concepts, such as the distinction between conversational and academic language, and the crosslinguistic interdependence between languages, I tried to be clear that these concepts didn't stand alone. The operation of these concepts could vary considerably depending on the social and educational context within which bilingual students were developing. However, it was only in 1986 that I began to explore in depth how the societal context influenced the linguistic and educational development of minoritized bilingual students.

The framework I proposed in 1986 and elaborated in subsequent years argued that relations of power in the wider society, ranging from coercive to collaborative in varying degrees, influence both the ways in which educators define their roles and the types of structures that are established in the educational system. Educational structures (e.g., policies, curriculum, assessment, and instructional realities), together with educator role definitions (i.e., teacher identity), determine the patterns of interactions between educators, students, and communities. These interactions form an interpersonal space within which learning occurs and teacher-student identities are negotiated. Power is created and shared within this interpersonal space where minds and identities meet.

Coercive relations of power refer to the exercise of power by a dominant individual, group, or country to the detriment of a subordinated individual, group, or country. For example, coercive relations of power are operating when teachers prohibit or punish plurilingual students for using their L1 in the school. Collaborative relations of power, by contrast, reflect the sense of the term *power* that refers to *being enabled* or *empowered* to achieve more. Within collaborative relations of power, power is not a fixed quantity but is generated through interaction with others. The more empowered one individual or group becomes, the more is generated for others to share. The process is additive rather than subtractive. Within this context, empowerment can be defined as *the collaborative creation of power*. Coercive relations of power devalue the identities of minoritized multilingual students, whereas collaborative relations of power affirm student identities.

What this analysis implies for educational practice is that minoritized students will succeed educationally only to the extent that the patterns of teacher-student interaction in school challenge the coercive relations of power that prevail in society at large. In other words, effective instruction requires that educators, individually and collectively within schools, be prepared to challenge the ways in which minoritized communities have been excluded from educational and social opportunity, often over generations. Thus, interactions between educators and minoritized students are never neutral with respect to societal power relations. In varying degrees, they either reinforce or, alternatively, challenge coercive relations of power in the wider society.

This analysis explicitly highlighted the fact that power relations are not just abstract conceptual constructs–they are enacted by real people in specific institutional contexts. Teachers have agency and can act to challenge the operation of coercive power structures. They can also remain passive and become complicit, intentionally or unintentionally, with these power structures.

Valérie and Reseda: You have highlighted the concept of 'identity texts' to illustrate the kinds of instruction that reflect collaborative relations of power. Can you explain what you mean by this concept?

Jim: Let me describe the concept of 'identity texts' with a concrete example that illustrates the instructional possibilities that emerge when students are enabled to utilize their background knowledge and multilingual repertoires as resources for learning. Shortly after her arrival in Canada from Pakistan, Grade 7 student Madiha Bajwa (age 13) authored a bilingual Urdu-English book entitled *The New Country* with two of her friends, Kanta Khalid and Sulmana Hanif. The 20-page book "describes how hard it was to leave our country and come to a new country." Both Kanta and Sulmana had arrived in Toronto in Grade 4 and were fluent in English, but Madiha was in the very early stages of English acquisition.

The three girls collaborated in writing *The New Country* in their Grade 7/8 classroom in the context of a unit on the theme of migration that integrated social studies with a focus on reinforcing students' knowledge of academic language. They researched and wrote the story over several weeks, sharing their experiences and language skills. Madiha's English was minimal, but her Urdu was fluent. Sulmana and Kanta were fluent and reasonably literate in both Urdu and English. In composing the story, the three girls discussed their ideas primarily in Urdu but wrote the initial draft in English with feedback and support from their teacher (Lisa Leoni). When the English draft was finalized, they translated it into Urdu.

In a typical Grade 7 classroom, Madiha's ability to understand instruction and participate academically would have been severely limited by her minimal knowledge of English. She certainly would not have been in a position to write extensively in English about her experiences, ideas, and insights. However, when the social structure of the classroom was changed to encourage collaboration among peers and use of students' home languages as well as English, Madiha was enabled to contribute her ideas and experiences to the story, participate in discussions about how to translate vocabulary and expressions from Urdu to English and from English to Urdu and share in the affirmation that all three students experienced with the publication of their story as a (hard copy) book and on the Internet.[5] The fact that instruction was conducted in English and the teacher did not know Urdu or the other home languages of students in her multilingual classroom was not an impediment to the

---

[5] www.multiliteracies.ca/index.php/folio/viewGalleryBook/8/42/0

implementation of crosslinguistic instructional strategies.

Kanta's account of what writing the story meant for her personally illustrates the intersection of identity and literacy that is the essence of the concept of 'identity texts.' Here is an excerpt of what she said in a presentation at the Ontario Teachers of English as a Second Language Conference, about two years after she and her friends had written 'The New Country':

> How it helped me was when I came here in Grade 4, the teachers didn't know what I was capable of. I was given a pack of crayons and a coloring book and told to get on coloring with it. And after, I felt so bad about that—I'm capable of doing much more than just that. I have my own inner skills to show the world than just coloring, and I felt that those skills of mine are important also. So, when we started writing the book, I could actually show the world that I am something instead of just coloring. And that's how it helped me, and it made me so proud of myself that I am actually capable of doing something, and here today, I *am* actually doing something. I'm not just a coloring person—I can show you that I am something.

As illustrated in Kanta's account, the term 'identity texts' describes the products of students' creative work or performances carried out within the pedagogical space orchestrated by the classroom teacher. Students invest their identities in the creation of these texts, which can be written, spoken, visual, musical, dramatic, or combinations in multimodal form. The identity text then holds a mirror up to students in which their identities are reflected back in a positive light. When students share identity texts with multiple audiences (peers, teachers, parents, grandparents, sister classes, the media, etc.), they are likely to receive positive feedback and affirmation of self in interaction with these audiences. This, in turn, fuels further literacy engagement. In the case of Madiha, Sulmana, and Kanta, the identity text became the vehicle for an identity transformation from 'English-as-a-second-language student' defined by their limitations in the school language, to an identity as creative authors defined by their creativity and competent oral and literacy skills in two languages.

Dual language identity texts such as 'The New Country' challenge coercive relations of power by affirming the legitimacy of students' home languages as tools for thinking and academic expression. This kind of project rejects the widespread assumption that students' home languages are irrelevant, or even an impediment, to their learning of the school language. The teacher-student identity negotiation that creates the instructional conditions for the creation of identity texts illustrates the definition of 'empowerment' as the collaborative creation of power.

Valérie and Reseda: A final issue that policymakers, educators, and school administrators are likely to be concerned about is how these theoretical concepts fit together. How do they translate into effective instructional practice? We know from the OECD PISA research over the past 20 years that many immigrant-background plurilingual students in countries across Europe and elsewhere continue to perform less well in school than their native-born peers. How can the research and theoretical ideas you have proposed help educators to develop whole-school policies and instructional practices that can reverse underachievement?

Jim: That's obviously a central and complex question that goes right to the heart of the quest for social and educational equity in many societies. It is also a question I tried to answer in my book *Rethinking the Education of Multilingual Students*. I suggested that a first step in considering this question is to ask ourselves: *Who are the students who are underachieving in our schools?* Or expressed differently: *What groups or categories of students experience underachievement?*

If we leave out students with special needs who are experiencing academic difficulty as a result of an individual condition or learning disability, the research points clearly to three overlapping groups of students who are experiencing disproportionate underachievement.

- *Plurilingual students who speak a home language that is different from the major language of schooling.* This home-school language switch requires students to learn academic content through a new language.
- *Students whose families are experiencing poverty or social disadvantage associated with low family income and/or low levels of parental education.* These families frequently experience

overcrowding, food insecurity, segregated housing, which results in segregated schooling and less access to cultural tools and experiences that cost money (e.g., mobile phones, books, visits to museums, and other cultural enrichment).
- *Marginalized group status deriving from societal discrimination and/or racism in the wider society.* Students from socially marginalized communities (e.g., Roma students in Europe, Indigenous students globally) are frequently stereotyped in negative ways, and their cultural identities are devalued in the wider society.

Some students experience opportunity gaps associated with all three categories (e.g., many Spanish-speaking students in the United States; many Turkish-speaking immigrant-background students in Europe), while others may fall into only one category (e.g., a middle-class Romanian immigrant student in France). These three sets of risk factors become realized as *actual* educational disadvantage only when the school fails to respond appropriately or reinforces the negative impact of the broader social factors.

International research on the education of plurilingual students has highlighted six overlapping sets of instructional strategies that respond directly to the causes of educational disadvantage among linguistically diverse, socially disadvantaged, and marginalized students. These strategies are:

- Scaffold comprehension and production of language.
- Reinforce academic language across the curriculum.
- Engage students' multilingual resources and encourage translanguaging.
- Maximize literacy engagement.
- Connect with students' lives and the knowledge, culture and language of their communities.
- Affirm students' identities by enabling them to use their language and literacy skills to carry out powerful intellectual and creative academic work.

The first three of these instructional strategies respond to students' need to learn the language of instruction at the same time as they are trying to catch up to their peers in L2 literacy and knowledge of academic context. Because of the challenges many immigrant-background students experience in catching up academically, it is essential that teachers take every opportunity to reinforce their awareness of how academic language works across the curriculum.

The strategy of maximizing literacy engagement is particularly important for students from socially disadvantaged backgrounds who have typically experienced significantly less access to print and opportunities to engage with literacy in their homes and neighborhoods than students from more advantaged backgrounds. An obvious reason for limited print access in children's homes is that parents who are experiencing economic difficulties don't have the money to buy books and other cultural resources (e.g., smartphones, tablet computers) for their children, and many may not be highly literate in their own languages. Research from around the world has demonstrated a *causal* relationship between literacy engagement and literacy achievement.

The instructional strategies of connecting instruction to students' lives and affirming their identities recognize that societal institutions such as schools in many countries continue to devalue the cultures, languages, and identities of marginalized or minoritized communities. In order to reverse this pattern, educators, individually and collectively, must challenge disempowering structures and ideologies by orchestrating patterns of interaction that enable students to mobilize their entire linguistic repertoire to engage in powerful communication involving the creation of identity texts.

So, in conclusion, what this framework is saying is that mainstream school policies have either focused on only one of the three sets of opportunity gaps or have addressed them in isolation from each other. For example, school systems in many countries have recognized that schools should support newly arrived students in learning the school language. However, there has been minimal acknowledgment that a large proportion of immigrant-background students who are learning the language of instruction are also experiencing the effects of social disadvantage and belong to communities that have been excluded from social and educational opportunity, often for generations. If multilingual and immigrant-background students are to succeed academically, it is essential that instruction incorporates evidence-based approaches that respond in a coordinated way to the effects of social disadvantage and marginalized status in addition to language differences. These instructional responses include maximizing students' opportunities for literacy engagement and enabling them to use language and other forms of self-expression to affirm their emerging academic and personal identities.

2.2. From Teaching Languages to Teaching Students: How Teachers of Bilingual Students Take Up Translanguaging Theory in Practice

Kate Seltzer and Ricardo Otheguy

The present chapter aims to answer a pragmatic question: What do teachers who have understood and come to own the tenets of what is generally known as translanguaging theory do? How do these teachers think about bilingual students, and how, as a consequence of this thinking, do they teach these students differently? What is special about the praxis of teachers who see their children through a translanguaging lens? In our attempt to answer these questions, we offer a brief theoretical preamble first and then turn our attention to bilingual children and adolescents, their teachers, and the languaging that is at the center of their lives in schools and classrooms.

The term *language* often implies the existence, in the minds of speakers—especially students—of a single, discrete linguistic system in monolinguals, two in bilinguals, three in multilinguals, and so on. (For simplicity, we use *bilingual* here to also refer to multilingual individuals.) This view, which treats the two languages of a bilingual as separate and distinct cognitive entities, is further reinforced by the use of different language names. We define a bilingual as someone who knows two languages, such as Arabic and French, Yoruba and Hausa, or German and Italian. Alternatively, as is the case with some frequency in Spain, Latin America, and the United States, it is Spanish and English. When language-related educational efforts are seen in the terms fomented by these language names, the mind of the student who is already bilingual is conceived of as possessing two linguistic systems. In contrast, the monolingual student who is learning a second or foreign language is seen as undertaking efforts to change from possessing only one of these cognitive systems to possessing two.

While there is little doubt that both monolinguals and bilinguals can be accurately characterized as having language, there is reason to question whether a cognitive difference exists between the two groups—specifically, whether bilinguals possess two distinct, separable linguistic systems or a single, unified one. That is, even though there is little doubt that, for example, the people we call English-only monolinguals and English-Spanish bilinguals both have language, there is reason to doubt that they differ cognitively in that the bilinguals possess two languages while the monolinguals have only one. When seen from an internalist cognitive perspective, that is, from the perspective of the individual speaker, there is every reason to believe that bilinguals are almost certainly the same as monolinguals: they have only one linguistic system. It is only from the externalist sociopolitical perspective that they have two. Understanding the reasons why the linguistic competence of bilinguals is thus best conceived of as *unitary* is important for educators no less than for theoreticians. This is not only because theoretical formulations always have large and small effects on praxis but because the unitary conception of the linguistic cognition of bilinguals can and has inspired teaching stances, instructional designs, assessment methods, and pedagogical shifts that are different from those derived from the familiar dual conception of the linguistic competence of bilinguals.[6]

Translanguaging: A shift in perspective

The approach that conceives of the linguistic competence of bilinguals as unitary and leads to teaching practices consonant with this conception has come to be known as *translanguaging*. The term was first coined in Welsh by Cen Williams, with reference to innovative educational practices in bilingual and second-language classrooms in Wales. Its current scope of reference—which also includes the speech behavior of *bilinguals* outside the school context—is discussed in García and Li Wei (2014). Details and extensive justification can be found in Otheguy, García, and Reid (2015, 2019). The term translanguaging refers, first, to a particular conception of the mental representation of language in bilinguals, specifically the unitary competence theory. However, it also refers to

---

[6] See García, Johnson & Seltzer, 2017.

a specific range of linguistic behaviors that are characteristic of bilingual communities, as well as a particular set of student behaviors in bilingual and second-language classrooms, and to the teaching practices that follow from these.

Translanguaging: A shift in practice

The shift in praxis stems from the fact that the familiar dual conception of the bilingual's linguistic system views the speaker solely from a social vantage point—that is, from the outside. In contrast, the unitary conception seeks to understand the bilingual from an individual, internal perspective. The implications for practice emerge when we ask: What would teachers do differently once they understood translanguaging? The translanguaging approach asserts that the unitary theory of translanguaging provides a linguistic understanding of bilingualism that has significant implications for the just education of bilingual, minoritized children and that opens up vistas of similar value for second and foreign language teachers.

Pedagogical praxis inspired by translanguaging theory begins by dispensing with the conceptualization of students, such as those in the Anglophone world, as *English language learners* and instead conceives of them as *emergent bilinguals*.[7] The idea of *emergence* emphasizes that the present possibilities of children and adolescents must be activated now—not deferred to the future—by teachers providing the appropriate affordances, as illustrated below.

The *translanguaging pedagogy* outlined by García, Johnson, and Seltzer (2017) enables teachers to offer such affordances. It works overall towards a more humanizing and equitable vision of bilingual education. The framework allows teachers to reimagine their classrooms and practices from the internal vantage point of their bilingual students, valuing the translanguaging of these students as an indispensable resource for learning. García, Johnson, and Seltzer use the metaphor of a *corriente* to describe the fluid current of languaging by bilingual students. In a body of water, there is always movement. Even when the water appears calm, one only has to put a hand below the surface to feel the flow of water moving beneath. In

---

[7] See García, 2009.

any classroom with bilingual students, a similar translanguaging flow of bilingual ways of knowing exists. Teachers who commit to a translanguaging pedagogy can bring that *corriente* closer to the surface and leverage it to further the students' learning and meaning-making. In a translanguaging classroom where the corriente rises to the surface, teachers of emergent bilinguals move away from teaching *languages* and toward teaching *students*, tapping into the linguistic repertoires they have already acquired before entering the classroom while also working toward the expansion of these repertoires, adding the new lexical and morphosyntactic resources, and the new communicative practices, that align with the tasks, genres, and literacies that students encounter in schools.

Teachers develop translanguaging pedagogies by weaving together three strands, which García, Johnson, and Seltzer (2017) refer to as *stance, design,* and *shifts*. We first describe each of these strands and then demonstrate them in action through three vignettes, each of which features teachers who have adopted this framework to approach their bilingual students in new ways.

The translanguaging stance

At the heart of a translanguaging pedagogy is a firm set of beliefs about bilingualism and bilingual students, which García, Johnson, and Seltzer describe using the word "juntos" to underscore the sense of togetherness and collaboration that is one of the hallmarks of translanguaging teaching. The *translanguaging stance*, comprising the "philosophical, ideological, or belief system that teachers draw upon to develop their pedagogical framework," encompasses several essential understandings. Teachers who adopt a translanguaging stance believe that students' communicative practices and linguistic repertoires are *juntos*, intertwined, and not rigidly separated into an L1 and an L2. These teachers, along with prominent linguists such as Torres Cacoullos and Travis (2018), have learned to question concepts such as 'the native language,' 'the matrix language,' and 'the second language,' and, along with these authors, discount the conventional belief in "the regime of ordered first and second language acquisition."[8] Teachers adopting the translanguaging stance also believe that students' families and communities are integral to their education and should work *juntos* with the school to develop students' education. Lastly, they view the classroom as a democratic space in which teachers are co-learners with their students, *juntos* in the learning process, and the struggle for social justice.

As empowered witnesses to the daily progress of children and adolescents, teachers adopting the translanguaging stance conceive of their students from the outset as successful acquirers of new lexical and structural resources that become integrated into their unitary competence rather than as only partially successful or failed acquirers of a second named language. It is unfortunate that traditional teachers—whose perspectives are rooted in the dual conception of the bilingual's linguistic system—are often compelled to focus on the perceived shortcomings of children and adolescents who have not yet mastered the second named language. In contrast, we celebrate teachers who look at the same students and who, inspired by the unitary conception sponsored by translanguaging theory, preside over the students' consistently successful process of additive expansion.

Translanguaging design

A *translanguaging design* emerges from an expansive, *juntos* stance and responds to the flows of the ever-present *corriente*. Translations into the practice of the translanguaging stance are evident in the purposeful design of classroom space (the physical organization of the classroom and the multilingual ecology that reflects the language practices of the students), in the design of instruction (lessons, units, and text selection), and in the assessments of student learning. All of these elements serve as "translations" of a translanguaging stance, communicating to students that all their language practices are integral to their learning and can be utilized at *all* times, regardless of the linguistic medium of instruction. In this way, teachers from any linguistic background can create translanguaging designs within any

---

[8] 2018: 66.

program and context and for any population of students, so long as they purposefully and explicitly make space for the translanguaging corriente to flow.

Translanguaging shifts

Flexibility and responsiveness are integral to effective teaching. For teachers of bilingual students, such flexibility can manifest in *translanguaging shifts* or the "unplanned moment-by-moment decisions that teachers make in response to the flow of the translanguaging corriente in their classrooms."[9] Like a translanguaging design, translanguaging shifts emerge out of a translanguaging stance; it is by perceiving bilingual students' languaging and meaning-making more expansively that teachers can change course and make moves that affirm and extend their learning. Whether providing students with opportunities to find translations of new vocabulary or encouraging them to turn and talk to a peer in a shared language about new content, such shifts can give teachers the means both to meet students' needs and to communicate their stance that students' translanguaging is a resource.

Theory into practice: What do teachers in translanguaging classrooms do differently?

We now turn to three short vignettes that offer insight into what teachers can do differently once they adopt a unitary theory of the bilingual's linguistic repertoire and take on translanguaging stances, designs, and shifts. We have purposefully chosen teachers who work in different settings and hold diverse positionalities to demonstrate how *all* teachers in *all* contexts can develop translanguaging pedagogies.

Transcending rigid named language structures in Carla's classroom.

Carla teaches in a dual language Spanish-English bilingual program in the Southwest region of the United States. Like Carla herself, her mostly Mexican- and Central American-origin students are bilingual in Spanish and English. However, they have various levels of comfort using their languages to accomplish school-based language and

---

[9] See García, Johnson & Seltzer, 2017: 77.

literacy tasks. In the following vignette, adapted from García, Johnson, and Seltzer (2017), we observe how Carla enacts her translanguaging pedagogy.

Although Carla's school's dual language bilingual program strictly separates students' learning into designated "English" and "Spanish" times, Carla sets aside a special part of the week that she calls a *Cuéntame algo* space. Here, students actively bring together their language practices by reading translanguaged texts, engaging in activities and discussions that hone their metalinguistic awareness, and creating texts that include both English and Spanish. For example, during a unit designed by Carla called *Cuentos de la tierra y del barrio*, Carla reads aloud the book *The Santero's Miracle* by Rudolfo Anaya. The book is written in both English and Spanish, with the two languages featured side by side on the page. Carla reads some paragraphs from the book in English and others in Spanish, and she and her students discuss the book regardless of the language in which she reads. Carla also draws students' attention to parts of the story where Spanish words appear on the English side of the text and engages them in discussions about why this might be the case. After reading the book, Carla strategically groups students based on their different language performances. She asks them to conduct research (using Spanish and English websites and interviewing family members bilingually) to author a research report on local holiday traditions. Carla instructs some groups to write in Spanish and others to write in English, but she also tells them to include quotes directly from their research in whatever language they have read or heard them. Carla reminds them that Rudolfo Anaya had chosen to render some words in Spanish in his English text and that they could do the same. She explains that they will use their research reports to make bilingual presentations to their school community.

Shifting assessment practices in Ella's classroom

Researcher Laura Ascenzi-Moreno (2018) describes how English as a New Language teacher Ella, who teaches in a suburb of a large city in the Northeast United States, makes what Ascenzi-Moreno calls responsive adaptations during formative reading assessments in English. These adaptations enable both Ella and her students to use all their linguistic resources in the assessment process, allowing students to "draw upon the full span of their language and social resources to make meaning of their literacy experiences" (p. 355). Such shifts aim to document the progress of emergent bilinguals as readers and provide Ella with a more holistic and nuanced understanding of what they know and can do. Ella identifies as an English speaker but is also fluent in Spanish and uses it with her students. In this vignette, we adapt one of Ascenzi-Moreno's findings[10] to illustrate how Ella employs responsive adaptations during a formative reading assessment to gain a deeper understanding of her student, Santiago.

Ella gives Santiago a copy of a book in English and asks him to read it aloud. As he reads to Ella, she notes his deviations from the text and divides them into the three categories typically used on such assessments: meaning-related, visual, and syntactical miscues. When working with emergent bilinguals like Santiago, Ella adds additional columns to her assessment form to note miscues related to language and pronunciation. When Santiago finishes reading to her, she does not simply end the assessment process there. She invites him into dialogue with her, collaboratively reviewing his miscues (i.e., "beard" for "bird" and "failen" for "fallen") and asking him to clarify his understanding of those words using any language he wants. When he provides the word *pájaro* 'bird,' Ella realizes that the miscue is not visual- or meaning-related, but due to pronunciation. She engages in a similar conversation with Santiago about his other miscues, allowing him to explain his reading experience. Rather than viewing his deviations from the text "neutrally" and adhering diligently to the traditional assessment script, such bilingual dialogue and attention to language-related miscues enable Ella to devise a plan for Santiago, including the language-specific features and practices he will need as he continues to expand his reading performances in English.

---

[10] 2018: 360-362.

Expanding approaches to English teaching in Ms. Winter's classroom

Ms. Winter teaches English Language Arts (ELA) in a large city in the Northeast United States. Although Ms. Winter identifies as a white, monolingual English-speaking woman, her secondary classroom is comprised of students of color from diverse cultural and linguistic backgrounds. In her work as an English teacher, Ms. Winter has devoted herself to unlearning many of the tenets that guided her teacher education experience, such as the belief that her role is to teach students the so-called standard language. Hence, they learn to speak and write like what her trainers called native speakers of academic English. As she unlearns, she moves away from seeing her role as a teacher of the named language, English.[11] Instead, she embraces what she has learned to see as the true language arts that her students bring with them to the classroom,[12] viewing her role as facilitator and guide as students encounter and integrate new linguistic features and practices into their existing unitary repertoires. In the following vignette, which Kate wrote based on her field notes from her study of Ms. Winter's classroom, we see how Ms. Winter pushes the traditional boundaries of the ELA classroom as she facilitates a multilingual whole-class Socratic Seminar on a topic labeled "standard English."

Students sit facing one another in a large circle. They gather their notes and prepare to engage in a Socratic Seminar, a structured, formal conversation on the question, "Should teachers at our school require students to use only standard English?" In the week preceding the Socratic Seminar, students engaged with a series of multilingual, multimodal texts from various perspectives, including essays, social media posts, videos, newspaper, and magazine articles, among others, all related to the central question. They helped students support their opinions with textual evidence. On the day of the Socratic Seminar, Ms. Winter begins by reviewing the guidelines for such discussions. Though English is the official medium of instruction for the class, Ms. Winter does not limit students to English only. Her guidelines include the explicit invitation for

---

[11] See Seltzer & de los Ríos, 2018.
[12] See Flores, 2020; Martinez, 2017; Seltzer & García, 2020.

students to participate in whatever language they like. One student, an emergent bilingual from Côte d'Ivoire, shares a quote from a magazine article she read and expands upon her thoughts in French. Although Ms. Winter and many students in the class do not speak French, they listen patiently, jotting down anything they understand (such as cognates from other languages or English words) or have questions about. After the student has finished sharing, Ms. Winter asks her and another experienced French/English bilingual student to try and summarize her comments in English. She does so, and another student picks up a thread of her ideas, sharing his own opinions and text-based evidence in English. After the Socratic Seminar is over, Ms. Winter introduces an argumentative writing project that is aligned with the standardized literacy exam students will take at the end of the year. She reviews the assignment, including students' tasks, audience, and role as writers. She helps them leverage the learning from the Socratic Seminar into an argumentative essay on the topic of "standard English" in schools.

Discussion

What can we take away from these brief glimpses into the classrooms of Carla, Ella, and Ms. Winter? What do we see these teachers doing differently? We can certainly see clear evidence of the three teachers' translanguaging stances, which stand in contrast to enduring, deficit-oriented thinking about emergent bilingual students. Carla, for example, believes that students' linguistic performances emerge not from two separate systems but from one unified, interrelated repertoire. This belief informs many of her translanguaging design choices. For example, although she recognizes and works within the norm of language separation in her dual language bilingual program, she also carves out space for students to transcend this separation and draw on their bilingual language and ways of knowing to engage meaningfully with content and develop their biliteracies together.

Ella, too, draws on her translanguaging stance to shape her approach to assessment. Like Carla, she recognizes that bilingual students' language practices and literacies cannot be understood in isolation from one another. However, Ella also knows that students like Santiago will be assessed using tools that conceptualize language and literacy in this binary way, casting their reading performances in a negative light. For this reason, her approach to assessment involves both planned and unplanned translanguaging moves. In a planned translanguaging design, Ella purposefully adapts the formative reading assessment itself, making it more inclusive of those "miscues" that might be related to language and pronunciation rather than meaning. Her translanguaging shifts, which are not planned but occur within her more expansive approach to formative reading assessment, occur as she invites Santiago into dialogue about his reading performance. Because she is highly attuned to his translanguaging, Ella is able to go with the flow of the *corriente* and, as such, gain a more accurate understanding of who Santiago and all of her emergent bilingual students are as readers.

Ms. Winter makes her stance known through several planned and unplanned translanguaging moves. First and foremost, Ms. Winter's translanguaging instructional design centers on topics and questions that explicitly draw students' attention to the intersections of language and power. By allowing students to question the very existence of "standard language," she communicates that, though she is their "English" teacher, she does not endorse a belief in its bounded nature or its hierarchy above students' ways of languaging.[13] Similarly, her translanguaging shifts – for example, enabling the student from Côte d'Ivoire to voice her ideas in French without regard for the "official" language of the classroom – communicate that Ms. Winter's comprehension is not paramount. She positions herself not as the sole "listener" of importance in the classroom but as *juntos* with her students—engaged in the learning process and in the collective pursuit of making meaning across and beyond named languages.

Conclusion

We return now to the question central to this chapter: what would teachers do differently once they understood a theory of unitary translanguaging? As we show in the previous three vignettes, teachers can do a great many things differently. They can leverage

---

[13] See Seltzer & García, 2020.

translanguaging in instruction, viewing all the various linguistic performances of students as valid and expansive ways of making meaning while limiting the real-world demands of named language separation to what is necessary for success in an educational setting. They can evaluate bilingual children for what they know how to do independently of the culturally dictated affiliation of their lexical, structural, and communicative resources. They can foster in students a critical lens on those ideologies that accompany named languages and tend to cast them in a deficit light. Translanguaging theory and practice ensure that educators prioritize bilingual children. These educators provide students with the opportunities to expand what is truly psycholinguistically fundamental—namely, their lexical, structural, and other semiotic resources. They acknowledge the importance of naming languages as boundary markers in schools and societies while also recognizing that these demarcations are sociocultural constructions that do not necessarily reflect students' cognitive-linguistic realities.

2.3. On Biliteracy and Theory(ies): A Bilingual Teacher's Journey
Cecilia M. Espinosa

Literacy has always been a collection of communicative and socio-cultural practices shared among communities. As society and technology change, so does literacy. The world demands that a literate person possess and intentionally apply a wide range of skills, competencies, and dispositions. These literacies are interconnected, dynamic, and malleable. As in the past, they are inextricably linked with histories, narratives, life possibilities, and social trajectories of all individuals and groups.
NCTE Position Statement, 21st Century Literacies, 2019

The word is a tool for understanding the world.
Paulo Freire, 1972

As members of particular communities, we all hold theories about what literacy is, as well as how literacy begins.[14] These beliefs are never neutral. In many settings, the vision of literacy upheld by society and institutions for individuals from marginalized racial, economic, and linguistic groups does not encourage them to draw on their languaging practices in school. Moreover, the literacy activities they are often invited to engage in rarely require them to reflect on or question their lived experiences. This stance toward literacy at school only invites them to memorize, engage in drills, and receive literacy as if it were already complete, created by someone else, and removed from the learner's experiences. They need to consume and practice it. They are only the recipients of it. In these settings, a person might be considered literate when they become officially *alfabetizado*. In many Latin American countries, this means being able to *deletrear*—in other words, to read by sounding out letters, often without paying attention to meaning. They are not invited to analyze the text critically or to bring their lived experiences to bear on their interpretation of the text.

---

[14] See Espinosa & Ascenzi-Moreno, 2021.

In contrast, literacy educator Kenn Goodman (1990) argued that at the core of literacy is the construction of meaning. Therefore, literacy has to have a purpose, he insisted. He wrote in the publication *Lectura y Vida*:

> Los niños aprenden el lenguaje oral en sus hogares sin que nadie lo divida en fragmentos pequeños. Lo aprenden cuando lo necesitan para expresarse y entienden lo que dicen los otros, siempre que estén con personas que utilicen el lenguaje con sentido y con un propósito determinado. (1990, p. n/a)

> [Translation: *Children learn oral language at home without anyone breaking it apart into small pieces. They learn language when they need it to express and understand what others say, as long as they are with people who use it with meaning and a particular purpose.*]

At school, Goodman (1990) argued that language is too often artificial and fragmented. It belongs to someone else, not the student. It lacks context, social relevance, and authentic purpose for the student, Goodman (1990, 2014) vehemently contended. Goodman (1990) questioned how literacy is often taught in schools, devoid of meaning and purpose, and therefore disconnected from its application in life, where it is rooted in purpose and authenticity. Literacy, Goodman (1996, 2914) proclaimed, changes and evolves depending on what people's needs are and what they are trying to do with them.

When considering biliteracy, learners have been asked to engage in similar drills and memorization practices for too long, often overlooking the languaging practices of students and how biliteracy exists in the world in authentic and usually multimodal ways.[15] In many instances, learners' biliteracy practices at school have been considered only from a deficit perspective and have been habitually rendered problematic and in need of remediation. The ultimate goal in many of these settings has been for bilingual students to become monolingual and use only English for literacy purposes.

---

[15] See Otheguy, García & Reid, 2015.

The field of biliteracy in the United States was initially built on Cummins' (1979) theory of Linguistic Interdependence. The biliteracy argument at the time was that what students learned in one language could be transferred to the second language.[16] While his theory supported the idea that the first language was critical in the development of the second language, it still kept each language as a separate system inside the person's brain.[17] For example, if a child learned to predict in Spanish, it was believed that the child would transfer this skill to English; this stance meant that languages were to be kept as distinct, separate linguistic systems. The idea of transfer from L1 to L2 was prevalent at the time.

In contrast, researchers García and Kleifgen (2019) present a 21st-century perspective on biliteracy. This is a transformative stance that views the bilingual person as having one linguistic repertoire and two (or more) named languages. These researchers argue that:

> Translanguaging pedagogy challenges existing ways of understanding and living bilingualism in schools. It invites us to question current beliefs we hold about how bilingual people use language in the world. It challenges ways in which particular ways of languaging have been silenced. Translanguaging centers the bilingual languaging practices. It focuses on meaning-making, inviting the whole child or adolescent into the biliteracy experience to capitalize on their entire linguistic repertoire, thus liberating their full potential to construct meaning. (p. 7-8)

Without a doubt, the question of what biliteracy is and what it involves is a question that encompasses ideologies about who is given the right to become fully biliterate and whose literacies are valued. What is the purpose of biliteracy? How does biliteracy exist in the world, and particularly in the communities of students? What are the languaging practices the students and families bring to the school? When considering biliteracy, it is impossible to separate it from the learning theories that a teacher holds about how children become

---

[16] See Cummins, 1979.

[17] It is important to note that at the time the field used the terms first (L1) and second language (L2). The field now uses terms such as home language and new language to refer to named languages.

biliterate. Undoubtedly, a teacher's beliefs regarding how children learn and the strengths (or perceived deficits) that they bring impact the teacher's biliteracy practices. Biliteracy is, after all, a political act. In this essay, I discuss how a teacher's theory(ies) of biliteracy are continuously reshaped by her experiences, as well as by the texts, dialogue, and experts she encounters. I describe the learning experiences of Carolina, a bilingual teacher of immigrant origin. The aim is to illustrate how a teacher's beliefs about biliteracy—and what it entails—directly shape their instructional practice. Next, I provide a brief overview of research on biliteracy practices, highlighting current findings. I begin by describing Carolina's experiences as a student developing biliteracy.

Biliteracy and the banking concept of education

Carolina grew up in Bolivia, South America, and attended elementary and high school from 1970 to 1982. In the setting where Carolina was a student, bilingualism and biliteracy were highly valued, particularly when they included learning European languages, such as English, French, and Italian. In contrast, indigenous languages were rendered invisible in most schools. While knowing two languages was deeply prized, the biliteracy practices (learning English as a new language) Carolina engaged in school mainly consisted of drills, i.e., conjugation of verbs in each tense and for each pronoun, isolated vocabulary words that were devoid of our experiences or interests, identification of each part of a sentence. Carolina and her classmates were never invited to listen to a song or poem, compose one in a new language, watch a movie in English, write a play, write a letter to an authentic audience, or listen to a read-aloud or read a book of their choice. They studied the new language (English) as if it existed outside of their lived experiences.

At school, there was no space for Carolina and her classmates to develop their questions or pursue their interests. The curriculum in the new language was already set. It was written by someone far away who had particular ideologies about how language is learned. The curriculum came prepackaged and ready to be used in the form of a teacher's guide and a textbook with fill-in-the-blank exercises for students. The guide provided the teacher with exact wording and step-by-step instructions. Each chapter in this textbook has a brief and decontextualized story or dialogue. Its focus was on a specific aspect of English grammar. There were a few examples to illustrate the grammar point that the writers of these texts elected to highlight. These were followed by a series of exercises that mainly consisted of answering simple questions or filling in the blanks. Carolina and her classmates could not ignore their home language, Spanish, during these drills. Yet, their translanguaging was never acknowledged, even though they were engaging in it while participating in repetitive exercises that failed to invite authentic meaning-making. Translanguaging García and Kleifgen (2019) write, "is a process that takes into account the sociocultural, sociolinguistic, and multimodal dimensions of learning" (p. 9). This represents a significantly different approach to the learning experiences that Carolina and her classmates participated in during their time as students.

As a student in this setting, Carolina was experiencing what Freire (1970) referred to as the banking concept of education. Examining these learning experiences through Freire's (1970) theory, Carolina and her classmates were the "listening objects," while the teacher served as the "narrating subject." Freire (1970) states:

> The teacher talks about reality as if it were motionless, static, compartmentalized, and predictable. Or else he [she] expounds on a topic completely alien to the existential experience of the students. His task is to "fill" the students with the contents of his narration -contents that are detached from reality, disconnected from the totality that engendered them, and could give them significance. Words are emptied of their concreteness or become a hollow, alienated, and alienating verbosity. (p. 71)

From this perspective, learning a new language and becoming biliterate means becoming a container the teacher fills. The student's role is to memorize, repeat, practice drills, fill in the blanks, and review the lesson from the previous day to demonstrate to the teacher the extent of their learning. The teacher posed the questions, and the students responded with their answers. There were no opportunities for the children to engage in creative acts in the new language. Carolina and her classmates learned that there is only one correct answer for each exercise. The questions the teacher posed were only those she already knew the answers to. These were evaluative questions rather than dialogical questions.

Teaching was not centered on critical dialogue about issues that affected the students, their families, and their communities. The teacher was the only one thought of as knowledgeable. She stood before the class and delivered a predetermined set of facts. The students sat in rows organized alphabetically by their last name or by height. Biliteracy learning was teacher-centered. The students were viewed as empty vessels whose job was to listen to the teacher's lecture and her corrections, as well as to copy and repeat what was written on the board. The biliteracy experiences the students learned in this context extended beyond their prior experiences. There was no space for wondering, questioning, developing metalinguistic awareness between Spanish and English, or studying a topic of interest that mattered to the students. Additionally, the students' and their families' funds of knowledge[18] were rendered invisible.

Funds of knowledge researcher Luis Moll (2019) describes it as a research stance, as well as a theoretical and a pedagogical sociocultural approach to document, re-present, and build upon the families' ways of knowing, resources and strengths that offer a counter-narrative to deficit orientations often so prevalent, particularly in the education of working class, immigrant-origin students. The first researchers to study families' funds of knowledge were Luis C. Moll, Cathy Amanti, Deborah Neff, and Norma Gonzales (1992), with their groundbreaking paper, "Funds of Knowledge for Teaching: Using a Qualitative Approach to Connect Homes and Classrooms." The primary purpose of this collaborative project across research disciplines (anthropology and education) was to "develop innovations in teaching that draw upon the knowledge and skills found in local households" (Mexican communities in Tucson, Arizona) (p. 131). Their claim, these sociocultural researchers added, was that "by capitalizing on household and other community resources, we can organize classroom instruction that far exceeds in quality the rote-like instruction these children commonly

---

[18] See Moll, 2019.

encounter in schools" (p. 131). From the banking concept of education, there is no space for the students' or their families' funds of knowledge. These are rendered nonexistent.

Languaging in a new country

When Carolina finished high school, she moved to the United States. She quickly learned that, despite the biliteracy experiences she had acquired in school in Bolivia over 12 years (elementary and high school), she was unable to fully engage in authentic and purposeful ways in her new language, English. In spite of her urgent need to participate as a full member in this new setting, she lacked authentic experiences in using English (to make new friends, go to the store, pass a driving test, ask for directions, talk about popular culture with peers, discuss the news, understand a joke, read the textbooks from her community college classes). Even though she was very literate in Spanish, she never felt empowered to tap into her home language. She kept English and Spanish separate. She used Spanish with her family and Latine friends and English at the community college. This was despite the fact that she was now living in Phoenix, Arizona—a city with a large Spanish-speaking population. Yet both the city and the state have historically had a complicated relationship with Spanish-speaking communities.

In Phoenix, Carolina learned that Spanish is a language of low regard. She learned from the local newspaper and the local TV news that Spanish speakers are perceived as not wanting to learn English; those who learn it are perceived as never quite speaking it correctly. This is in contrast to Carolina's experiences at the university, where she helped speakers of English as a second language learn Spanish. She became a highly regarded tutor. The Spanish that the college students learned at the university held a high status. As a university student and a resident of Phoenix, she recognized that the issue of low status was linked to the Spanish spoken by certain individuals and in specific communities in Phoenix. These were insights that unsettled Carolina. Still, it took many years for teachers like Carolina to learn about raciolinguistics, a critical theory developed by Flores and Rosa (2015), who state that it is the white listening subject whose gaze imposes a perspective of deficit upon racialized emergent bilinguals. These arrogant perceptions of the other are fictional—but they are a very real fiction, rooted in ideologies that portray others as deficient and in constant need of urgent remediation.[19]

Becoming a teacher of biliteracy

Once Carolina graduated from university with a teaching degree in early childhood and elementary education, along with a bilingual certificate, she was hired as a bilingual teacher in a large, urban, progressive bilingual school. A brave new principal was determined to transform the bilingual program into one that built on the children's, their families', and communities' assets and thus took a perspective of strength. The research Carolina was reading in her teacher preparation program[20] indeed advocated for quality biliteracy practices for bilingual students. She read, for example, the groundbreaking study, *Writing in a Bilingual Program,* by Edelsky (1982). She learned from Edelsky's research that "what a young writer knows about writing in the first language forms the basis of new hypotheses rather than interferes with writing in another language" (p. 227). Edelsky challenged the notion that the child's first language would confuse them as a writer in the new language. Her findings opened possibilities for teachers to offer biliteracy experiences to young bilingual writers. Later on, researchers Sarah Hudelson and Irene Serna (1994) added:

> Becoming bilingual/biliterate children whose native[21]-language literacy development has been valued and supported, as has been the case in this whole language bilingual program, have confidence in themselves as readers and writers. As they begin to view themselves as readers and writers, they begin to experiment with their new language, in this case, English. Their experimentation involves using the resources of their native languages to

---

[19] See Lugones, 2003.
[20] See Edelsky, 1986; Faltis & Hudelson, 1997; Freeman, 1988; Freeman & Freeman, 2000; Hudelson, 1987; Hudelson & Serna, 1994; García & Flores, 1986 among several others.
[21] At the time the field used the words native language. This idea has been questioned now by bilingual educators. A recommended term now is home language.

figure out how to express themselves in their new language. The children who are the most fluent readers and writers in Spanish are the ones engaging in the most experimentation with English or adding on to English. (p. 293)

These biliteracy researchers at the time invited practicing bilingual teachers and prospective teachers to take a perspective of strength about the students, their families, and their communities. They insisted that biliteracy at school needed to reflect the biliteracy children witnessed and experienced outside of school. Perhaps it was reading a menu at a restaurant, translating for someone else, receiving a letter in Spanish from a relative in Mexico or Central America, making a shopping list, listening to an adult read aloud at home, hearing an oral story, singing or listening to a song, or presenting their learning to an audience who spoke only English, only Spanish, or both.

These researchers insisted that children needed to be in control of their learning, including learning to read and write in English. They encouraged teachers of bilingual students to celebrate children's experimentation as writers. Their research demonstrated that children used what they knew in Spanish to write in English.[22] They explained to bilingual teachers the importance of offering children spaces to develop a strong literacy in their home language and access to rich content. They described the children in their research as active, filled with wonder, and fully capable of using language to express and learn. These researchers encouraged teachers to recognize the value of inviting children to use both English and Spanish to facilitate their learning. They also reminded teachers that they needed to create learning spaces where children could become readers and writers who understand the power of literacy for multiple and authentic purposes in and out of school.[23]

At the time, the field of biliteracy was centered on the idea that what bilinguals did was add language and support bilingual students in sustaining their bilingualism and biliteracy. As described earlier, researchers of the time had demonstrated the value of using students'

---

[22] See Hudelson & Serna, 1994.
[23] See Hudelson, 1987.

home language as an essential resource for learning to read and write in a second language, English, in the United States. This strong advocacy helped to ensure that children would first acquire literacy in their home language and informed teachers' practice in particular ways. For example, bilingual teachers initially engaged children in literacy experiences mostly in their home language. The assumption was that children came to school speaking only a language other than English, i.e., Spanish; it was never assumed that the child could come to school with bilingualism as their home language. Within a few years, the expectation in most schools was that the children would transfer the literacy they developed in their home language to English, and in most cases, they were never expected to use Spanish again at school. This was a belief about biliteracy that the teachers and administrators at Carolina's school, as well as bilingual university researchers, were striving to resist. Instead, they proposed a biliteracy program that would sustain the children's bilingualism over time.

New understandings about bilingualism, such as the notion that a bilingual person has a single linguistic repertoire, have yet to emerge. It was assumed that what children had was two separate named languages.[24] Despite what Carolina now recognizes regarding the conceptualization of the separation of named languages within the bilingual speaker as a limitation, these researchers and teacher educators challenged her to pose more profound questions about what biliteracy is and what it entails. Bilingual teacher educators did research in their school. They followed bilingual students for five years at Carolina's school.[25] In their child studies on biliteracy, they documented how the children's biliteracy developed over time.

As a new kindergarten teacher, Carolina brought years of experience to her pedagogy, having encountered literacy drills lacking meaningful context during her schooling in Bolivia. She recalls that perhaps a couple of months into the school year, she decided the bilingual children in her classroom were "drawing too much" and needed to shift their focus to letters and learn the alphabet

---

[24] See Otheguy, García & Reid, 2015.
[25] See Hudelson & Serna, 1994.

in preparation for reading. Carolina implemented a regimen of alphabet drills, beginning with the letter A, without considering which letters held meaning for the children or which ones they might already be familiar with. Unsurprisingly, the children became tense, and a few even cried, distressed by the loss of drawing as a way to express their feelings.

The bilingual and biliterate researchers visiting Carolina's class asked why she felt it was essential to make this change in the biliteracy experiences she was offering the children. Carolina explained her rationale: *"I cannot see how they are going to learn the letters with all this drawing."* The researchers listened attentively to her perspective and her understanding of what biliteracy entails. Through thoughtful questioning, they helped her recognize that the children were deeply engaged in constructing meaning as they drew and conveyed their messages using inventive spelling.[26] The researchers sat beside Carolina and, together with her, examined the children's journal entries over time. They invited her to consider how much learning was taking place as the children drew and wrote using inventive spelling. With their support, she began to notice that a child who had initially only drawn was now writing his name, along with the beginning letters of words in messages he wanted to convey. She started to recognize the importance of adopting a biliteracy stance that begins with the messages and words that matter to the children. She came to understand that at the heart of biliteracy lies the construction of meaning. Gradually, Carolina's understanding of what biliteracy is, what it entails, and its purposes began to shift.

Soon after, a study group was formed at this progressive school, bringing together all the kindergarten teachers. They read and discussed current professional literature on biliteracy, examined children's work, and studied their development of biliteracy over time. The biliteracy researchers often joined the group, contributing their insights and observations. With support from the school administration, the teachers began to reflect more deeply on their practice. Administrators, too, started to question how children

---

[26] See Edelsky, 1982; Ferreiro & Teberosky, 1982; Hudelson & Serna, 1994; Hudelson, 1984; Teale & Sulzby, 1986.

become biliterate through sharing their lived experiences with teachers—and how educators might help them learn to "read their worlds."[27] Additionally, the teachers at the school participated in a decade-long professional development initiative led by Patricia Carini, whose work on Descriptive Processes—developed in collaboration with her colleagues in Vermont—introduced a radically different way of thinking about teaching and learning to Carolina's school. Carini writes:

> The [descriptive] processes can enact and translate a vision of human possibility: a vision of children as complicated, interesting, and active in making meaning of the world and their own lives.[28]

Carini invited Carolina and her colleagues to create classroom spaces where children could learn in multimodal ways through the use of open-ended materials that offered them multiple entry points. Carini insisted that:

> Meaning is usually derived from firsthand experiences—to know something firsthand is to know it through yourself—therefore, it makes knowing and knowledge highly personal and places the person's meaning and interests squarely at the center of what we call learning.[29]

Carolina and her colleagues studied together children's biliteracy development over time by engaging in Descriptive Reviews of the Child as well as Descriptive Reviews of Children's work.[30] As teachers, they rediscovered that they—and the parents—knew a great deal about the children and were continually learning more through observation and daily interaction in their biliteracy classrooms. They developed a deep understanding of what it means to invite the whole child into the classroom, honoring diverse modes of thinking and learning, as well as the families' funds of knowledge. Carolina and the other teachers learned to address each child's development with deep care, observing and responding pedagogically to the unique

---

[27] See Freire, 1970.
[28] See Carini, 2001: 17.
[29] See Carini, 1977: 14.
[30] See Strieb *et al.*, 2011.

strengths and needs of every learner. They began to describe children from a perspective of strength rather than deficit.[31]

Over time, Carolina's kindergarten class evolved into a multi-age, Kindergarten-to-second-grade bilingual class. As the years passed, her theory and the other kindergarten teachers' theory of what biliteracy is and what it involves evolved. They began to understand how biliteracy could help the teachers and the students engage in an organic curriculum that reflected the socio-cultural and linguistic experiences of the students. The teachers at the school searched inside and outside the United States[32] for children's literature that offered them windows and mirrors[33] into who our students were. They fine-tuned their skills as teachers to engage the children in rich conversations about children's books. They developed critical insights into what Peterson and Eeds (2007) mean by the statement, "Literature is the illumination of life" (p. 18). The children made connections to their lived experiences as readers; they wondered and posed questions about their worlds, built relationships with authors by studying their work, and wrote their own stories, poems, songs, and letters.

They also engaged in integrated thematic studies that focused on local issues, such as the Arizona desert, and required them to examine their relationship with it critically. Carolina invited audiences to listen to the children's presentations during a museum day when the children engaged in multimodal presentations.[34] The bilingual children wrote and presented plays that challenged issues of gender, languaging practices, and female beauty. They learned about the work of Cesar Chavez and Dolores Huerta, leaders of the migrant workers' movement, and their commitment to addressing the injustices faced by farm workers in the Southwest. The teachers drew on the parents' funds of knowledge to enrich and affirm the children's learning.[35]

---

[31] See Carini & Himley, 2010.
[32] See Hudelson, Fournier, Espinosa & Bachman, 1994.
[33] See Sims Bishop, 1990.
[34] See Espinosa, Moore & Serna, 1998.
[35] See Moll *et al.*, 1992.

Carolina's experiences as a bilingual classroom teacher—including the rich professional dialogue at the elementary school where she taught in Phoenix, Arizona—helped her reframe her theoretical understanding of biliteracy and its implications. Most importantly, she learned that literacy and biliteracy are never neutral and can constantly shift depending on what one is trying to accomplish and what the person or group needs.[36] Carolina learned that careful observation of children's actions as biliterate learners mattered. She also learned that it mattered that she took a perspective of strength.[37] Carolina also learned to critically examine mandates and practices that offer a narrow view of what biliteracy is, i.e., biliteracy begins with the study and memorization of letter sounds out of context and without consideration of meaning for the individual child.

In contrast, she learned from Hudelson's work (2008), which stated, "a meaning-based view of phonics learning and teaching proposes that comprehending is the core of reading. It follows that the focus of children's beginning reading instruction should be on experiences that have meaning and purpose for them. Phonics teaching and learning is part of children's literacy development, but this development always occurs within the context of purposeful reading and writing experiences" (p. 656). The biliteracy researchers whose work she read argued vigorously for a meaning-based perspective for bilingual readers.

Translanguaging as a transformative stance in biliteracy

After a few decades, Carolina stopped teaching. During these years, the field of Biliteracy did not remain static. Understanding of this critical field continued to evolve and shift as researchers arrived at radically new conceptualizations of bilingualism and biliteracy. Over time, these new ideas have begun to be integrated into some teacher preparation programs.[38] Consequently, translanguaging pedagogy, as an integral component of biliteracy, is becoming increasingly accepted in classrooms, and an increasing number of teachers are

---

[36] See Goodman, 1996.
[37] See Carini, 1986.
[38] See Espinosa, Ascenzi-Moreno, Kleyn, Sanchez, 2020.

incorporating it into their practice. In what follows, I describe what Carolina's engagement and understanding of biliteracy might be like now in light of the current research on biliteracy development.

Carolina's understanding of what biliteracy is would continue to evolve and radically shift as she develops a vision for biliteracy that views bilingual children as having one linguistic repertoire. At the same time, "reject[ing] the notion of separate, bounded languages as defined by nation-states and their institutions and instead capture the meaning-making potential of the fluid semiotic practices of multilinguals."[39] These researchers emphasize the need to center and privilege the capacities of bilingual and biliterate speakers, writers, readers, composers, creators, and listeners.[40] It matters that bilinguals bring their entire linguistic and semiotic meaning-making capacities, as well as their bodies, their biographies, and geographies to each biliteracy encounter, García and Kleifgen (2019) insist. Bilingual educator Ofelia García (2021) writes about her grandchildren's translanguaging capacities as a vivid illustration of how children challenge that bilingualism exists in a binary. García writes:

> When they hear a new word used in meaningful ways for them, whether that word is said to be from "English" or "Spanish," they repeat it, pick it up, and add it to their linguistic repertoire. Their linguistic repertoire is not divided into two boxes – a box that contains Spanish and a box that contains English. Instead, their semiotic repertoire consists of a broad communicative network. That network consists of elements that some may call "linguistic" and others "paralinguistic," and that some may call "Spanish," whereas others call it "English." Regardless of the ways that are named as categories, they do not experience them as categories. They experience them as meaning-making resources that are always available for them to play and communicate with, although sometimes only some of the resources are used and not others. (p. 65)

---

[39] See García & Kleifgen, 2019: 4.
[40] See García & Espinosa, 2020.

García and Kleifgen (2019) and García (2021) remind us that these biliteracy practices are often profoundly influenced by power structures, including socio-political and economic factors. How they are understood, interpreted, measured, and valued by others depends on the white gaze of the listening subject.[41] It is not the language in isolation that is in question, but what is in place is a raciolinguistic ideology, Rosa and Flores (2015) assert. Enacting a translanguaging pedagogy is a political and transformative act, García and Kleifgen (2019) posit. This transformative theoretical and pedagogical stance centers on learners' rights to fully engage themselves in the classroom.[42] This is a conception of the bilingual student as a dynamic learner deeply involved in constructing meaning. It can only occur when their languaging practices are legitimized and capitalized as resources rather than being compared with an ideal but fictional[43] monolingual, García and Kleifgen (2019) argue. This stance positions biliterate students not from a deficit perspective but as learners filled with capacities to learn, to express, and to transform the curriculum as they engage in reading not just the word but the world.[44]

In Carolina's classroom, bilingual children would continue to engage in purposeful and authentic biliteracy engagements. Her pedagogy will center on the children and their capacities to construct meaning more fully through translanguaging. In her classroom, bilingualism will be the norm. The following biliteracy principles can guide her theoretical and pedagogical stance on biliteracy:

- Listening, talking, reading, writing, and multiple modalities are tools for thinking, learning, wondering, and expressing that are central to the development of literacy(ies). To construct meaning fully, students need to leverage their entire linguistic repertoire in literacy events, such as reading, drawing, dramatizing, and discussing a poem.

---

[41] See Flores & Rosa, 2015.
[42] See Espinosa & Ascenzi-Moreno, 2021.
[43] See Lugones, 2003.
[44] See Freire, 1970.

- Students must have opportunities to engage with texts that allow them to participate in more complex and deeper thinking. Relying solely on the new language limits their ability to participate. Additionally, children require access to texts that offer diverse perspectives and multiple entry points.
- Students need to be involved right from the beginning in literacy events and be encouraged to engage as thoughtful and critical thinkers, readers, writers, and creators. Translanguaging allows this engagement in learning to happen.
- Translanguaging opens doors not only for students' linguistic repertoire but also for families' and communities' ways of knowing, making them partners in children's literacy development. Translanguaging builds connections between the worlds of school, family, and community.[45]

Additionally, Ascenzi-Moreno, Espinosa, and Lerner-Quam (2022) challenge the notion that "when children are given the time and space to engage with texts through play and exploration, they seamlessly engage in the higher thinking skills that are valued in literacy instruction" (p. 126). These researchers emphasize that children need experiences that not only affirm and deepen their understanding of themselves and others but also help them build connections to their sociocultural backgrounds—while critically examining narratives that portray others from a deficit perspective. They add, "When literacy is expanded to include room for multilingualism and multimodalities, children have more time to explore creatively and to forge deep and dynamic connections to texts (p. 126)." These researchers remind us to question dominant assumptions about what constitutes academic and age-appropriate content in biliteracy engagements. They argue that it is essential to invite the whole child into the literacy event—physically, emotionally, socially, intellectually, and linguistically. Critical translanguaging and multimodal experiences enable teachers to create richer contexts for the development of biliteracy. Carolina, for example, could expand

---

[45] See Espinosa & Ascenzi-Moreno, 2021: 23.

her pedagogical repertoire by integrating translanguaging and multimodal practices into her daily work as a biliteracy teacher. Gort and Hamm Rodriguez (2022) emphasize that teachers can support "a vision of literacy that is expansive, purposeful, multimodal, and multilingual" (p. 203).

As Carolina's expertise in adopting a translanguaging stance grows, she might also create a learning environment where children can become critical language ethnographers—exploring the dynamic language practices within their communities.[46] In this study, the researchers documented how teachers, alongside their young bilingual students, explored not named languages but the dynamic ways in which language exists in communities—and the roles these practices play in the lives of community members. Through this community study, teachers and children examined the languaging practices of those living in the neighborhood where the school is located. This exploration led them to recognize issues of power and invisibility within the school, particularly regarding certain community-based language practices that were present among families but remained unacknowledged in the school setting. The supremacy of English reinforced this invisibility, as well as the partial visibility of Spanish and the constraints of a dual-language program that centers only on these two named languages.

Through this inquiry project, teachers blurred the traditional boundaries between school and community, which often remain disconnected. Students engaged as ethnographers, spending time outside the classroom to research the community's languaging practices. They participated in authentic biliteracy experiences grounded in translanguaging, asking questions, interviewing community members, and recording their observations and findings. Back in the classroom, they discussed and documented what they had learned, deepening their understanding of language in lived contexts.

These engagements led students to think critically about the hegemony of English and to question why translanguaging practices in their communities were not reflected in their schools. They began to advocate for viewing these practices not as exceptions but as the

---

[46] See Sánchez, Espinet, & Hunt, 2022: 152.

norm. As Sánchez, Espinet, and Hunt (2022) write, "Students and teachers were not only able to access their full language repertoire freely but also were able to recognize that practice in themselves and others" (p. 145).

Similarly, Carolina could create space in her classroom to study the languaging practices of families and other community members. Her biliterate students could engage in transformative inquiry that examines how language exists in their lived experiences, families, and communities. Such an approach would ensure that traditionally invisible languaging practices become present, welcomed, and affirmed in the school. It would also challenge the limitations of a dual language model that rigidly privileges only Spanish and English, ignoring the rich, multilingual realities of students, their families, and their communities.

The potential to enrich and develop a more complex and relevant curriculum that supports students' biliteracy has also emerged in classrooms where students engage in Freire's (1970) problem-posing education. Poza and Sites (2022) describe an ethnographic study conducted in a dual-language setting with two eighth-grade social studies classrooms. In this study, the teacher approached a unit on Westward Expansion—a district-mandated topic in U.S. history—by centering students' voices and choices through a problem-posing education stance.[47] The teacher engaged students in the social studies curriculum on Westward Expansion by integrating a current, locally relevant issue—gentrification in their community—into the historical study. In this unit, students were positioned as subjects rather than objects of learning, and the teacher adopted a dialogical stance toward the curriculum. As Poza and Sites (2022) describe, students examined both primary and secondary sources—including print materials, videos, and audio—related to both Westward Expansion and gentrification. They explored these topics from multiple perspectives, drawing on their full linguistic repertoires to construct deeper meaning. Through this process, students agentively analyzed and evaluated the implications of both historical displacement—through the study of Westward Expansion in the United States—and

---

[47] See Freire, 1970.

contemporary displacement, as seen in the gentrification of their community.

These researchers describe how translanguaging allowed them to "grapple with points of tension in the overly facile critiques of both gentrification and Westward Expansion with which they entered the unit."[48] Their findings challenged assumptions they had when they started the study about race, class, and gentrification. Students presented their findings to the school community and district personnel by preparing multimodal presentations, including slideshows, essays, animations, and other formats. Throughout the study, students' identities as biliterate thinkers filled with agency shifted. Students not only acquired a deeper and more complex understanding of these topics, but they also developed their voice and agency. Similarly, Carolina could explore with her students a current issue the neighborhood is facing by designing a study based on Freire's (1970) problem-posing education. Likewise, according to the study developed by Poza and Sites (2022), Carolina could help her students position themselves differently in relation to their biliteracy identities.

Given the demands of the 21st century, Carolina might ask herself how she can bring a purposeful and relevant pedagogical and theoretical stance on computational literacies into her classroom. These are literacies that many of her students already know and need to critically engage with in their day-to-day lives as part of the biliteracy experiences required in the 21st century. Computational literacies researchers Vogel, Hoadley, Castillo, and Ascenzi-Moreno (2020) invite educators to consider the ethical questions regarding computer science (CS), multiliteracies, and translanguaging within the context of equity and justice. They insist on a computer science pedagogy that centers on learners constructing meaning and communicating for authentic purposes and expression.

Vogel et al. (2020) argue vehemently that educators need to adopt a translanguaging and multiliteracies stance toward computing education, ensuring that learners can capitalize on their entire linguistic repertoire, not only to participate more fully but also to

---

[48] See Poza & Sites, 2022: 88.

transform the field of CS and make it more equitable and just. These researchers argue for a stance toward CS that ensures a multiplicity of voices that capitalize on students' translanguaging capacities. These researchers contend that:

> As much as computing literacies are shaped by digital technologies, they are also socially constructed and shared by discourse communities that evolve over time. As more people, especially those who are members of racial, economic, and gender groups who have been excluded from and marginalized in computer science, participate in computing literacies, not only do they learn the discourses of computing communities, but they shape and transform those communities and discourses. (n/p)

In the study by Vogel et al. (2020), bilingual middle-grade students were invited to remix the telenovela genre with their creative ideas, including their biliteracy talents and semiotic repertoires, and utilize the Scratch interface and code to experiment, program, and design their telenovelas using the Scratch script and codes. Carolina could engage as a teacher first by becoming a learner of these computer literacies, thereby bringing her understanding of computational science up to date. Next, she could develop her pedagogy to integrate these 21st-century practices into her daily practice, ensuring that her students have the power and potential to transform CS communities where bilingualism is the norm. It is, after all, by engaging critically in this discourse that young biliterate learners can disrupt the silencing of voices that often privilege just a few, particularly when it comes to computational literacies. Akin to these researchers, Carolina can ensure that "code is not something to be learned in a vacuum."[49] Coding then becomes a form of expression within a community that is never static, that is purposeful, useful, and socially constructed. Carolina's students might further complement the research by Vogel et al. (2020) by inviting them to critically analyze the role of gender and issues of colorism in Latin American telenovelas, as she encourages her students to integrate CS while adopting this critical perspective from a biliteracy stance.

---

[49] See Vogel *et al.*, n/p.

Finally, with the possibilities and challenges that Artificial Intelligence (AI) brings to the field of biliteracy, Carolina would need to continue dialoging with other educators who are asking what biliteracy is for in light of these new technological developments. What purposes does biliteracy serve? What possibilities does AI offer multilingual writers and readers as a tool for thinking and as an aid to develop new ways of composing in creative and relevant ways?

Conclusion

In this chapter, I have strived to describe the importance of considering a teacher's theory(ies) of what biliteracy is and what it involves. Theory(ies) about biliteracy that centers on purpose and authenticity needs to be nurtured within the teacher's daily practice and professional development. We cannot assume that these can be imposed or consumed by teachers. I illustrate how these shifts in understanding occur within a dialogical space that centers on the teacher's emerging questions and issues of practice. As I described in Carolina's stories, biliteracy pedagogy emerges from a teacher's own experiences as a learner, her evolving theories of how children learn, the interactions she has with colleagues, as well as other more knowledgeable learners,[50] including the texts she reads. A theory of biliteracy is also integrally connected to the teacher's ability to develop a curriculum that is relevant, meaningful, purposeful, and authentic. Bilingual learners must have opportunities to engage in problem-posing education experiences where their sense of agency and voice as biliterate citizens can be heard and strengthened. When working with emergent bilingual students, this curriculum emerges as the educator grows in her understanding of the transformative power of translanguaging and critical perspectives regarding raciolinguistic ideologies.

The field of biliteracy has undergone a radical shift and continues to evolve. The research on translanguaging, raciolinguistic ideologies, computer science, and multimodalities has challenged the field of biliteracy to stop creating narratives of deficit regarding the languaging practices of bilingual students. Instead, these theoretical

---

[50] See Vygotsky, 1978.

principles emphasize creating learning spaces that liberate the creative, resourceful, and critical capacities of emergent bilinguals. These are spaces where bilingual students can do more than subsist; they can blossom, as researcher Betina Love (2020) vehemently argues. Educator Paulo Freire (1970) adds that:

> Education as the practice of freedom—as opposed to education as the practice of domination—denies that man [people] is abstract, isolated, independent, and unattached to the world; it also denies that the world exists as a reality apart from people. Authentic reflection considers neither abstract man [people] nor the world without people, but people in their relations with the world. (p. 81)

The biliteracy stance (theory/ies) a teacher takes determines the experiences they provide their bilingual students. It matters that she helps them develop as biliterate citizens who are fully awake and engaged in the world. Young bilingual learners can only do this if the biliteracy engagements teachers invite them to challenge them to understand and act in the world by taking a critical and subjective agentive stance.[51] Bilingual educator Ofelia García (2021) reminds us that "it is essential to ensure that children can use language to play, tell a story, express feelings, solve problems, ask and answer questions" (p. 67). As educators of bilingual students committed to preparing them for the demands of the 21st century, we must continuously (re)examine our theories about biliteracy as we seek practices that enable us to acknowledge, build, sustain, and critically engage in complex biliteracy practices.

---

[51] See Lugones, 2003.

2.4. Equitable Assessment Practices for Emergent Bilingual Students
Marcela Ossa Parra

David is a second-grade Spanish-English emergent bilingual student in Lucy's English-only classroom. He attended a 6-hour early childhood program from the age of 2 to 6 before moving to the United States. Lucy conducts oral reading assessments throughout the school year to gauge her students' reading development and design instruction informed by their strengths and areas for growth. In addition to the students' reading level, she considers their interests and linguistic strengths when selecting the assessment texts. For David's assessment, Lucy chose "El Perro con Sombrero," A Bilingual Doggy Tale by Derek Taylor Kent. She knew David would love this book because he had just gotten a puppy, and he would be able to put his Spanish skills to use. Lucy took Spanish courses in high school, during which she mainly developed listening and reading skills. She leverages her Spanish skills to understand the holistic reading development of her emergent bilingual students. David first read the Spanish version of the book fluently, with only a few self-corrections. During the English oral reading, Lucy noticed that he had difficulties decoding letter combinations such as "ew, ow, ou, th." She also noted that he omitted words such as "of, the, a, in." After reading the book in both languages, David drew from his entire linguistic repertoire to retell the story. Lucy noticed that, in comparison with the earlier oral reading assessment, David included more English sentences in his retelling. Based on this assessment, Lucy decided to provide extra phonics instruction on the letter combinations unfamiliar to David, as they do not exist in Spanish. She also plans to teach David to follow the reading with his finger and watch out for short words. Finally, she is excited to see David's reading progress in both languages and plans to continue encouraging him to read bilingual books.

The above vignette illustrates Lucy's holistic approach to oral reading assessments in which she considers what her emergent bilingual (EB) students know and can do across their languages. These assessments guide Lucy's reading instruction by providing accurate information about her students' knowledge and skills. Like many teachers in immigrant-receiving countries, Lucy teaches in a monolingual program where many different languages are represented, and she has adapted her assessment practices to tap into her EB students' linguistic resources. Unfortunately, in many cases, assessment practices for EB students have had detrimental consequences on their schooling since they are expected to perform monolingually in a language they are just learning.[52] To design equitable and accurate assessments, it is necessary to shift from a monolingual to a multilingual perspective that holistically encompasses EB students' linguistic repertoires, knowledge, and skills.[53] Adopting a multilingual perspective does not require teachers to know their students' additional languages. While sharing a language with students can be an asset, it is unrealistic to expect teachers to be fluent in all the languages present in super-diverse classrooms.

This chapter focuses on language and literacy assessments in monolingual elementary programs that serve a multilingual student body in which some students are learning the language of instruction (e.g., English). While I present specific examples from research on language and literacy assessment practices, I also provide suggestions on how these examples may be extended to other content areas. The chapter begins with the theoretical underpinnings that inform a multilingual perspective on assessing EB students, followed by a presentation of research on holistic literacy assessments for elementary students. After this, I propose four research-based, equitable assessment practices and end with suggestions for professional development.

Multilingual perspective on assessment

Current research on the education of EB students is stimulating an educational paradigm shift from monolingualism to multilingualism. From a multilingual perspective, becoming bilingual is conceived as a dynamic rather than an additive process.[54] Additive approaches to bilingualism are informed by monolingual perspectives, which view bilinguals as the sum of two monolinguals with distinct language

---

[52] See García & Kleifgen, 2018; McClain *et al.*, 2021.
[53] See Chalhoub-Deville, 2019; García & Kleifgen, 2018.
[54] See Cenoz & Gorter, 2011; García & Sylvan, 2011.

systems.[55] From an additive approach, bilinguals are expected to function monolingually in each of their languages. For example, it is assumed that true bilinguals have native-like language proficiency and can deactivate their additional languages to perform like monolingual speakers.[56] These assumptions inform the use of monolingual assessments, which are normed for monolingual populations, to assess EB students.

A dynamic approach to bilingualism informs the design of more accurate assessments for EB students since it highlights the flexible and complex ways they use language.[57] Rather than being conceived as having separate languages, bilinguals are viewed as having a unified linguistic repertoire that is always active, even when they are using a single language.[58] From a dynamic perspective, bilingual development is a gradual process through which learners build on their current language practices, knowledge, and skills to expand their linguistic repertoires.[59] Furthermore, bilingual development is tied to the available contexts of language use and the myriad of language practices in which bilinguals engage. Translanguaging is one of these language practices in which bilinguals flexibly use their linguistic repertoires without separating their languages to accomplish their communicative and meaning-making purposes.[60]

Assessment from a dynamic perspective entails documenting the complexity of EB students' language and literacy performances by creating a holistic picture that captures their skills and knowledge across their linguistic repertoires.[61] In this sense, the learning of EB students must be understood on their own terms, without being compared to that of their monolingual counterparts.[62] The following section presents research on elementary school literacy assessments

---

[55] See García & Sylvan, 2011; Ortega, 2013.
[56] See Ortega, 2013.
[57] See García & Kleifgen, 2018; García & Sylvan, 2011.
[58] See Otheguy *et al.*, 2019.
[59] See García & Li, 2014.
[60] See Otheguy *et al.*, 2019.
[61] See Bauer *et al.*, 2020; Butvilofsky *et al.*, 2021; Espinosa & Ascenzi-Moreno, 2021; Van Viegen & Jang, 2021.
[62] See García & Kleifgen, 2020; Noguerón-Liu, 2020.

that address EB students' dynamic language and literacy development.

Holistic language and literacy assessments

As illustrated in the introductory vignette, holistic literacy assessments view literacy as a unified process encompassing students' entire linguistic repertoires.[63] Furthermore, a holistic approach entails recognizing that all assessments always have a language component.[64] Literacy, social studies, math, and science, among others, have language demands that confound EB students' knowledge and skills. For example, by using a bilingual book, Lucy, the teacher featured in the introductory vignette, could distinguish David's reading comprehension from his English learning process. In addition, the distinction between language and content knowledge and skills is an opportunity to assess language in a contextualized manner.[65] Traditional approaches view language in assessments as a decontextualized, static, and individual performance, while from a multilingual perspective, language is considered dynamic, situated, and collective.[66] In this sense, holistic assessments provide opportunities for EB students to use their entire linguistic repertoires in the context of meaningful and relevant tasks.

Another important distinction is whether the evaluation focuses on the general or specific linguistic performance of EB students.[67] A student's general linguistic performance encompasses their ability to use any language feature in their linguistic repertoire to complete a task. In contrast, their language-specific performance refers to the ability to use the features assigned to a particular named language (e.g., English, French). This distinction enables teachers to make informed decisions about the use of their students' linguistic repertoires in the assessment process. For example, in the introductory vignette, Lucy wanted to know what David could do with language in general, so she selected a bilingual book and

---

[63] See García & Kleifgen, 2018; Kabuto, 2017.
[64] See Fine & Furtak, 2020; Noguerón-Liu *et al.*, 2020.
[65] See Fine & Furtak, 2020.
[66] See Chalhoub-Deville, 2019.
[67] See García *et al.*, 2017.

stimulated him to use his entire linguistic repertoire during the retelling. However, as David expands his linguistic repertoire, she might want to know more about his specific performance in the new language, so she might ask him to retell the story in English only.

García and Kliefgen (2018) propose several ways to include students' linguistic repertoires in assessments. For example, assessments may be administered in both languages. In this case, the test is first administered in the language of instruction, and the items that the student did not answer correctly are re-administered in the student's home language. This approach enables teachers to assess students' knowledge and skills independently of the language used in the test. Another approach to bilingual assessments is to present the questions in one language and allow students to respond in their other language. With this approach, teachers have the flexibility to adapt the assessments to their students' strengths and evaluation purposes. For instance, suppose the purpose of the assessment is to gauge students' knowledge, skills, and general linguistic performance. In that case, the evaluation questions may be presented in the language of instruction, and students answer them in their home language.

In contrast, if the goal is to assess language-specific performances, the questions may be posed in the home language to ensure that students understand them and that the answers are provided in the language being assessed. Finally, translanguaging is another approach to assessment design that encourages students to utilize their entire linguistic repertoire during the assessment. In this case, the design of the evaluation questions is adapted to the students' language strengths, and they are encouraged to utilize their entire linguistic repertoire to demonstrate what they know and can do.

The remainder of this section presents three holistic language and literacy assessments for elementary students, illustrating how teachers can provide a more comprehensive and nuanced portrayal of their EB students' knowledge and skills.

Oral reading assessments

The introductory vignette is an example of an oral reading assessment. These formative evaluations capture elementary students' contextualized reading behaviors and habits, contributing essential information to inform instruction.[68] In these assessments, reading is viewed as a meaning-making process guided by three language cueing systems: meaning, syntactic, and visual.[69] Miscues, defined as observed responses that differ from the expected response (e.g., word substitutions/omissions/insertions, self-corrections), provide windows into readers' meaning-making processes. The analysis of readers' miscues offers qualitative and quantitative data on their oral reading performances and retellings.[70] Miscue analysis typically has four components: (1) introduction to the text, (2) listening to and documenting student reading, (3) retelling, and (4) feedback..[71] In addition, miscue analysis can serve as a culturally relevant assessment tool for studying reading across different spoken and written languages, as it provides a multidimensional perspective on how bilingual readers construct meaning.[72]

Ascenzi-Moreno's (2018) research with three elementary teachers who served EB students in different program types (monolingual and bilingual) revealed how these teachers enacted responsive adaptations to address the role that their students' language and cultural knowledge played in their reading performance. These responsive adaptations opened new possibilities for the teachers to tap into their students' language resources and interpret how they leveraged their entire linguistic repertoires in their reading. For example, during the text introduction, teachers may encourage students to connect their prior knowledge and the text and, when possible, use their additional languages to open a space for translanguaging. Translanguaging enables EB students to provide more detailed and complex retellings since they have access to their entire linguistic repertoires. When teachers are unfamiliar with students' additional languages, they may have them write a retelling rather than an oral one and then seek translation support from a

---

[68] See Ascenzi-Moreno, 2018.
[69] See Goodman, 1996.
[70] See Kabuto, 2017.
[71] See Ascenzi-Moreno, 2018.
[72] See Kabuto, 2017.

colleague or community member.[73] As Noguerón-Liu and colleagues (2020) propose, "understanding linguistic repertoires can be a collective effort where the adults in the child's life can explore how various resources come together when children learn to read" (p. 431).

When listening and documenting student reading, expanding the miscue analysis form to include columns for registering potential pronunciation and language miscues, such as vocabulary,[74] is relevant. These miscues are debriefed after the oral reading to establish distinctions between language and literacy skills. For example, a Spanish-English bilingual student systematically substituted the word "cart" with "car" during an oral reading. When the evaluator debriefed the student on this miscue, she learned that shopping carts are called "cars/carros" in Spanish.[75] Ascenzi-Moreno (2018) presents another example in which a boy read "beard" instead of "bird." When the teacher asked him about this word, she discovered that it was a pronunciation miscue in which he had sounded out the word in Spanish. By being attentive and responsive to how EB students leverage their entire linguistic repertoires in the reading process, teachers gain a more nuanced understanding of their students' reading abilities and identify opportunities for offering targeted feedback that addresses students' reading strengths and weaknesses across languages and their specific language skills.

Biliterate writing assessments

Biliterate Writing Assessments are formative assessments conducted throughout the school year to achieve a holistic understanding of EB students' literacy development by capturing their reading and writing skills across their linguistic repertoires.[76] In addition to reading, it is

---

[73] See Ascenzi-Moreno, 2018.
[74] Miscue analysis forms typically include four columns for documenting self-corrections, meaning, syntax and visual miscues. See Kabuto (2017) for an in-depth description of the miscue analysis procedure, and Ascenzi-Moreno (2018) for a detailed presentation of responsive adaptations.
[75] See Noguerón-Liu *et al.*, 2020.
[76] See Butvilofsky *et al.*, 2021; Escamilla *et al.*, 2014.

also relevant to include writing assessments, as they provide another window into how students make meaning of print as they produce their texts. The Biliterate Writing Assessment consists of having students respond to three similar but not duplicative prompts in two named languages (e.g., English and Spanish), addressing different genres studied across the school year (e.g., informational, opinion, and narrative). The set of texts produced by the students for each genre is jointly analyzed to determine their understandings of language in the discourse (stages of the genre, transitions, punctuation, capitalization), sentence/phrase (types of sentences, cohesion between sentences), and phonemic/orthographic levels (phonemic and graphemic awareness).[77]

Butvilofsky and her colleagues (2020) compared the performance of a group of EB second-grade students in these assessments with their performance in the Dynamic Indicators of Basic Literacy Skills (DIBELS)[78] which is a formative assessment widely used to inform literacy instruction in the United States. While these students performed below benchmarks in the DIBELS throughout the school year, the examination of their biliterate writing revealed their literacy knowledge and skills, as well as their growth during the year. The DIBELS results indicated that these students required remedial reading instruction due to deficiencies in phonemic awareness and decoding skills. However, their writing samples in the biliterate writing assessment showed their knowledge of phonemic and orthographic principles across languages and their ability to connect words and ideas in meaningful ways.

While Biliterate Writing Assessments are more suited for bilingual programs due to their high language and literacy demands in two named languages, they can also be adapted for use in monolingual programs. For example, rather than having students write in both languages, they might be encouraged to use their entire linguistic repertoire and visual resources to create the writing samples. These writing samples can be analyzed to gain a deeper understanding of

---

[77] See Chapter 7 in Escamilla *et al.*, 2014 for a detailed description of this writing assessment.
[78] See Good & Kaminski, 2002.

how they approach texts at the discourse, sentence/phrase, and phonemic/orthographic levels.

Bilingual language assessments

A common indicator of children's language development is their vocabulary knowledge. Additionally, vocabulary knowledge is closely tied to reading comprehension.[79] Vocabulary assessments are typically conducted using monolingual measures normed for monolingual populations. When the vocabulary knowledge of EB children is measured using monolingual tests, it appears that their monolingual counterparts have a vocabulary advantage.[80] However, this monolingual vocabulary advantage disappears when the vocabulary knowledge of EB students is accounted for in both languages. To gain a complete picture of EB students' receptive vocabulary knowledge, it is necessary to assess their total receptive vocabulary (the number of words in both languages combined), their conceptual vocabulary (the number of concepts for which the child has a word in either language), and translational equivalents (concepts for which the child has a word in both languages).[81]

McClain and colleagues (2020) compared the performance of Spanish-English bilingual second- and fourth-grade students in three receptive vocabulary assessments: English-only, Spanish-only, and conceptually scored bilingual. They used the Peabody Picture Vocabulary Test[82] as the English-only measure, normed for English-monolingual children—the *Test de Vocabulario de Imágenes*—as the Spanish-only measure, normed for monolingual Spanish children, and the Receptive One-Word Picture Vocabulary Test—Spanish Bilingual Edition as a conceptually scored measure, normed for Spanish-English bilingual children. These receptive vocabulary tests measure whether students can identify a word by showing them four pictures and asking them to point at the picture of the target word (e.g., apple). In a conceptually scored receptive vocabulary test, students receive credit for knowing the concept, regardless of whether

---

[79] See McKeown, 2019.
[80] See Gampe *et al.*, 2018; McClain *et al.*, 2021.
[81] See Gampe *et al.*, 2018.
[82] See Dunn & Dunn, 2007.

it is expressed in one language or the other. Questions are first presented in one language (e.g., English). If the student cannot identify the picture of the word in that language, they are asked again if they can identify it in another language (e.g., Spanish).

The results of comparing EB students' performance across three different tests (English-only, Spanish-only, and conceptually scored) revealed that the conceptually scored test made a significant difference in portraying EB students' receptive vocabulary knowledge.[83] While the monolingual assessments normed for monolingual populations represented EB students as lagging behind national monolingual norms, the conceptually scored evaluation demonstrated that, on average, the EB students in the research study schools were performing better than the national bilingual norms. In this sense, the conceptually scored vocabulary assessment enabled students to demonstrate their linguistic knowledge. When the study results were presented to the teachers, their perceptions of their EB students changed.[84] They were no longer seen as deficient compared to their monolingual peers but as having rich linguistic knowledge that teachers could tap into to guide their learning.

Equitable assessment practices

Based on the research described above, I propose four equitable assessment practices for elementary EB students that can be extended to other content areas (e.g., math, science, and social studies).

Learn about your students' multilingualism

A starting point for broadening the view of language and literacy in the classroom is to learn about EB students' language backgrounds, practices, and bilingual development trajectories.[85] Teachers may gather information from their students and parents to create a multilingual profile that provides insights into their linguistic realities and resources and how these can be leveraged in their learning process.[86] The multilingual profile encompasses information such as

---

[83] See McClain *et al.*, 2021.
[84] See McClain *et al.*, 2021.
[85] See Briceño, 2021; García *et al.*, 2017; Guzman-Orth *et al.*, 2017.
[86] See García *et al.*, 2017; Guzman-Orth *et al.*, 2017.

the following: (1) demographic characteristics (e.g., country of birth, time at the receiving country, parents' country of birth); (2) language experiences (e.g., languages that the child has been exposed to, student's language use, household language practices); (3) bilingual development (e.g., simultaneous, sequential); (4) literacy experiences (e.g., home literacy practices – reading letters, religious practices, language brokering for parents); and (5) educational experiences (e.g., participation in prior formal and informal educational programs).[87] In addition, creating a multilingual profile helps appreciate the diversity among EB students. Even within the same language group (e.g., Spanish), there is significant variability in terms of country of origin, socioeconomic status, culture, age of exposure to two languages, fluency in both languages and the languages spoken by parents.[88]

Design culturally and linguistically appropriate assessments

School curricula, in general, and assessments, in particular, perpetuate social hierarchies by representing only dominant knowledge, language, and culture (e.g., white, monolingual, Eurocentric, middle-class norms). To achieve more equitable assessment practices, it is necessary to ensure that they are culturally and linguistically appropriate. This entails expanding the notion of what constitutes valid knowledge in the curriculum to include the perspectives of the community and family. To achieve this, teachers can establish partnerships with community members to build on the cultural values and knowledge EB students bring to the classroom.[89] These partnerships enable teachers to gather information for designing assessment tasks related to the students' community's realities,[90] select culturally relevant texts and prompts, and integrate families' knowledge and participation in the assessment process.[91] For example, families and community members are essential resources for translating and interpreting literacy assessments.

---

[87] See García *et al.*, 2017; Guzman-Orth *et al.*, 2017.
[88] See Guzman-Orth *et al.*, 2017; Noguerón-Liu, 2020.
[89] See Fine & Furtak, 2020; Noguerón-Liu *et al.*, 2020.
[90] See Fine & Furtak, 2020.
[91] See Noguerón-Liu *et al.*, 2020.

Additionally, it is necessary to review assessment items to ensure that they are culturally and linguistically appropriate. Culturally appropriate items do not include referents or content that could have unintended meanings for different students (e.g., represent stereotypical views of various cultural groups) and do not give an unfair advantage to one cultural group over another (e.g., presuppose prior knowledge of the dominant culture).[92] Linguistically appropriate items are formulated with accessible language for multilingual students. For example, the items do not contain complex syntactic structures or vocabulary that would be unfamiliar to EB students compared to their peers who have more expertise in the language of the assessment.[93]

Use contextualized tasks and include mediation practices

EB students may be deemed unable to engage in complex content because they are not yet proficient in the language of instruction. However, it is possible to design contextualized and authentic tasks based on relevant, real-life situations. These tasks are performance-based in the sense that they ask students to make a product or perform an action (e.g., reading, writing, explaining, interpreting) and enable them to leverage different skills to show what they know and can do.[94] In addition, to ensure that the task description and instructions are accessible to EB students, teachers may integrate scaffolds and modifications such as reducing the complexity of linguistic structures, using bullet points to break apart ideas, using bold type for emphasis, dividing prompts into smaller units, and using graphic organizers, rubrics, and checklists to make the task expectations clear.[95] Furthermore, it is relevant to integrate mediation practices to create a supportive assessment environment in which students' linguistic and cultural resources and experiences are integrated. Mediation practices enable the evaluator to consider student performance independently and with moderate assistance.[96]

---

[92] See Fine & Furtak, 2020.
[93] See Martiniello, 2008.
[94] See Fine & Furtak, 2020; García & Kleifgen, 2018; Guzman-Orth *et al.*, 2017.
[95] See Fine & Furtak, 2020.
[96] See García *et al.*, 2017; Guzman-Orth *et al.*, 2017.

Conduct conceptual scoring to distinguish language from content

As mentioned before, content assessments not only provide information about students' content knowledge and skills but also about their language skills.[97] Conceptual scoring helps teachers disentangle content from language by focusing on what EB students know and can do when they have access to their entire linguistic repertoires. In this sense, teachers assess students' understanding of the content without regard to the language in which the student gave the response.[98]

Professional development

The above practices provide a starting point for reflecting on the design of equitable assessments for elementary EB students. To transform these practices into action, it is essential to engage in ongoing professional development that focuses on building assessment literacy, which encompasses the knowledge, skills, and strategies for engaging in classroom-based language assessment.[99] Educators need to be knowledgeable about their EB students' language and literacy development to understand what they know and can do holistically.[100] It is also necessary to grapple with ideologies about race and language and how they shape how culturally and linguistically diverse children's languages are viewed.[101]

Conclusion

There is agreement in the research on EB students' assessment about the need to consider their entire linguistic repertoires to gain a full picture of what they know and can do. This entails adopting a more dynamic and holistic approach to language, one that acknowledges the varied ways in which EB students draw upon their linguistic resources. In this approach to assessment, teachers are encouraged to build networks with collaborators who support them in translating or

---

[97] See Fine & Furtak, 2020; Noguerón-Liu *et al.*, 2020.
[98] See Guzman-Orth *et al.*, 2017; Lopez *et al.*, 2017.
[99] See Van Viegen & Jang, 2021: 295.
[100] See Guzman-Orth *et al.*, 2017.
[101] See Ascenzi-Moreno & Seltzer, 2021; Guzman-Orth *et al.*, 2017.

serving as interpreters when collecting information from EB students who speak additional languages. These networks also provide opportunities for learning about the students and the community. This knowledge informs the design of culturally relevant assessment tasks that provide strengths-based perspectives, focusing on what students know rather than what they lack.

2.5. The Linguistic Repertoire from the Perspective of Lived Experience[102]
Brigitta Busch

Over the last twenty years, several hundred people in Carinthia, the Balkans, South Africa, Vienna, and elsewhere have entrusted me with their language biographies through interviews or autoethnographic accounts. To begin, I have selected a text from these narratives written by a student during a seminar. Since the author initially believed that she grew up monolingual, this text is not about what is generally understood to be multilingualism. I will refer back to this text periodically to illustrate this point.

The student describes in hindsight the moment when she changed schools—moving from a small town to a secondary school in the state capital—as the first time she consciously experienced not belonging: "It was a very hierarchically structured school, most of the students came from the 'upper classes' and I felt very insecure and a little inadequate with my rural, colloquial language compared to the 'big-city High German' spoken there."

It is an experience that everyone is familiar with: belonging or not belonging due to diverse ways of speaking. Accordingly, only those who have never had this experience, who have never felt themselves to be "different" when speaking, would be considered monolingual. From this perspective, the focus is not on how many or which languages someone speaks—that is, whether they can claim an L2, L3, or Ln in addition to their first language (L1), using linguistic terminology. I am particularly interested in demonstrating how linguistic variation constructs notions of belonging or difference and, above all, how such constructions are experienced as linguistic exclusions and inclusions.[103]

Even a short excerpt like the one just quoted makes it clear that several factors need to be considered when analyzing linguistic

---

[102] This chapter is based on the 2012 inaugural lecture held at the University of Vienna.
[103] See Busch, 2021a.

practices. For one, speakers participate in different social spaces at various times or even simultaneously—in the example of the student, these include the town, the city, the family, and the school. In each of these spaces, different rules of language use and different habits apply; in sociolinguistics, one would say that different language regimes characterize them. Others are language ideologies, i.e., discourses about language and "correct" language use, which express and establish hierarchies—in our example, the power differential between the "standard language" of the capital and the rural dialect. Finally, the linguistic repertoire that speakers bring into a specific interaction context must be considered, which is the actual topic of this chapter.

First, the concept of the linguistic repertoire as it was developed in sociolinguistics must be addressed. Then, I will explore how today's perspective can expand the concept of repertoire by taking the lived experience of language (*Spracherleben*)—that is, the perspective of the speaking subject—as a starting point. In particular, I am interested in how bodily, emotional, and historical-political dimensions of the lived experience of language are manifested in the repertoire. In the final section, I use the example of a nine-year-old's language portrait to illustrate how children represent and discuss their linguistic resources and aspirations.

The concept of repertoire

The concept of the linguistic repertoire goes back to the anthropologist and linguist John Gumperz. Based on his analysis of linguistic interactions, Gumperz (1964) developed the concept of linguistic repertoire from his research in the 1950s and 1960s in two medium-sized rural communities: Khalapur, eighty miles north of Delhi, and Hemnes in the Norwegian Rana Fjord, both of which were in the process of becoming more urban. As a framework for his analysis, Gumperz employs the concept of the speech community—not defined in essentialist terms, but rather as one established through regular interaction over an extended period of time. The linguistic repertoire, says Gumperz, "contains all the accepted ways of formulating messages. It provides the weapons of everyday communication. Speakers choose among this arsenal in accordance with the meanings they wish to convey."[104]

The repertoire is understood as a whole that encompasses those languages, dialects, styles, registers, and codes, in short, all routines that characterize interaction in everyday life. It thus includes the entirety of the linguistic means available to speakers in a speech community to convey (social) meaning. According to Gumperz, although it is up to the individual speaker to decide on the use of linguistic means, this freedom of choice is subject to both grammatical and social constraints. It is limited by generally accepted conventions that serve to classify ways of expressing oneself as informal, technical, literary, or humorous. "The social etiquette of language choice is learned along with grammatical rules, and once internalized, it becomes a part of our linguistic equipment" (ibid.).

Gumperz's concept represents a significant step. It does not focus on individual languages or varieties as a given but starts from the possibility of variation that prevails in linguistic interactions. Gumperz concludes from this that once acquired, a repertoire is available like an "arsenal," a toolbox that can be accessed at any time. This instrumentalist character that Gumperz ascribes to the repertoire must be questioned from today's perspective, however, because language choice is not only guided by rules and conventions but is also influenced by what we call the lived experience of language. Gumperz, who had to emigrate to the USA in 1939 to escape National Socialism and was thus exposed to a new linguistic environment, was aware of this. He notes that "stylistic choice becomes a problem when we are away from our accustomed social surroundings" (ibid.).

Lived experience of language

In his concept, Gumperz assumed relatively stable speech communities with a clearly defined repertoire. A possible change of environment, which can lead to problems in language choice, appears to be a special case, so to speak. This assumption, which

---

[104] See Gumperz, 1964: 138.

was justified in the 1960s, can no longer be upheld today. Steven Vertovec (2007) coined the term *super-diversity* to describe the phenomenon of globally expanding mobility, which gives rise to new, increasingly complex social formations and is linked to processes of inclusion and exclusion. Network practices are emerging beyond traditional affiliations, resulting in speakers often participating simultaneously in different, temporarily established, and territorially disconnected networks.

Just starting school or, as in the text quoted at the beginning, changing schools can be experienced as a language choice problem in Gumperz's sense: a surprising, confusing, sometimes shocking perception that one's language repertoire does not "fit" or does not quite "fit." A feeling of being out of place, of being a misfit, of being in the wrong place with the wrong language. In many of the language biographies I have collected over the years, the moment of starting school is identified as such a key experience, as a triggering moment of confusion with one's language repertoire. The constellations in which this confusion manifests can vary significantly in specific cases, particularly when starting or transitioning to a new school. For some, it is the experience of being confronted with the normativity of standard language for the first time in class. Yet for those with a near-standard family language, conversely, the challenge can lie in encountering a peer group defined by a local dialect that refuses to accept them. Still, others are placed in an environment when they start school where they understand virtually nothing and cannot make themselves understood. And some are astonished to discover that others only have one family language and not one for their mother and one for their father, as they do.

All of these cases concern the lived experience of language, with accounts of how people perceive themselves and how they are perceived by others when interacting through language. Speakers usually become aware that they have a linguistic repertoire, albeit *ex negativo*, namely when they have the feeling that they are perceived as having a "different language" by those around them. Such language experience is not neutral. It is linked to emotional experiences, to whether or not you feel comfortable in a language or in speaking it. Emotionally loaded language experiences are an aspect that has long received little attention in the study of multilingualism, as the focus has been, and far too often still is, too exclusively on language skills and testable, measurable performance.

Every portrayal of language experience is unique. Nevertheless, some basic axes can be identified, which are also evident in the initial example of changing schools.

For one, it is about the relationship between *self-perception and others' perception*. The student reports how she tried to meet the expectations of her new environment and speak "High German" as a young person. "I can still remember today," she writes, "how I almost listened to myself speak from the outside and felt like an actress. My speech seemed so fake." The linguistic adjustment that the student makes in the hope of no longer being perceived as "different" in the eyes of others means that she now perceives herself as different, as a stranger.

Furthermore, it is a question of *belonging or not belonging*. This can include both the desire to identify with a group and the experience of being identified with a stigmatized group by others without being asked. In our example, both factors come into play: the narrator's identification by her classmates as someone "from the country" and, simultaneously, her desire to belong to the class community and not be excluded.

Finally, it concerns the experience of linguistic *power or powerlessness*. In our example, the power imbalance and linguistic hierarchy lead the students to feel "very insecure and a little inadequate," and they prefer not to speak at all in certain situations. Conversely, those well-off students who set the tone in the class are not only able to devalue others because of their speech but also to reproduce and consolidate their privileged position through linguistic distinction. The silencing that the student reports is a reaction referenced in many language biographies—not always, or not only, as being silenced, but sometimes also as an attempt to establish defiant silence as a form of resisting power.

The focus on the lived experience of language brings the speaking and experiencing subject back into linguistics, where it was ignored for a long time due to a purely structuralist understanding of language. Since the 1990s, a steadily growing body of linguistic biographical research has emerged. It focuses on the subjective experiences of speakers to gain a deeper understanding of questions such as motivations for language learning, language retention or language change, or the connection between languages and identity construction. In contrast to language attitude research, which (usually with the help of quantitative sociopsychological survey methods) investigates socially and cognitively entrenched attitudes toward specific languages, varieties, and groups of speakers, language biography-oriented research is primarily interested in how linguistic-ideological evaluations by others are experienced and reflected in one's linguistic repertoire.

Only when we include the level of language experience in the concept of repertoire can we also consider dimensions that cannot be adequately grasped from an external perspective —that is, through mere observation of interactions. In the following, I explore the dimensions of the language repertoire that extend beyond internalized syntactic and pragmatic knowledge, including the bodily, emotional, and historical-political dimensions.

The bodily dimension

Experience presupposes a perceiving, experiencing subject. It can only be examined if there is a shift in perspective—from an external, observational viewpoint (as adopted by Gumperz) to that of the subject. In other words, from the third person to the first person. This change of perspective can be conceived of in light of Edmund Husserl's phenomenology, which was further developed by the French philosopher Maurice Merleau-Ponty, among others. Merleau-Ponty (1962) sees the foundation of the subject as a bodily being. Our body, he says, is always there with us. It situates and localizes the subject in the world. Merleau-Ponty makes a conceptual distinction between the physical body (*corps physique*) as an object that is observable and measurable and the lived body (*corps vivant*) as the subject of feeling, experiencing, acting, and interacting. He illustrates the ambiguity of the body as both toucher and touched, using the example of the left hand (as subject) touching the right hand (as object).

According to Merleau-Ponty, the body's movement is the basis of the ability to relate to the world and engage with it. The hand that reaches for an object "knows" what and where it is reaching for, even without our consciousness having to calculate the points that the hand passes through in a space-time diagram. A movement is learned by the body "getting it" through assimilation. According to Merleau-Ponty, it is not the "I think" (*je pense*) that stands at the beginning of our being-in-the-world, but an "I can" (*je peux*).[105]

The relevance of this approach to understanding the linguistic repertoire stems from the fact that, according to Merleau-Ponty, speech is also grounded primarily in the body. Like gesture (and emotion), language is mainly a way of relating, a projection toward the other, and only then a cognitive act of representation and symbolization. Language is anchored in bodily-emotional gestures and is part of intersubjectivity, that is, the projection from an "I" to a "you." Thus, it belongs to the domain that Merleau-Ponty refers to as intercorporeality.

The linguistic repertoire, it could be concluded, is not arbitrary and also not readily interchangeable; it is attached to the bodily subject embedded in it. Past experiences remain inscribed in the body and can unexpectedly resurface through a posture, a gesture, a taste, or a sound. This bodily component of language experience and language repertoire also comes to light in the biographical text cited above, when the student reports on how, at school, she felt like she was listening from the outside when speaking "High German" and felt like an actress. In other words, she had the impression of not being in her body and speaking with her body but of slipping into a strange role and observing her speaking self as an object-body from the outside.

The emotional dimension

Traditionally, conceptions of language acquisition and language processing were characterized by mentalism; that is, they were

---

[105] See Merleau-Ponty, 1962: 159.

based on models that did not focus on the intersubjective of the social but on the cognitive performance of the individual. The language–emotion connection is barely addressed. This dearth of research is not only evident from linguistic-biographical studies. Insights gained from other disciplines—particularly in the philosophical study of emotions, as well as in language acquisition research and the neurosciences, and, of course, in psychoanalysis—also suggest that cognition and emotion are closely linked in language acquisition and language production. In an updated repertoire concept, it will, therefore, no longer be possible to ignore emotional evaluations that influence the ability to utilize linguistic resources.

The language–emotion connection is multifaceted. Language not only plays a role in naming and talking about emotions, but emotionalization is also expressed or evoked in speech. Emotional processes can affect all levels of speech production. On the phonetic/phonological level, for example, through vowel elongation or the use of onomatopoeic words, on the morphological level through intensifying or diminutive affixes, and on the lexical/semantic level through metaphors. On the syntactic level, through exclamations, or on the pragmatic level, through sociolectal interjections, irony, and similar means. At the paraverbal level, for example, it can be observed that anxiety causes not only irregular and increased breath and heartbeat but also a change in voice intensity, pitch, vocal rhythm, and emphasis. We also know from everyday observations that excitement can lead to stuttering, muddled speech, and breaking off, among other phenomena, and that these issues are largely beyond our control.

From a philosophical perspective, as Demmerling and Landweer (2007) explain, feelings are seen as acute experiences that take hold of us physically without us doing anything. They have an intentional content—intentional in the sense of being directed: they are related to an object, a circumstance, a person. I am afraid of something, I am happy about something, I love someone. Feelings have a subjective dimension because they affect us both physically and emotionally. At the same time, they also have an intersubjective-social dimension because they can interact with the feelings of others. Joy or fear can be contagious, and love reciprocal. Finally, feelings also have a socio-cultural dimension, as the experience is also linked to how feelings are discussed and perceived within a particular culture.

The *psychoanalytic perspective* also argues for the connection between emotion and language. The work of Julia Kristeva, who combines psychoanalytical and linguistic-semiotic approaches, is fascinating in this respect. She assigns two distinct dimensions to language. On the one hand, for Kristeva (2002), meaning, sign, and signified are connected in an essentially cognitive manner, which she refers to as the symbolic function. By entering into the normativity of language and through the capacity for symbolization, the subject is established as such. This symbolic function contrasts with a semiotic dimension characterized by heterogeneity in relation to sense and meaning, as well as indeterminacy or ambiguity. This semiotic dimension—associated with the preconscious or unconscious, the bodily-affective, which Kristeva traces back to early childhood babbling and rhythmic intonation—is increasingly displaced by the symbolic function as one grows up, but remains present in all speech, according to Kristeva. She finds residues of the semiotic in "psychotic discourse," for example, when the dissolution of semantic function threatens the subject. This dimension is, however, also present in what she calls "poetic language": the playful fantasizing that can undermine and override the regularity and standardization of language. As Jacques Hassoun[106] puts it, pre-linguistic articulation is the "bearer of our oldest, strongest feelings" (my translation)— physical touches, inarticulate sounds, words that the child hears without understanding and that the adult suddenly finds again in a linguistic turn of phrase or a sudden change of emotion.

Such lines of thought are different from the idea of the linguistic repertoire as a kind of toolbox from which one selects the "right" or "appropriate" language according to the context and situation. Instead, the repertoire can be seen as a space of potentiality that is both expanded and restricted by a sedimentation of bodily-

---

[106] 2003: 35.

emotional experiences. The choices available to a speaking subject are limited not only by grammatical rules and social conventions but also by emotional factors—specific languages, codes, or ways of speaking may carry such emotional weight that they are inaccessible, or only partially accessible, at particular moments. The repertoire is not only determined by what a speaking subject "has" but sometimes precisely by what is not available, becoming all the more noticeable in a given situation as a void, threat, or desire: languages that are associated with a deep desire to unite or identify with another; languages of longing from which one has been expulsed through exile, by prohibition, by voluntary or forced assimilation; languages that one shies away from for fear of exposing oneself, or because one fears that they could displace another thereby replacing it; languages that one avoids or fears because they are associated with adverse or even traumatic experiences, with the loss of autonomy and agency.

The historical-political dimension

Let us recall once again the confusion described at the beginning, caused by a change from a rural to an urban secondary school and the associated experience of immersion in a new linguistic environment. Due to her manner of speaking, the student is identified as not belonging. Her rural accent functions as a shibboleth—a linguistic differentiator used to categorize "us" and "them." *Shibboleth*, the Hebrew word meaning "ear of corn," was used as an identifier, according to the Old Testament book of Judges. Anyone who pronounced it as *Sibboleth* was identified as a fleeing Ephraimite and killed; only those who could pronounce the "sh" sound were allowed to pass. In the case of the schoolgirl, as the text excerpt says, she is confronted with a hierarchical peer group in which classmates from the upper classes set the tone. The power constellation is produced and reproduced with the help of language ideologies, i.e., discourses about language and "correct" language use. The mismatch between self-perception and the perception of others makes the student aware that she is someone who is assigned to a particular category—to the "naiveté of the countryside"—and that she is, to use Judith Butler's (1997) words, discursively or performatively established as a subject of a particular kind.

In her work on gender, discrimination, power, and performativity Judith Butler begins with the ambiguity of the concept of the subject, according to which the subject is primarily not an autonomously acting one but a subjugated one, a sub-jectum, whereby the subjugation to the power of already existing discourses, already spoken language, precedes action and makes it possible in the first place. Butler (1997) refers to the formation of the subject through the discursive power of language as subjectivation: it shapes thinking, speaking, feeling, and even bodily being. One becomes a subject through the repeated assignment by others and by oneself to predetermined categories such as male–female, domestic–foreign, heterosexual–homosexual, and so on. Any recognition is, at the same time, a misjudgment because it is based on exclusion and reduces heterogeneity to either/or categories.

Social, ethnic, national, and other affiliations are constructed through language ideologies. In terms of the linguistic repertoire, this means that the restrictive power of linguistic categorizations is particularly felt when language is not readily available, for example, when people are not recognized as legitimate speakers of a particular language or do not perceive themselves as such. As we have seen, this can be the case when they change their linguistic environment, that is, when they enter a social space in which linguistic practices other than those to which they are accustomed prevail.

A feeling of dislocation, a sense of not (or no longer) speaking the "right" language, can also arise without speakers changing their place of residence. A change in political power constellations can lead to specific languages or ways of speaking being evaluated differently than before. In Germany, for example, certain terms or designations that had become naturalized in the GDR[107] in contrast to the use of language in the Federal Republic became a distinctive feature after reunification, identifying speakers as so-called "Ossis."

---

[107] German Democratic Republic (note from the editors).

The dissolution of the former Yugoslavia in the early 1990s not only led to the emergence of new nation-states but also to a reconfiguration of language policy. Instead of Serbo-Croatian or Croato-Serbian, which had been constructed and codified in the 19th century as a common standard language with a wide range of regional variations, three new national languages were proclaimed: Bosnian, Croatian, and Serbian. Montenegrin was added later. Each of these languages was then codified in a way that made it as distinct as possible from the others.[108] As can be seen from numerous language biographies, such political changes force speakers to reposition themselves in relation to the changed linguistic categorizations, all the more so if they are required to commit to a "new mother tongue" as a sign of loyalty.

Even if language ideologies are subject to constant change, this does not alter the fact that new categorizations continue to emerge. These categorizations exert power because they are repeatedly invoked and continually enacted. They cannot simply be wished away.

The language portrait as a representation of the repertoire

As an approach to exploring linguistic repertoires, the language portrait is gaining popularity in multilingualism research, just as it is in education and psychotherapy. Research participants are invited to use a given body silhouette (or a self-drawn body outline) to visualize their linguistic repertoire or different communicative resources, utilizing colors, and then discuss them. For the development, use, and methodological justification of the language portrait, see Busch (2021b).

The following language portrait (Figure 1) was created during a workshop with students from a multilingual class at the Slovenian secondary school in Klagenfurt/Celovec.

---

[108] See Busch, 2021a.

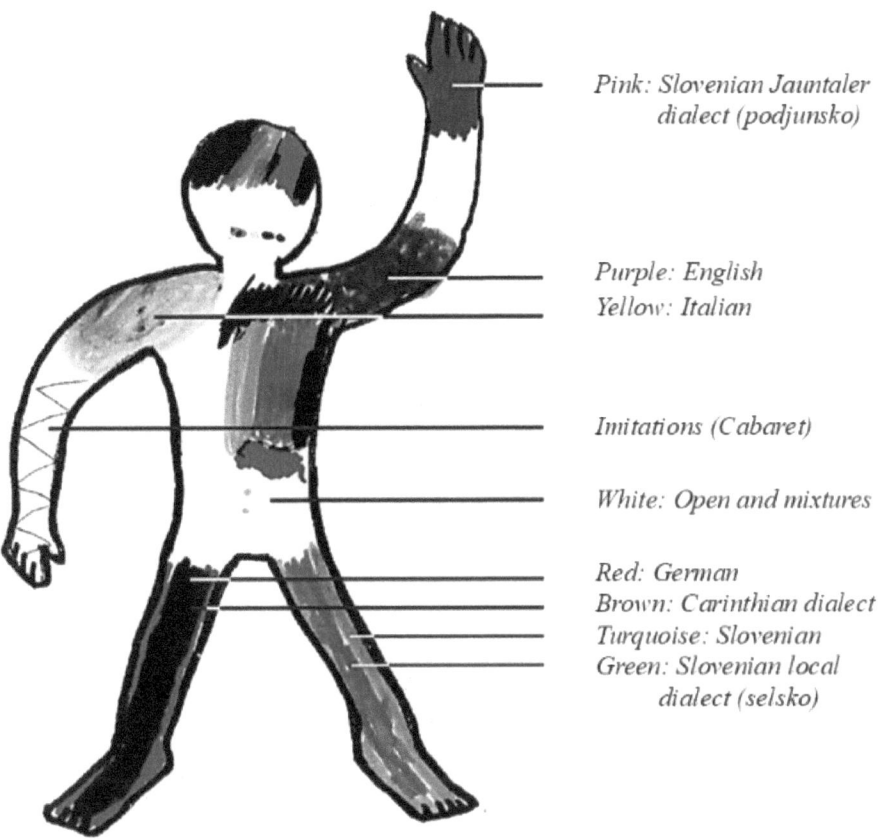

Figure 1: Portrait of Peter

The languages of teaching and learning are Slovenian, German, and Italian, depending on the subject. Established in 1959 for the Slovenian minority in Carinthia, the secondary school is now attended by students with a wide range of different family languages. At the time, the students involved in the workshop were one year away from graduating. One student, whom we will call Peter, begins the presentation of his language portrait as follows:

> So, the feet are/ one foot is German, and one foot is Slovenian, those are the two pillars, the brown is the Carinthian dialect and the green/ that is my home dialect. And that actually is strongest. That means that when I speak,

> I don't speak High German, but instead, my two dialects, yes. One is my mother. One is my father. My father speaks German, and my mother speaks Slovenian.

The two dialects, the German-Carinthian regiolect and the Slovenian dialect of his home village, are each drawn inside a leg, surrounded by the standard German and Slovenian varieties (red and light blue, respectively). Through the symmetrical arrangement, Peter emphasizes that he wants to give both "pillars" the same value. These four colors appear again in both the torso and the head, but no longer as two distinct, symmetrically arranged blocks. Instead, they are interlocked, forming a repertoire of diverse ways of speaking that Peter associates with various contexts and places, held in a taut relationship between emotion (the heart) and reason (the head). While Slovenian dominates the heart, the opposite is true of the head:

> The German language actually dominates in my head because pretty much everything in Carinthia is German anyway, the media, and so on. That is why I mainly think in German, unfortunately.

Peter attributes this imbalance to the sociolinguistic situation in Carinthia, where "pretty much everything is German anyway," while the minoritized language is primarily relegated to the private, non-public sphere. With the elliptical comment "unfortunately," he self-critically evaluates his statement that he thinks predominantly in German, implicitly referring to a widespread ethnic group discourse according to which the minority language should be consciously cultivated.

Peter places Italian and English, which he learns at school, on his shoulders because they are a "burden" but also a "backpack" that can be unpacked when needed, for example, on vacation. He also mentions another local Slovenian dialect that he has drawn in his raised hand. He learned to speak it in order to "reach out to my younger cousin." Beyond these "nameable" languages and varieties, Peter states that the zigzag line in his arm stands for "imitations and parodies," and the space left white for his "own mixtures," "own creations," and "for everything that is yet to come."

During the almost four minutes that Peter explains his drawing, he provides an account of his linguistic repertoire from a current perspective and within the context of the workshop. He describes an arc in time that encompasses the past, growing up in the languages of his mother and father, through to the present and future, symbolized in the picture by the open areas left white. He traverses various social spaces, including family, village, school, extended family, and vacation. He discusses the emotional connotations he assigns to specific ways of speaking. He illustrates these—as the body outline suggests—with the help of body metaphors: the pillars, the burden on the shoulders, and the outstretched hand. Lastly, he also relates his repertoire to the linguistic and ideological positions circulating in society.

Summary

Starting from how language is experienced, I have approached the linguistic repertoire from the perspective of the speaking subject, its inherent intersubjectivity, and discursive nature, focusing in turn on the bodily, emotional, and historical-political dimensions of language. In the linguistic repertoire, the biographical is intertwined with the historical and political. Bakhtin's (1938/2008) concept of the chronotope—the co-presence of different space-times within a single literary text—can also be applied to the linguistic repertoire. With every linguistic action situated in the here and now, we position ourselves not only in relation to what is directly present (i.e., our interaction partners and the immediate context) but also implicitly in relation to what is absent. This includes what resonates in the background and subtly enters the present: other people who are significant to us, other spaces and times, and other discourses or values to which we orient ourselves, whether intentionally or not. Bakhtin writes:

> Chronotopes can be connected to one another, coexist with one another, intertwine with one another, replace one another, be juxtaposed comparatively or contrastively, or be in complicated interrelationships with one another.[109]

---

[109] 1938/1981: 252.

In any case, they interfere in the here and now and contribute to the fact that the linguistic repertoire cannot be understood as a toolbox from which speakers can draw as needed. Instead, it represents a heteroglossic realm of possibilities: different languages and ways of speaking sometimes come to the fore, then recede again; they observe each other, keep their distance, interfere with, or intertwine to form something new, but in one form or another, they are always present. Because language is dialogical, to use Bakhtin's words,[110] because it moves "on the border between oneself and the other," the linguistic repertoire reflects the synchronous coexistence of different social spaces in which speakers participate. It refers diachronically to various levels of time: not only backward to previous ones in which it has been formed and reshaped but also forward to what is to come and for what one is preparing.

---

[110] 1935/1981: 293.

Note: The body silhouette can be downloaded at:
www.heteroglossia.net/Sprachportraet.123.0.html

2.6. Transculturality and Plurilingualism
Jürgen Erfurt

1. Outline of the problem

"Should the German Johann stop making tacos?"[111]—under this headline, author Michael Allmaier reported in the weekly newspaper "Die Zeit" that the debate about cultural appropriation has reached the kitchen and culinary culture. "Suddenly Pad Thai and Spaghetti Carbonara have the makings of a shitstorm" (ibid. 59). He introduces a person called Stefan from Oldenburg, who, back from a vacation in Thailand where he rode an elephant through a village and took a cooking course, decided to open a restaurant where one could experience "what Thai cuisine really tastes like." The author admits that, although Stefan is a fictional character, there are real-world role models who can relate. In the last two years, British celebrity chefs have experienced that a recipe for Jamaican "Jerk Rice"[112] or the opening of a restaurant with "authentic Asian street food" brought them massive accusations of cultural appropriation.

In Berlin and many other places, recipes and gastronomy have become fields for political debate, where the authenticity of the dishes and their ingredients are being politicized and negotiated. There is more at stake here, namely the legitimacy of those who prepare and/or sell these meals and their professional existence in a market where people with migrant biographies compete with others who, like Stefan, are usually privileged white people. As appropriation critics put it, "Who are you to think you can cook our food?" And, it is not okay "when fully mainstream members of the majority population adorn themselves with other people's feathers" (ibid. 60).

Allmaier's stories about Stefan, the Italian restaurant owner Guido Mondi in Regensburg, and the Thai chef Khamlao, who co-founded a network of non-white restaurant workers in Berlin, do

---

[111] See "Die Zeit", No. 21, May 19, 2022, 59-60.
[112] See the BBC's report at bbc.com/news/newsbeat-45246009.

not need to be retold in detail. The punchline of the text alone does the job: "Dear Stefan from Oldenburg, no more elephant rides, okay? But I'm looking forward to your food. By the way, I had my first Tom Yam Gung while I was in Frankfurt. At a Vietnamese restaurant. I think the galangal was missing. But it had pineapple in it" (ibid.).

If you read this text on the appropriation debate from a different angle, it is not just about how cuisine and gastronomy, cultural phenomena per se, are confronted with questions of political correctness. It also tells stories of the mobility and migration of individuals, of their cultural contacts and interdependencies, which, in one way or another, are an expression of globalization. These stories contain elements of conflict because their protagonists share their experiences of cultural differences and social and economic inequality. They are seen as agents who are both mobile and creative and whose actions give rise to something new along the lines of: Why not prepare the sour, salty, and spicy Thai cuisine classic Tom Yam Gung with pineapple?

Seen through the eyes of a transculturality researcher, the stories of the people in this text provide the central keywords for an analysis of transculturality and transcultural processes. We are talking about contact and entanglement, migration and mobility, individuals and conflicts, inequality, difference and emergence, mixtures, and transformations, to name but a few. They will be defined in more detail below, and their connections with language and language learning will be outlined. This argumentation is flanked by another.

For many decades, interculturality has been regarded as one of the central concepts not only in the management of cultural conflicts and cultural understanding but also in education, communication, and learning. This is also reflected in disciplines such as intercultural education, intercultural communication, and intercultural learning. The diverse approaches to bilingual education often reference interculturality. The broad acceptance of interculturality should not, however, obscure the fact that this concept has become problematic and is no longer appropriate for a variety of contexts. The social and cultural developments of the last two to three decades call for a different approach. Something the perspective of transculturality attempts to adopt.

2. Interculturality vs. Transculturality

2.1. Interculturality as a concept of conflict management

The concept of interculturality can be juxtaposed with biculturalism and multiculturalism. Bi-, multi-, and interculturality are concepts for coping with cultural diversity and managing cultural conflicts. All three concepts have their place, one way or another, in the struggles of cultural (minority) communities in nation-states seeking recognition from the dominant culture.

Many nation-states pursue strategies of conflict management to negotiate cultural differences. Canada is one example. During the emancipation movement of the marginalized French-speaking population—also known as the "Silent Revolution"—the Royal Commission on Biculturalism and Bilingualism (1963–1969) recommended the recognition of the interests of French-speaking Canadians by, among other things, declaring their language to be the second official language of the Canadian Confederation. Since 1969, Canada has been officially bilingual. In this way, the state pursues a policy of biculturalism and bilingualism. The Indigenous (or autochthonous peoples), however, remain largely excluded. The recognition of biculturalism in conjunction with the official bilingualism of the state is considered a relatively effective form of conflict management that helps to defuse conflicts between minoritized and dominant communities in many states and (autonomous) regions: Belgium, Finland, Haiti, Ireland, until 2018 Israel; autonomous regions such as the Aoste Valley and South Tyrol in Italy, or the Basque Country, Galicia and Catalonia in Spain can be cited as examples.

Since the 1970s, a different approach to conflict management has gained significant traction, particularly in Anglo-Saxon countries like Great Britain, Canada, and the U.S.A., where immigrant communities and Indigenous peoples are demanding recognition for their cultures and opposing assimilation by the dominant culture. In 1971, multiculturalism was declared a state principle for the first time in Canada to respond to the repeatedly virulent legitimacy disputes surrounding immigrant cultures. Here, we see one of the classic immigration countries experiencing its special form of bilingual multiculturalism.

Whereas the discourse surrounding multiculturalism often uses the image of a mosaic with a multitude of groups living side by side, interculturalism propagates the image of mutual exchange, interaction, and dialog aimed at respecting shared values.

The history of the term reveals that the concept of interculturality emerged in very different historical contexts. Vogt[113] first refers to the work of the U.S. anthropologists Edward and Mildred Hall, who, based on their earlier research, were commissioned by the U.S. government in the 1950s to train diplomatic personnel. Their publications represent an important reference for the field of intercultural communication.[114] But even prior to their work, nation-building processes were already underway in Latin American countries in the 1940s to overcome the "states' internal otherness"[115] with the aim of forming a homogeneous citizenry of Indigenous, Mestizo, and Iberian origin desired by the state. Finally, Vogt cites the situation in France after the end of colonialism, where since the 1960s, educational strategies had to be developed specifically catering to an ever larger group of immigrant communities from the former colonies.

The French philosopher and sociologist Jacques Demorgon points out that there have been contact, relationships, and exchange, intentional or unintentional, peaceful or violent, between individuals and groups throughout human history, and that human activity is also designed for interaction, and thus for "interculturation." The intercultural represents the matrix of human history.[116] Demorgon distinguishes the intercultural perspective, which emerged in the second half of the 20th century, from the fact of the intercultural—"l'interculturel factuel." The former developed in areas such as international relations, business and management, migration and education research, and the field

---

[113] See Vogt, 2018: 189f.
[114] See Hall, 1959.
[115] See Vogt ibid.
[116] See Demorgon, 2008: 559.

of aesthetic and media creativity. The intercultural perspective would not have existed if the individualizing differences among people, groups, and societies had not come to light due to the pressures of globalization. The intercultural perspective has set itself the task of uncovering the permanent and always contradictory processes of human adaptation and their "interculturation" throughout history.

Demorgon's understanding of interculturality sets itself apart from earlier and other ideas of interculturality, which are concerned with the management of potential conflicts in intercultural encounters and culture-related misunderstandings. This means that, for example, a culture A, which represents the "own," interacts with a culture B, which represents the "foreign." The emphasis lies on the interaction between the cultures—and not, as in the case of multiculturalism, on their coexistence—while at the same time recognizing cultural differences. Nevertheless, cultures are still represented as largely homogeneous and distinct from one another. Interculturality also assumes that the representatives of the two cultures are in a symmetrical relationship and that they have the same degree of curiosity, openness, and tolerance.[117] More recent understandings of interculturality, for example, in intercultural pedagogy and intercultural communication,[118] take a critical view of these positions. They differ from older standpoints in that: a) they focus on power relations; b) they do not view cultures as homogeneous, monolithic, or ethnocentric but rather assume heterogeneity; and c) they understand culture in terms of its processes of constitution, negotiation, and transformation.

There are, however, considerable doubts as to whether the concept of interculturality can accommodate the developments that have shaped demographic, cultural, and linguistic conditions since the early 2000s in the wake of rapidly changing lifestyles, migration, mobility, and diversity. This by no means applies uniquely to urban centers, for which the anthropologist Steven Vertovec (2007) developed the concept of "superdiversity." The findings from

---

[117] See also Langenohl, 2017: 55.
[118] See Demorgon, 2014; Gogolin & Krüger-Potratz, 2010; Mecheril, 2014.

sociology and border studies on individualization,[119] the erosion of borders,[120] and the dynamics of the dissolution of borders in the conflict between globalization and regionalization[121] also point to new processes and changes. Finally, the processes of culturalization[122] in late capitalism should be mentioned, which once again shows that the basic assumptions on which the concept of interculturality[123] is based are less and less applicable.

2.2. Transculturality as a concept of scientific description

As a concept, transculturality is related to the other cultural concepts of bi-, multi-, and interculturality mentioned above, as they all refer to inequality and difference. At the same time, transculturality[124] differs from these concepts in a categorical way in that—at least so far:

first, it is not a concept of political or pedagogical negotiation and the management of cultural conflicts but one of scientific description and recognition of social and cultural processes. It is, therefore, committed to a different logic than a concept of political negotiation;

second, it usually focuses, mostly retrospectively and reconstructively, on the forms and practices of staging cultural entanglements;

third, the associated processes and structures can be described and explained not only in terms of difference theory—as in the case of bi-, multi-, and interculturality—but also in terms of

---

[119] See Berger, 2010.
[120] See Beck, 2002.
[121] See Schiffauer *et al.*, 2018.
[122] See Kleeberg & Langenohl, 2011.
[123] The fundamental assumptions of the concept of interculturality are as follows: a) interaction between a culture A, which represents the "own" and a culture B, which represents the "foreign," b) the two cultures are considered to be (relatively) homogeneous internally and externally demarcated, c) the representatives of the two cultures are in a symmetrical relationship, and d) bring the same degree of curiosity, openness, and tolerance (see Erfurt, 2021: 67–68).
[124] The following three aspects are explained in a broader context in Erfurt, 2021: 99.

emergence theory;[125]

fourth, unlike bi-, multi-, and interculturality, which have their frame of reference in the nation-state, transculturality unfolds their special dynamic under the conditions of globalization and the erosion of borders that previously separated states, markets, civilizations, cultures, life-worlds, and people.

Transcultural research focuses on the processes and structures of cultural exchange, negotiation, and entanglements. These (presumably) run through the entire history of humankind and have —growing more systematic in recent years—been uncovered retrospectively and reconstructively by historical sciences such as anthropology, archaeology, ethnology, history, historical migration research, religious studies, linguistics, and literary studies, translation studies, and others.[126] From this author's point of view, the concept of transculturality can be defined by the following aspects[127] depending on who deals with the problem of transculturality from a linguistic and cultural studies perspective, in particular, the learning and practice of languages in the context of migration and mobility:

a) Transculturality in cultural and linguistic studies means that communities and individuals with their languages, literatures, media, and other cultural manifestations do not form and move in ethnically closed, linguistically homogeneous, and territorially delimited spaces. They are entangled with other communities and individuals across borders, and their contacts arise in essence from the migration and mobility of the actors.

b) Transculturality assumes that cultures encounter each other in

---

[125] If difference theory aims to describe and explain processes and structures of power and hegemony and the hierarchies they produce, emergence theory focuses on the development of new forms and processes, that is, those that arise spontaneously without being premeditated or planned, for example, as side effects of other actions from which something new arises unintentionally and unpredictably.

[126] Unlike in Europe, the concept of transculturality plays a much greater role in the health and nursing sciences in North America, although this will not be discussed in this article.

[127] The following list of points a to f can be found in slightly modified form in Erfurt, 2021: 101-102.

their diversity and that contact between them is dependent on negotiation. This initiates diverse processes of mixing, the erosion of boundaries, transcultural memory, appropriation and conflict, transfer, and mediation, which in turn are integrated into processes of power, hegemony, and exploitation.

c) Transculturality assumes that cultures do not meet *en bloc*. Instead, it is individuals and groups with their norms, values, views, languages, religions, and so on that come into contact. This calls for a change of perspective: from the cultures of communities to individuals and their cultural practices. This change of perspective also means shifting the emphasis from the homogeneity assumed for communities to distinction, difference, and heterogeneity within and between individuals and groups.

d) If the subject of transculturality is the study of processes and structures of cultural exchange, negotiation, and entanglement, and the emphasis is on processes of distinction, difference, and heterogeneity within and between individuals and groups, then it must also be assumed that unforeseeable, unexpected, unintended, and thus new cultural forms and practices always emerge in these entanglements and interactions. In theoretical terms, this means that transculturality must be modeled not only from the perspective of difference theory (as with bi-, multi-, and interculturality) but also from that of emergence theory.

e) The growing prevalence of the term transculturality is directly related to the increasingly diverse forms of socialization in the age of globalization, the internet, and computer technologies on the one hand, and processes of culturalization in late capitalism on the other. In this context, transculturality stands for individual mobility profiles and individual forms of expression and appropriation of cultural practices – in other words, every individual has a culture.

f) The concept of transculturation goes back to the studies of the Cuban anthropologist Fernando Ortiz (1940). He speaks of "transculturación" – which he introduced – in contrast to the term "acculturation," which was predominant in U.S. anthropology at the time, for the process of change in cultures and cultural relationships. If, following Ortiz, "transculturation" stands for the process of change, then "transculturality" refers to the structural aspect of this process. Key concepts in the analysis of transcultural processes are inequality, above all, social, economic, linguistic, and educational inequality of the actors; difference, especially the cultural, social, and ethnic difference of the actors in the structure of hierarchies, power, and hegemony; and, emergence, that is, the emergence of something new in the course of contact and entanglement.[128] Central fields of cultural and linguistic analysis are processes and phenomena of mixing and hybridity, diaspora and diasporic reading, transcultural memory, migrant writing, the transfer of knowledge, and translation.

2.3. Transculturality, the individual, and linguistic repertoire

For the purposes of further argumentation, I would like to highlight the aspects of the definition of transculturality mentioned above under parts c and e, respectively, and discuss them in more detail.

In the context of transculturality, the focus is decidedly on individuals as learning, speaking, writing, reading, remembering, or cooperating persons who enter social relationships of various kinds with others. The focus on the "individual" and "individuality" in no way represents a rejection of the fundamental social dimension of language and culture. The emphasis is on the positioning of the actors. Or, in the words of Schulze-Engler, the concept of transculturality shifts the "traditional [...] question of what different cultures do with people to the new question of what different people do with culture" (2006: 46). Regarding language, the focus on the individual represents a corrective to linguistic approaches that take a bird's eye view by classifying and homogenizing languages as separate systems and formulating "external expectations of speakers about the 'typical' linguistic

---

[128] See Erfurt, 2021: 80-97.

performance of certain ethnic groups."[129] Individuals, people who learn, speak, write, etc., are mobile. They move in space and time, within societal orders, through them, and beyond their borders. This movement often manifests as migration, which is the trigger, or also the framework, for language learning and the restructuring of linguistic repertoires. The observation of linguistically active individuals is thus an expression of the actor—and repertoire—centered perspective in current sociolinguistics. It sets a different emphasis than the competence-centered bilingualism research of the 1990s and 2000s.

The individual perspective is also linked to the concept of the linguistic repertoire, which refers to the totality of an individual's available linguistic resources. As such, it focuses attention on their (potential) plurilingualism.[130]

From a temporal perspective, the term linguistic repertoire stands for the individual's lifelong learning of linguistic forms and structures. In this way, it is to be understood as complementary to the concept of language biography wherein the experiences with language, the learning of language through to linguistic emotions in biographical contexts are illuminated retrospectively and reconstructively.

In the context of migration, but not limited to this, a wide range of areas of conflict, barriers and blockages, traumas, and breaks in language biographies arise, which can extend to the "forgetting" of a language that was once learned as a mother tongue. In this context, the dynamics of learning and growth can be seen as a restructuring[131] of the linguistic repertoire. Restructuring of the repertoire means that —during migration, social upheavals, or other incisive events—the previous linguistic resources are limited or no longer sufficient for coping with the demands of life, and learning processes become necessary to be able to participate linguistically in the new circumstances. As a rule, the restructuring of the repertoire does not apply equally to all registers. In the

---

[129] See Androutsopoulos, 2018: 213.
[130] See Blommaert & Backus, 2013.
[131] On the restructuring of linguistic repertoires, see the detailed description in Weirich, 2018.

context of migration, the previous linguistic resources of the intimate/familial register can continue to be functional, while those for the domains of informal public communication and the formal register are no longer functional and largely devalued under the new circumstances.

3. Transculturality and plurilingual learning

Language and plurilingualism are prominent door openers for research into transculturality.[132] Transculturality is highly dependent on the processes of exchange between actors and the entanglement of their actions associated with language. Transcultural processes and viewpoints also change the perception of language. Increasingly, attention is shifting from language(s) as separate systems to "speakers on the move,"[133] that is, to linguistically interacting, mobile subjects in spaces characterized by plurilingualism. From the spectrum of questions and problems that arise in connection with transculturality and language learning, I would again like to single out two: first, the discussion about translanguaging, and second, the problem of plurilingualism.

3.1. Translanguaging

In addition to the sociolinguistic discussion on the concept of the linguistic repertoire mentioned above (e.g., Blommaert & Backus, 2013), the concept of "translanguaging" as prominently introduced by Ofelia García and colleagues (see Seltzer/Otheguy this volume; García, 2018), has provided a breath of fresh air into the research and didactics of plurilingualism[134] in recent years. It has much in common with the concept of "compétences plurilingues et pluriculturelles" developed by Coste, Moore & Zarate (1997/2009).

To illustrate the translanguaging approach, the following situation should be mentioned. Traditionally, when learning languages, a distinction is made between mother tongue and

---

[132] See Erfurt, Hélot, Leroy & Stierwald, 2022: 12.
[133] On the linguistic-historical dimension of this approach, see Erfurt & Gessinger, 2022.
[134] The following comments take up ideas from Erfurt & De Knop, 2019, in particular pp. 13-20.

foreign language, language of origin and school language, source language and target language, first language L1 and second language L2. Teaching and learning arrangements are also geared toward these. This applies not only to traditional foreign language teaching but also to concepts of bilingual learning based on the principle of immersion or bilingual subject teaching (CLIL). In this logic, which is still based on the idea of human monolingualism, not only are the languages strictly separated from each other, but they are also the languages from the speakers or linguistic actors. Furthermore, language is usually only understood as the normative or standard variety. The fact that all these ideas have little to do with the linguistic realities of modern societies and today's ways of communicating and living does not need to be explained any further. A reference to the widespread prevalence of individual and social multilingualism, particularly in urban settings, should suffice to indicate the paradigm shift. The starting point for the concept of translanguaging is the actual or intended bilingualism or plurilingualism of individuals in an educational context. Translanguaging as a pedagogical practice means using two—and even several—languages simultaneously in order to promote the expansion of learners' linguistic repertoires.

As the concept of *translanguaging* became more widespread, it was no longer only used to describe the learning strategies and linguistic practices of bilingual or plurilingual individuals. It now prominently stands for a conception of language that is diametrically opposed to the modeling of bilingualism as two separate and autonomous language systems in the mind of the individual.[135] Similar to Jim Cummins and others earlier, the proponents of the *translanguaging* concept assume that the linguistic knowledge of plurilinguals cannot be modeled additively as the sum of knowledge bound in multiple individual languages. Instead, it is, to a considerable extent, available as cross-linguistic knowledge for speaking, writing, and understanding several languages.[136]

A linguistic concept both didactic and theoretical in nature,

---

[135] See the detailed description in Erfurt, Weirich & Caporal-Ebersold, 2018.
[136] See Otheguy, García & Reid, 2015: 283; Streb, 2022.

translanguaging refers to processes of permeation and entanglement of different languages in the sense of expanding the individual's linguistic capacity to act.

3.2. Pluriliteracy

There are many ways and modes of expanding one's linguistic repertoire and expanding and rebuilding one's linguistic register over the course of a lifetime. One of these is learning in two languages at school simultaneously. For example, in the socially dominant language and in a minority language[137] as practiced in the context of migration in reciprocal immersion schools (also two-way immersion).[138] Even learning in three languages, as practiced in the trilingual Ladin schools in South Tyrol with Ladin, German, and Italian,[139] is indicative of successful school results for pupils.

Bilingual learning at school means that not only the forms and structures of oral language are learned in a second or third language but also those of written language. This may involve learning a different alphabet and/or a different writing system, as in bilingual programs for Arabic and French, for German and Russian, or for Spanish and Chinese. Learning different alphabet systems is one aspect of plurilingualism. The term draws attention to the often-neglected writing dimension of plurilingualism and plurilingual people.

The fact that plurilingual people not only speak their languages but also write them—insofar as they are literate—has only recently come to the attention of plurilingualism research.[140] Compared to studies on plurilingualism, studies on pluriliteracy remain significantly underrepresented.

The phenomenon itself is widespread and has been known for a long time. It is conspicuous among writers, scientists, and other intellectuals who write their literary and scientific works in several languages and/or write in languages other than their first language.

---

[137] See the studies in Hélot & Erfurt, 2016 on the various constellations of bilingual education in France.
[138] See Budach, Erfurt & Kunkel, 2008; Streb, 2016; Fialais, 2019/2021.
[139] See Franceschini, 2013; See also Risse in this volume, chapter 3.5.
[140] See Hornberger, 1989; Lüdi, 1997; Maas & Mehlem, 2005.

The list of authors is both long and prominent: Samuel Beckett, Maryse Condé, Mircea Eliade, Jorge Semprún in the 20th century, Alexander and Wilhelm von Humboldt, Karl Marx or Adalbert von Chamisso in the 19th century, and further back via Rabelais and Erasmus of Rotterdam to Dante and Alfonso X, also known as the Wise.[141] Their pluriliteracy shows that a virtuoso use of several languages and the creation of great literature cannot be tied without reservation to a native linguistic sensibility and that important works can also be created by authors in second or third languages. Nevertheless, the pluriliteracy of cultural elites should not be the measure of all things.

Schoolchildren in Japan, India, or Georgia learn several alphabets or writing systems in succession without much effort in order to write a language, just as they learn to use these writing systems simultaneously for writing and reading other languages. The reverse case, namely that one alphabet is used for writing many languages, can be shown using the example of the Latin alphabet for Germanic, Scandinavian, Slavic, or Romance languages, whereby language-specific writing systems have been established depending on the language, for example, in the form and function of diacritical marks. Writing practices also differ both culturally and socially, for example, when we think of handwriting traditions and conventions in France or Germany, handwriting in cursive and printed script, the Sütterlin script, the primary Latin script, and so forth.

To illustrate the problem of multiple scripts with an example,[142] we can draw on the experience of bilingual school projects in Frankfurt am Main, in particular, bilingual two-way immersion programs in German and Italian or German and French, which we have studied in Frankfurt am Main in recent years.[143] The fact that children also learn the graphic differences within a writing system can be seen when learning German and Italian.

---

[141] See Kremnitz, 2015.
[142] I have taken the following example from my book on transculturality, see Erfurt, 2021: 241.
[143] See Budach, Erfurt & Kunkel, 2008; Erfurt, Leichsering & Streb, 2013; Streb, 2016; Fialais, 2019/2021.

Problematic cases are graphemes or bi- or trigraphs such as <ch>, <sc>, and <sch>. They not only represent different sounds in German and Italian but also different syllabic segmentations when the trigraph <sch> is pronounced as [sk] vs. [ʃ]: cf. it. mas-chera (mask), ris-chio (risk), where it is spread over two syllables, while in German, it is pronounced in one syllable as [ʃ] as in Fischer. In other words, <sch> before -e/i or <sc> before -a/o/u is pronounced in Italian as in [pes-care] (fish), i.e., syllable-segmented, while <sc> before -e/i, for example in it. il pesce (the fish) is pronounced as [pe-ʃe] (cf. Streb, 2016).

Up to this point, the analysis has been at the level of writing and pronunciation in German and Italian. It becomes an analysis of transcultural processes when, following Streb's research (2016), we take a broader view and consider the children's linguistic learning. Streb meticulously observes individual linguistic and social behavior over a period of four years. Her aim is to "identify factors that explain the heterogeneity of linguistic repertoires and the different strategies for expansion [...]" (ibid. 533).

The simultaneous literacy of the children in both languages represents a central aspect of reciprocal immersion. Discussing the linguistic differences in the written forms promotes the children's linguistic analytical skills and thus their knowledge of individual languages and cross-linguistic knowledge, as well as the transfer of knowledge beyond these two languages to other languages. This is because English from third grade onward and additional family languages are also part of the children's repertoire. Transculturality should be considered here at the level of the transfer and circulation of knowledge. It is also significant to look at how—and at the same time how differently—the individual children act linguistically, both individually and with each other in class, how they deal with orthographic conventions in class, and in doing so, mobilize very different linguistic resources and expand their repertoire.

When analyzing plurilingualism, further aspects of transculturality come into discussion, such as questions of inequality, difference, and emergence. For example, German and Italian are not on equal footing in the German school system. Italian is the language of a minority. Furthermore, the children and grandchildren of Italian immigrants in Frankfurt am Main generally do not have the same resources as their German-speaking classmates, which are valorized by the school institution. Social marginalization and failure at school are far more common in this group than among children from the majority society. In this context, reciprocal immersion learning opens new avenues for psychological and cognitive effects to come into play. This means that the children who speak the minority language are seen as experts, which they experience as recognition of their language and culture – and not least of themselves. The minority language becomes a legitimate language for all children in the class when it is used outside the family context as a medium of oral and written communication and for the acquisition of knowledge at school, which is beneficial when using this language. It also shows that the simultaneous use of both school languages promotes linguistic transfer between the languages and the children's meta-linguistic knowledge.

4. Conclusion

Let us return to the problem outlined at the beginning. The discussion of appropriation, as introduced here using an example from the restaurant business, is rife with potential conflict. Inequality engenders experiences of difference and emergence among individuals and groups, which in turn are embedded in processes of migration and mobility, interdependence and contact, the culturalization of the economy, the marketing of culture, and more. In principle, none of these are entirely new processes. In the second half of the 20th century, many states and institutions reacted with corresponding strategies of conflict management. While the strategies of bi-, multi-, and interculturality had their frame of reference in the nation-state, transcultural entanglements unfold primarily under globalization and the erosion of borders that previously separated states, markets, civilizations, cultures, life-worlds, and people. The consequences for people's lives and cultural practices are considerable: terms such as "multiple modernities," "superdiversity," "transcultural memory," or "hybridity" refer both to the effects of colonial and postcolonial structures, to the growing migration and mobility of actors, and to the new cultural and communicative practices emerging through digital media and networks. Language is the central medium here; plurilingualism is to be understood as an important gateway into transcultural processes.

2.7. Language and Education Policy: Power, Prestige, and Bilingualism
Anne-Marie de Mejía

Introduction

When we refer to bilingualism and bilingual education, it is interesting to see the diverse ideas put forward by teachers, coordinators, parents, and students. In Colombia, as in other Latin American countries, such as Brazil, Ecuador, and Argentina, some people refer to the teaching and learning of foreign languages, that is, languages that are not generally used in the immediate context but are taught in schools and educational institutions. These programs, in particular, focus on English but can also provide instruction in other languages, such as French and German, and do not necessarily include the students' first language(s). Other people focus on bilingual or multilingual education in Indigenous or immigrant communities. In this chapter, I will discuss some issues that are particularly important to consider when language and educational policy guidelines are referenced, especially in school contexts. I hope the discussion will help teachers and coordinators come to terms with some of the many complexities and challenges involved in this type of educational provision.

In 2005, I referred to the traditional divide that exists between policy, practice, and research into bilingualism for so-called majority language speakers and modalities offered for so-called minority (or minoritized) language speakers in Colombia and other South American nations. I noted that "This separation leads to a necessarily limited view of the progress of bilingualism and bilingual education within the country as a whole" (p. 48). It appears that the situation remains essentially unchanged today. Not all bilinguals are considered equal. If you are bilingual in your first language and a prestigious international language, such as English, French, German, or Spanish, in Latin America, this is generally considered a positive attribute. However, if you are bilingual in an Indigenous or immigrant language as well as the dominant language in the country, your bilingualism is generally invisible, as many people do not consider this an advantage for career prospects. This is illustrated in the following observation by Lopez-Gopar[144] in the Mexican context, when he notes that "since many parents and children in Oaxaca have bought into the public and media discourse that English 'opens doors" and "changes your life," they prefer English over Indigenous languages." In this respect, Hélot (2012) laments, "the lack of recognition of migrant languages and different forms of bilingualism developed outside of the school context" (p. 214).

What are some key points that schools should consider when implementing bilingual education policies and practices? I will focus on the following issues:

- The status and role of the first language in bilingual programs
- The importance of including considerations about intercultural sensitivity in bilingual programs
- Policies and practices of inclusion in bilingual programs

The status and role of the first language in bilingual programs

The question is: How should teachers and students utilize the two (or more) languages present in a bilingual or multilingual school? Some people believe that each language should be kept separate and never mixed, as they consider this to affect the purity of the different languages. Jim Cummins, in a chapter published in 2008 entitled, *Teaching for transfer: Challenging the two solitudes assumption in bilingual education*, has described this position in the following way, "It is assumed that instruction should be carried out, as far as possible, exclusively in the target language without recourse to the students' first language" (p. 65) and described this as the "two solitudes" assumption. In other words, the student's first language is to be kept apart from the target language in the process of teaching and learning.

But is this realistic? Studies on bilingual interaction have shown that it is normal for bilinguals and multilinguals to draw on both or all of their languages (their entire linguistic repertoire) when communicating with another bilingual speaker. Therefore, if the traditional separatist approach in bilingual education is discarded

---

[144] 2016: 11.

and a more flexible position on bilingual language use is adopted, then a wider panorama opens up. As Jim Cummins argues:

> When we free ourselves from exclusive reliance on monolingual instructional approaches, a wide variety of opportunities arise for teaching bilingual students through bilingual instructional strategies that acknowledge the reality of and strongly promote cross-language transfer. (p. 65)

Consequently, it is crucial to value the use of the first language in the process of helping students become bilingual, particularly through the notion of cross-language transfer. This can be accomplished in various ways, depending on the students' age and language proficiency level. For example, teachers of the first language (e.g., French in France) can coordinate their language program with teachers from the foreign language department so that students can relate what they are learning in English, Spanish, or German with what they have already learned about their first language. This can then be formalized in a bilingual language policy document for the institution. Furthermore, students can be encouraged to become more aware of the similarities and differences between the first and target languages, such as the differences in the position of adjectives in relation to nouns in French and English. Another strategy involves introducing students to interdisciplinary projects, which utilize two or more languages, as well as other curricular areas, such as Mathematics or Science. Cummins assures us that "it is not only language items that can be transferred but also aspects such as phonological awareness and metacognitive and metalinguistic strategies."

A bilingual school policy that explicitly includes all the languages taught in the curriculum helps students recognize that their home languages are valuable assets in their education. This awareness enables them to understand that these languages, particularly immigrant and Indigenous languages, are just as important as the national or dominant language(s) in the country. Furthermore, it can be argued that "translanguagings are multiple discursive practices in which bilinguals engage in order to make sense of their bilingual worlds."[145] Therefore, teachers should not be over-worried if students use translanguaging to convey meaning in bilingual classrooms. They should, instead, create a bilingual classroom language policy that covers interaction in particular grades, specifying when the first language should be used and for what purposes. In this respect, the City University of New York-New York State Initiative on Emergent Bilinguals (CUNY-NYSIEB) website features videos of school administrators and teachers discussing this topic.

The importance of including considerations about intercultural sensitivity in bilingual programs

A teacher in Colombia who works in bilingual education recognized the importance of bilingual teachers collaborating with their students to develop intercultural sensitivity. After participating in a project to help teachers become more aware of intercultural contact and understanding as part of his Master's studies, he acknowledged that "...a successful English teacher needs much more than... technical ability...Teachers have the ability [to] reinforce and perpetuate hatred or stimulate diversity and inspire students to create a better world."[146] This is very important in all parts of the educational system, but particularly in the private sector in Latin American countries where students come from the wealthier social strata and sometimes do not appreciate the value of diversity both within their own countries as well as at international level, often resulting in the unquestioning acceptance of "prestigious" language varieties. This notion, as Flores and Rosa[147] argue, "reflects a form of linguistic normativity anchored in raciolinguistic ideologies [...] unrelated to empirical linguistic practices" and may influence how these language and cultural practices are interpreted by teachers in the process of establishing which languages are considered "prestigious" and how they address intercultural topics.

Many schools and teachers continue to believe that the best way to teach languages is to concentrate on grammar and vocabulary, despite the advent of the Communicative Approach in the 1980s,

---

[145] See García, 2009: 45.
[146] See Jaime Durán, Universidad de los Andes, 2018.
[147] 2015: 160.

which focused on developing communicative competence in foreign language learning. However, there has been a recent increase in recognition that developing linguistic competence for language teachers and students is important but not sufficient. Claire Kramsch (1993) was one of the first researchers to claim that while many approaches to language teaching have focused on linguistic features of language teaching and learning, the connections between discourse and culture have been insufficiently explored. In 2009, she argued that the inclusion of the intercultural dimension should be taken as a revitalization and renovation of language teaching and learning from a critical and reflexive position.

Kramsch and Huffmaster (2015) recommend "a pedagogy focused on fluid relationships between different ways of meaning-making [in which] we can raise students' awareness of the meaning-making processes at work in the construction of social and cultural experience" (p. 134). Liddicoat and Scarino (2013) acknowledge, for their part, that despite growing recognition of the fundamental importance of integrating intercultural capabilities within bi/multilingual language pedagogy, one of the challenges has been to move from this recognition to the development of practice. So, we may ask, how can teachers and administrators respond to this challenge?

In 2019, the Universidad de los Andes in Bogotá and Université Paris III conducted an interinstitutional project aimed at sensitizing in-service language teachers to the importance of incorporating an intercultural dimension into their teaching. In Paris, as in Bogotá, teachers were asked to read and discuss articles about interculturality and identify a related topic in their teaching contexts to create intercultural didactic sequences tailored to their specific contexts. They were then asked to implement these with their students. The aim was to challenge the participants to unpack, deconstruct, and negotiate meanings related to stereotypes, their preconceptions about what teaching culture entails, and their own experiences, attitudes, and behaviors as language teachers. Participants were guided towards a permanent reflection on their teaching views, pedagogical practices, and awareness of the role of the intercultural dimension in language education. In the following comments, I will focus on some of the findings from the teachers in Bogotá.

These participants selected a range of topics for their didactic sequences, including gender, regional differences in Colombia, urban and country life, college life in the U.S. and Colombia, interculturality through art, institutional policies of inclusion and deaf and blind students, and bullying. Thus, it can be seen that they went beyond focusing on national and international issues to highlight aspects they had identified as related to interculturality in their encounters within their contexts. One important theme that emerged from the analysis of the pedagogic sequences created by the participants for the institutions where they worked was their gradual deepening of consciousness regarding issues concerning identities, diversity, and multilingualism. Another was related to the growing understanding of how a focus on interculturality can help language students and teachers identify different perceptions of the Other.

Dervin highlights the importance of developing intercultural sensitivity among students[148] in the following terms, "In a world where racism, different kinds of discrimination, and injustice are on the rise, time spent at school should contribute effectively to prepare students to be real *interculturalists* who can question these phenomena and act critically, ethically, and responsively." This reinforces the need for bilingual education programs to adopt an intercultural perspective as part of their language policies and practices.

Policies and practices of inclusion in bilingual programs

In this section, I discuss initiatives that explicitly address the notion of inclusion with respect to the populations they target. As Hélot (2012) has argued, "The linguistic exclusion of bi- and multilingual students of immigrant background and speakers from socially deprived backgrounds remains one of the main challenges for researchers and practitioners today" (p. 226).

The first of these projects, focused on inclusion, is the Didenheim Project, conducted by Christine Hélot and Andrea Young at a primary school in Alsace from 2000 to 2003. After collaborating with

---

[148] 2016: 2.

teachers, parents, and students, they concluded, "We want to argue that diversity of linguistic and cultural situations is not an impediment to developing a shared classroom culture and that, on the contrary, such diversity can be used as a source of learning."[149] Many of the students came from families with migrant backgrounds. They spoke languages such as Arabic, Turkish, Polish, Portuguese, and Italian, as well as children from Alsatian-speaking homes, and there had been problems of racism noted among the school population.

The project involved teachers inviting parents to present their languages and cultures to children from six to nine years old. They prepared presentations, showed videos, cooked specialties from their country, and shared their personal stories. In this way, the languages and cultural practices of children from non-French backgrounds were "recognized and put on the same level as any other language and culture, including the school culture" (p. 251). The contributions of the parents to this initiative were seen as especially valuable as they presented the children with illustrations of different lifestyles, both traditional and modern, in various cultural contexts. The researchers evaluated the project's results positively, noting a transformation of the school's existing diversity into a learning resource for students, teachers, and parents. The teachers, in particular, became increasingly aware of what it meant to be bilingual, and a multilingual space was created within the school where differences were viewed in a positive light. The researchers concluded that "by making diversity visible in the school, through valuing all languages and cultures equally, they have transformed it into a shared resource to combat racism and intolerance" (p. 255).

The second initiative I include here is the modality known as "Dual Language" or "Two-Way" bilingual education. This has been developed in the United States, originating in Dade County, Florida, in 1963. The idea is that the programs involve equal numbers of students who come from families with a dominant language background, such as English in the U.S., and those who speak other languages, such as Spanish, Japanese, French, and Korean. The aim

---

[149] 2005: 243.

is that the two groups placed together should serve as language and cultural models for each other.

Each language is programmed for 50% of the teaching and learning activities, sometimes on alternate days, and both languages are given equal status.[150] In addition, speakers of the two school languages are integrated into all lessons, and a bilingual ethos is established throughout the school, evident in classrooms, corridor displays, and notice boards in both languages. The aim of these bilingual education programs is not only to produce bilingual and biliterate graduates but also to "enhance intergroup communicative competence and cultural awareness" (p. 224). Each student is a native speaker of one of the school's languages, which leads to the possibility of authentic and meaningful communication, resulting in increased respect for members of the other language group through "child-centered education that builds on the child's existing language competence" (p. 225).

In a recent study conducted by Gort and Sembiante (2015) with teachers and preschool children in Miami-Dade County, US, the researchers documented "show and tell" classroom activities. They concluded that:

> Given the school's language policy of "one teacher/one language" and the presence of two teachers who enacted monolingual and bilingual performances of the instructional languages, the focal classroom became a vibrant bilingual space where children and teachers displayed a dynamic bilingualism that allowed them to use their entire linguistic repertoire flexibly, meaningfully, and competently. (p. 23)

There are approximately 3,600 dual-language schools in the U.S., located in 45 states. About 80% of these programs are related to Spanish and English, and 8.6% involve Chinese and English.[151] According to Lindholm-Leary (2001), they have been evaluated as successful in promoting high levels of language proficiency, academic achievement, multicultural competencies, and positive attitudes toward learning among students. However, to continue

---

[150] See Baker, 2011.
[151] See American Councils Research Center, 2021.

achieving their goals—bilingualism and biliteracy, cultural competence, and high academic achievement—teaching, and learning must be linguistically and culturally responsive and differentiated to meet the individual strengths and needs of each student.[152] Some of the implications of these programs for bilingual language and education policy include recognizing the importance of understanding and respecting pluralism in education, which fosters mutual understanding and tolerance within the school community. This, in turn, may help to come to grips with the notion of hybrid and multiple identities.

Conclusion

In 2010, Menken and García argued that teachers are at the epicenter of language policy in education, and they can function as agents of change in the various policies they have to translate into practice. In other words, rather than passively implementing policies that language teachers receive from the national government or educational institutions from a top-down perspective, they will be able to negotiate and enact policy in their classrooms, empowering both themselves, their colleagues, and their students, and necessarily questioning the verticality of centralized policies.[153] In this case, they will need to understand how bilingual processes differ from monolingual teaching and learning and be able to adapt these to their particular contexts.

In 2013, García and Kleyn proposed three ways forward for language teacher education curricula in the 21st century. One of these aspects involves co-constructing with teachers, spaces, and opportunities to develop multilingualism based on social justice and equity, as well as social practice, which the authors view as connected to students' worlds and identities. If, as we have evidenced in our interinstitutional study, understanding the relationships between language teaching and learning, interculturality, and the construction of identity can be seen as a relatively new development for bilingual and multilingual education programs, there is an obvious need for both pre-service and in-service teacher education to face up to the

---

[152] See Franquiz & Ortiz, 2018.
[153] See Ball *et al.*, 2012.

challenge of incorporating a critical intercultural agenda within foreign language and bilingual teacher education programs.

Another key point has to do with the need to establish clear institutional language and education policies that guarantee continuity in the processes of bilingual teaching and learning and help to ensure the permanence of both teachers and students to be able to project the results of the evaluation of the implementation of bilingual education in the long term. For these bilingual language policies to be successful, the entire school community must understand what it means to be a bilingual school, as there are often many misunderstandings in this regard. Furthermore, it is equally important to promote an integrated vision of bilingual teaching and learning among all the different agents involved in these processes, including the Ministry of Education, school administrators, teachers, students, and parents. One way to help ensure this is to establish an institutional bilingual committee to coordinate the development of bilingualism and bilingual education throughout the school. The participants should include representatives of parents and students, as well as teachers and representatives of the school administration, to consolidate bilingualism and bilingual education as a transversal school project at all levels.

I want to conclude by referencing an insight from Joshua Fishman, who wrote about the sociology of bilingual education in 1977. He argued that enrichment—unlike subtractive bilingual education—offers an additional window into the world and seeks to expand both intellect and personality. I would suggest that this kind of intellectual and personal growth is just as valuable for bilinguals from Indigenous and immigrant communities as it is for those from upwardly mobile, middle- and upper-class backgrounds.

3. Practice

3.1. Making Space for Teachers' Voices to Research Together on Teaching and Learning Issues in an English Immersion School Setting

Aurore Isambert, Damien Céné, Delphine Jeandel, Véronique Lemoine-Bresson, Anne Choffat-Dürr, Valérie Fialais, and Latisha Mary

Introduction

In this chapter, we present our PRIMERA research project, titled 'Immersion practices and autonomous research' (Pratiques en immersion et recherche autonomisante), which was conducted in a primary and lower secondary school in the Académie de Nancy-Metz, utilizing a French-English bilingual teaching model. The study was conducted by a multidisciplinary group comprising primary and secondary school teachers, Department of Education supervisors, and four researchers from Education, Training, and Language Sciences at the University of Lorraine and the University of Strasbourg. PRIMERA is part of a network of associated educational areas (AEA) supported by the *Institut Français d'Éducation* (IFÉ) of the *École normale supérieure* (ENS Lyon) for a three-year period from 2021 to 2024.

The Collective shares a common concern for understanding and recognizing the linguistic and cultural diversity of all students to implement plurilingual pedagogies that fulfill the official expectations of English immersion teaching. PRIMERA is based on a bottom-up conception of research, without ignoring the theorization of emerging educational phenomena, and on founding principles such as collaboration between research and school professionals who *research together*. Darchy-Koechlin (2022: 329) rightly points out that an AEA "rests on fragile balances and complex alchemies." The methodological protocol designed, therefore, takes on specific qualities to create both "room to breathe" (an expression dear to Yves Reuter) and a space that enables us to co-problematize, to *work together* (absence of hierarchization and instrumentalization, or condescending oversight), to seek solutions that awaken in both teachers and researchers "the powers to act that routine can weaken."[154] The initial work employed an empirical method, incorporating classroom observations, video-stimulated recall, interviews, focus groups, and sessions to examine both experiential and academic knowledge, as well as practical classroom trials and initial theoretical reflections. These efforts supplied the PRIMERA collaborative space and challenged the Collective to step out of its comfort zone. The Collective developed questions, such as the inclusion of all students in the immersion system, and attempted to better understand what may hinder this contemporary challenge.

The effects of *researching together*[155] led to the emergence of a new way of working: *writing together* and, above all, making room for teachers' voices in the research space. Three teachers filled this role: Aurore (also the head teacher), Delphine, and Damien. All three had received immersion training in the United States: Utah for Delphine and Damien, and Louisiana for Aurore. According to some aspects of Marcel's position theorization (2023), the position of the three colleagues is viewed as an issue that aims to grant them academic legitimacy, thereby securing a place in research. The position also becomes an objective, i.e., the Collective must take a stance on societal issues where the issues of social justice and the success of all students are crucial.

This chapter is a trial-and-error-based collaborative effort in the PRIMERA Collective. It belongs to an under-explored theme, both in France and internationally, concerning the co-writing process between researchers and teachers involved in research.[156] The text, therefore, does not follow the classic guidelines of a scientific text. It is, however, backed by the theoretical principles of collaborative research, which establish a space of safety and communication,[157] allowing Aurore, Damien, and Delphine to express themselves freely.

---

[154] See Sensevy, 2022: 12.
[155] See Dias-Chiaruttini *et al.*, 2021.
[156] See Promonet & Lemoine-Bresson, 2025; Natland, 2021.
[157] See Mottier-Lopez, 2015.

At this stage, this research arrangement aims to account for multiple voices surrounding selected objects, encompassing the principles of collaboration, professional development, and beliefs about teaching and learning in bilingual settings. The chapter is protean; it is presented as an interview between the four researchers (CRP, Collective of Research Professionals): Aurore, head teacher and primary year 1 teacher; Delphine, a teacher in year 2; and Damien, a teacher in year 3. The CRP chose five discussion points rooted in theoretical reflections and submitted them to the three teachers, who were then asked to respond openly and individually. Aurore, Delphine, and Damien then conducted a group interview (recorded and transcribed) to *negotiate* their positions *together*. This chapter presents five points of theoretical reflection, followed by the teachers' reactions. Parts of the group interview, inserted by the CRP, punctuate these reactions and document the individual remarks. Each of the five sessions concludes with a reflective pause from the PRIMERA AEA, providing theoretical insights into the teachers' points of view, as well as an opening up to emerging issues at the heart of the PRIMERA Collective.

Collective of research professionals:

The CRP has sought to establish a research project with you based on the principle of collaboration, in which it was essential to accommodate your daily practices in English immersion to work together on this subject. While this kind of "research together" is likely to bring about changes in classroom practices, the CRP aims to both empower and reassure teachers and encourage questioning based on observed practices. What are your thoughts on this collaborative space?

Aurore: In the early days of research support, the researchers set out to establish a benevolent, non-judgmental framework. They made this explicit. In addition, the absence of a hierarchical superior also helped to break down this trainer/teacher, teacher/learner relationship. Little by little, a sense of trust was established. Over time, long-term support gave way to a more symmetrical relationship between researchers and teachers. The form of the meetings also facilitated this trust-building. First of all, the meetings were scheduled at the school, a shared place. The setting was relaxed, and informal social times were made a priority. In my opinion, it was this benevolent, reassuring, and long-term setting that enabled us to create space for discussion, to reassess our practices, and then to question them. The recordings were made voluntarily. Nothing was imposed. In front of the camera, even when I was a little stressed, I personally never felt judged in my work. I was very curious to see what went on in other teachers' classrooms. I dreamed of being a fly on the wall to observe my colleagues and learn from their practices; the camera made it possible. We created a community of sharing where everyone learns and continues to learn from one another. Feedback on the recordings was given after some time had passed, requiring anamnesis and distancing. At selected moments during the recording, the teachers filmed were able to pause the video and comment on specific moments in class. In this way, the teachers made their pedagogical choices explicit and their expertise visible. We worked in different small groups. The teacher being filmed would then take the floor, which made space for discussion and allowed common issues to emerge.

How can we help students with learning difficulties in English? Does the exclusive use of English exacerbate comprehension problems in mathematics? How and what to assess? What about science difficulties in English for students who arrive mid-course in upper elementary school (Cycle 3)? What can we say about the lack of emotional involvement possible when speaking with students in English? Gradually, a common malaise began to emerge. What remained was to define it and understand its origins. In our training culture, pedagogical sessions are often top-down, offering highly pragmatic and model-based pedagogical formulas. Likely developed in response to teachers' expectations, these training sessions provide temporary satisfaction but do little to empower us.

Damien: (A remark by Damien appears to confirm a perceived lack of agency when a significant challenge was at stake). With the all-English approach – some kids got stuck, and I was not doing it – using French or other languages – because I did not allow myself to.

Aurore: The experience of being accompanied by research gave me a new way, not of being trained, but of being accompanied to reflect and make a conscious choice. This collaborative space, which invited me to engage in research, prompted me to reflect on my representations of languages and the world. In this way, through the school's management and my teaching practices, I can choose what resonance I want to be reflected in the Jean Jaurès school community. From now on, the school's challenge is to train teachers from around the world to share, disseminate, and support the implementation of plurilingualism, thereby promoting the success of all students.

AEA PRIMERA reflective break:
This feedback acknowledges the collaborative nature of the shift in our perspective on immersion practices, ourselves, and others. It highlights the importance of building an open community comprising researchers, the teaching team, and research contributors to foster a renewed professionalization through various subjects (all participants in collaborative research) in related activities. The choice of a methodological protocol that draws on experience to "collaboratively develop knowledge and resources"[158] brings about changes in both teaching practices and those of the researchers. This process means that everyone's practices are constantly being reconfigured, and working together is viewed more as support than training.[159] Gathering data through interviews, observations, video-stimulated recall, and focus groups enables us to better identify the needs of those involved, reflect on our activities, and note the effects on students, including their learning and perceptions of identity. While this statement appears to emphasize the need to create a safe space for research and sharing, it also underscores the fact that this space is well-equipped to welcome critical reflection on the practices, beliefs, and choices made by different actors.

Collective of research professionals

The first step in the collaborative process was to develop a common project among ourselves. We conducted classroom observations and group discussions. Together, as researchers and teachers, our

---

[158] See Mottier-Lopez, 2022: 336.
[159] See Savoie-Zajc, 2010.

Collective identified the difficulties encountered in the classroom and the points to be addressed during the research project. As a CRP, we tried to foster collaboration based on trust and the creation of safe spaces in which you could express yourselves without the presence of your institutional hierarchy. In the CRP's view, this was particularly important given the nature and importance of the administrative hierarchical structure in the French education system. How do you relate to these statements?

Aurore: During discussions with the lower secondary school (collège), the school's English teacher repeatedly mentioned a significant discrepancy between the students' oral production, whether continuous or interactive, and their written production. At the time, we insisted that English was a tool for learning but not an object of learning.

> Jean Jaurès Elementary School is a public French/English immersion school. Children living in the school's geographical area are enrolled. From Grades 1 to 5, students are taught in English (40-50% of the teaching time, depending on the class level) and French (50-60% of the teaching time, depending on the class level). Teachers do not teach English but teach in the English language. Depending on the class level, subjects such as math, music, geography, and science are taught in English. Teachers follow the official programs of the French Department of Education.

This extract from the welcome booklet given to families on their arrival at the Jean Jaurès school leaves little room for metalanguage. We realized that our students were limited in their ability to learn. Oral expression alone was not enough. Written skills were necessary to enable our students to progress further, including orally. Gradually, the need arose to create a medium that supports and structures English language learning. We called it a "toolkit." During many working evenings when the researchers were absent, we drew up an English grammar progress chart that would enable students to structure their metalanguage. The toolkit would also serve as linguistic support for students arriving mid-year, giving them a "survival kit" to draw on. Working on metalanguage with students means enabling them to compare languages in order to understand universal linguistic features—such as plurals, negation, or verb endings like -s in the second person singular in French and -s in the third person singular in English. Initially, we made comparisons between the school's two languages of instruction (French and English), and gradually, along the way, we came to integrate the other languages present in the classroom, those spoken by the children.

AEA PRIMERA reflective break:
One of the most critical points to emerge was the need for the team's English and French teachers, both in primary school and *collège*, to work together as resources. Various categories of resources can be identified, including reference resources (such as welcome manuals and official texts) to justify teaching choices and a meta-resource (toolkit) to reflect on teaching in English and integrate the reflection points co-constructed within the PRIMERA collective.

Collective of research professionals

In particular, PRIMERA plans to highlight specific classroom practices and teachers' beliefs about bilingual education and bilingualism, encouraging them to reflect critically on their practices and evolve. The CRP first recognized and valued your individual and collective expertise, then drew on these experiences to make connections with current research in the field of bilingual education, with the aim of articulating theory and practice. How would you describe these beliefs and their effects?

Aurore: One of the beliefs handed down to us by our institutional heritage was the exclusive use of the target language for learning a second language.

Delphine: (insists on this point) When I arrived in the program, we had witnessed this ideal model experience. We wanted to copy what we had done and what we had experienced in Utah.

Aurore: So, we spoke only in English, including with students who had arrived mid-way through the program or students with learning difficulties. Even tutoring sessions outside class time were conducted in English. The program was innovative. Only one school in Nancy offered English immersion. The majority of students made spectacular progress in English. We were often in the limelight as a model for foreign and national delegations. This influence meant there was little room for discussion and reflection on how to challenge the two parallel monolingual systems.

Damien: (supports this comment) I was convinced that the American system, with its strict separation of languages, was the only one, the singular, the best, and that everything else was haphazard.

Aurore: The original idea was to take the model of bilingual education in Utah and replicate it in Nancy. It was an ambitious and innovative project. My aim is not to disparage it—quite the contrary—but to show how difficult it was to allow oneself to deviate from it. The strict separation of languages materialized spatially by the classrooms and was temporally defined in the timetable. One teacher, one language. One classroom, one language. One half-day, one language. In other words, two languages are evolving in parallel without any link between them. There is no link between classrooms. There is no link between English and French teachers. The school's reputation put the spotlight on English-speaking teachers, leaving French-speaking teachers to feel undervalued. We had to deal with divisions sometimes. During our research, we discussed, identified, listed, and classified the difficulties we observed in our students. One day, when we were ready for the scientific insights, the researchers provided us with some reading material. The text by Roussel and Gaonac'h was my first trigger. I remember this revelation clearly. According to a study by Roussel, Tricot, and Sweller, the first group of law students received their course in their L1 (language 1) and L2 (language 2), the second group only in their L2, and finally, the third group in their L1. This study showed that the best-performing law students were those in groups 1 and 3 who had studied their course in their L1 and L1/L2, and those who developed greater language skills were those who had received the course in both languages. A diagram of a brain symbolizing the embedding of learners' L1 and L2 illustrated the point.

At that moment, I understood the links and transfers that were taking place between the languages. I then allowed myself to consider a place for French in English to decompartmentalize languages, enabling students with difficulties to overcome linguistic blocks or to ensure their comprehension. This research provided a platform for the French language and retrained teachers. As a result, bilingual children's literature projects involving both English and French teachers were born. At my career review meeting, I submitted this article to the inspector. The hierarchy needed to know how the brain works and about language transfer. The inspector was very attentive to my presentation and to the changes that reading the article had brought about in my practices.

Damien: My first steps in bilingual immersion teaching led me to a strict representation of bilingual immersion teaching. I practiced as a French language teacher in the Dual Immersion program in Utah. It worked in the following way: two teachers, one specializing in the English language and one in the French language, with an equal distribution of teaching time in both languages. The French teacher had to speak only in French, no language bridges. The students had to believe that I did not speak a word of English.

Delphine: (recalls an anecdote that struck her) Before one of the first school swimming lessons, the headteacher at the time had called the pool manager, telling him that I was not going to speak French, that I was not French, and that she hoped they would speak English. It was a completely crazy situation.

Damien: (emphasized this point with some humor) And the kids were drowning, and we were like, *"Breathe," "Grab the edge of the pool."* There was something a little surreal about it. (Recalls another anecdote that seemed to stay with him) We were on an outing, and one of the students' father was accompanying the class. When it came time to randomly form the groups, the student whose father was a chaperone was not assigned to the group with his father. He cried and cried, *"I want to be with my dad! I want to be with my dad,"* but the kid was French, so he cried in English because he was with me, and he would never have allowed himself to cry in French. The students were also required to express themselves exclusively in English, including when communicating with one another. As their progress was "spectacular" and the use of another language was not perceived as a constraint, I long considered this system to be the most effective, if not the only valid one, and to regard other ways of teaching languages as "the easy way out" or "low-cost immersion." One issue in particular led us to question our target-language teaching methods: how do we integrate new students, especially from year 3 (CE2) onwards? Is it reasonable to believe that by being immersed 50% of the time in a class where the students and teacher speak only English, these new students will catch up? And what about struggling students? It did not take long for the methods we had been using to reveal their limitations. We had to find ways to adapt, but we needed to find the right way to do so. In the end, the idea of building bridges with the students' language(s) seemed obvious, and our certainties had never led us to it.

LéA PRIMERA reflective break:
Damien and Delphine's words highlight the proactive educational policy pursued in Utah, one that is not based on the initiative of parents or academics but on the conviction of politicians about the benefits of bilingualism. Notably, this initiative was led by Jon Huntsman Jr., a polyglot governor, and Howard A. Stephenson. Upon their return to France, guided by pedagogical guidelines enshrined in the ideological program of Dual Language Immersion, both attempted to replicate the 50/50 model in their new teaching context, with two teachers, one teaching exclusively in French and the other entirely in English. This example illustrates that many bilingual programs are rooted in the assumption that a second language is acquired in the same manner as the first, i.e., through linguistic immersion, which involves maximum and exclusive contact with the target language. Furthermore, teachers often have limited awareness of bilingual language development research, which can lead to the risk of basing their pedagogies on popular myths about second-language acquisition. The principle, known as One Person One Language (OPOL), is undoubtedly the most widely adopted method in formal educational contexts. It serves as an answer to the questions raised by political decision-makers and educationalists concerning the distribution of languages, teaching, and teachers in all bilingual education models due to the presence of two languages of instruction. This principle, which dates back to the work of Grammont and Ronjat in the early 20th century, was initially

conceived for the bilingual education of children in mixed-language families:[160]

> According to Grammont, language input must come from both parents, each in their own language, so that the language other than the dominant one has sufficient space within the family unit to be jointly acquired. The separation of languages according to people, in this case, the parents, assumes that the child can acquire both languages naturally in this way and that language mixing can be avoided.

The OPOL principle in the classroom primarily serves to separate languages in the context of consecutive bilingualism, as opposed to simultaneous bilingualism, which is often the case in mixed-language families. This choice of OPOL is based on the fear of language mixing or delayed acquisition of one or both languages; in other words, a fear of bilingualism.

Collective of research professionals

During the initial observation phases, the CRP noted that several English teachers had numerous questions about their practices and doubts about the legitimacy of their role as bilingual English teachers, being so-called "non-native" English speakers. What is your stance on this observation?

Aurore: When I arrived at the Jean Jaurès school, I was greeted by a teacher with an English language teaching profile. While explaining how the school worked, he tried to reassure me about my English level. He then trivialized teacher error, telling me that it was an everyday part of the classroom. He also gave me some advice and suggested that if I did not know a word, I should ask the English-speaking students in the class for help. However, for my very first English-language classroom sessions, I remember scrupulously preparing the script for my sessions. Although I feel a little more at ease today, the question of legitimacy as a non-native speaker remains a salient concern.

Delphine: My first immersion teaching experience was in Utah, in the *French dual immersion program*. I was 26 at the time, and it was

---

[160] See Fialais, 2019/2021.

also one of my very first professional experiences. My job was to teach exclusively in French in an American public school. To achieve this, the state of Utah invested heavily in its Spanish, French, and Chinese immersion programs. We had frequent training seminars with researchers specializing in second-language acquisition processes. Utah was opening more classes and formalizing the teaching methods adopted elsewhere, becoming a benchmark in immersion teaching. These immersion classes are seen as a key argument for attracting businesses and supporting the state's economic growth. In addition to the economic argument, the development of these classes has a particular resonance in Utah due to the strong presence of the Mormon Church, which encourages its followers to undertake a two-year mission in a foreign country. All these socio-economic and religious issues made my immersion teaching experience feel massive, colossal, even grandiose... in short, disproportionate. When I returned to France to teach English, I tried to copy this immersive model. Since our superiors considered that we had been trained in the USA, they gave us a lot of latitude. I never doubted my legitimacy to teach my students in English, especially since I hold a degree in English. Still, I soon realized that for my teaching to make sense, the context in which my students were immersed had to be authentic. I tried to make my writings and albums as idiomatic as possible, using personal photos and videos taken in Utah. Still, I always found that what I was proposing to my students "sounded fake," whereas, in Utah, I could never have doubted the authenticity of what I was proposing to my students. The fact is, I am not American but French, and that made all the difference. Language is full of feelings. When you teach a language, you embody it. You represent it. Besides, I am no more American than I am British or a New Zealander, so why teach in US English? Perhaps because my other colleagues had also been trained in Utah. In conclusion, this professional experience was both exemplary and challenging to reproduce in France.

AEA PRIMERA reflective break:

These reflections reveal two elements that can contribute to the perpetuation of language teaching reification. On the one hand, there is the question of the model evoked by Delphine, and on the other, the native spectrum to which Aurore refers. Delphine shows how Utah's language policy provides a clear roadmap to follow, with its reassuring aspects for the teacher who knows where they must go and how to get there to achieve a precise goal. Delphine's words, as well as Damien's, clearly indicate a myth surrounding the single path to immersion teaching. The comfort felt by teachers who follow a strict course of action, with formulas at their fingertips, can be contrasted with the questions emerging today around the long-term effect of this method on personal development and issues of inclusion for all students. This one-size-fits-all method appears to overlook the challenges faced by teachers in complex, heterogeneous contexts such as Utah, as well as by students with diverse cognitive, linguistic, and cultural backgrounds. Aurore raises the figure of the native in language teaching, even though the supposed superiority of the native has been widely criticized in the scientific literature in English, not least because it implies the inferiority of the non-native, whose language is considered deficient compared to the native.[161] However, this spectrum does not seem to have hindered Delphine, who believes herself sufficiently competent, citing her experiences in Utah, as well as her diploma in English. Her way of thinking demonstrates her reflective stance toward the interconnectivity of both experiential and academic knowledge, particularly in her practices and search for solutions, as well as her ability to consider herself an expert in her field.

Collective of research professionals

The CRP also identified a critical need to foster collaboration between English and French teachers. The CRP had noticed that the teaching collective was keen to understand the impact of their practices on children's bilingual learning and development, and to develop their knowledge and skills to meet students' needs better. How has your thinking on this evolved? Would you say there has been a shift?

Aurore: Today, our understanding of languages has evolved beyond bilingualism. For me—and for several others—we now

---

[161] See Kasper & Kellerman, 1997.

envision a bridge that has been built, notably through insights gained from research on translanguaging. This marked the second, and perhaps the most significant, turning point in my journey. With 10 years of experience in priority education areas and having worked to promote co-education, I would often invite parents into the classroom to share a story or sing a song in their native language as part of my teaching practice. I was aware of social inequalities and was sensitive to them. When I arrived at the Jean Jaurès school, I was somewhat blinded by the excellence of the French/English bilingual teaching, which overshadowed the other languages present.

Delphine: That is what they—the institution—were looking for from us. They were expecting us to be the model; we are the model.

Aurore: I had not been aware of this language hierarchy. Now, I find myself wondering: When will we see the first French-Arabic bilingual public school? Thanks to this collaboration, I am now convinced of the political power of languages. As headteacher, I can make multilingualism a priority in our immersion school. Teachers and principals have the opportunity to give their schools a humanist dimension by integrating the languages present.

> This project serves the success of ALL students. Building "bridges" between languages aims to integrate existing languages to the benefit of both target languages (English and French) through a social justice lens. Developing a positive relationship with family languages not only enables all students to build on their learning using existing skills but also enables all children to benefit from the linguistic and cultural diversity of the classroom. Our students develop metalinguistic skills that are effectively applied in both French and English. The aim is no longer to train language speakers but to cultivate citizens of the world.

This excerpt from the minutes of the school council meeting on 13 October 2022 was sent to the school's parents and aims to raise awareness of these humanist values throughout the educational community.

Today, our collaboration with research extends beyond the scope of mere "training"—it has taken on the dimension of becoming a devoted advocate for me. Our school is becoming an increasingly effective vehicle for promoting inclusion and acceptance of those who are different from others. Students at our school now exhibit a notable level of open-mindedness as future citizens. They understand that a student at Jean Jaurès does not necessarily speak French at home. French and English are the languages of schooling, but our students do not impose a hierarchy among languages. Armela speaks Albanian, Salma speaks Arabic at home, Arno speaks Armenian, and William speaks English. It is simply a fact. They understand that French and English are the common languages of education but not everyone's native language. They recognize the added value this linguistic diversity brings—both individually and collectively.

When Stella's father visits the class to read a children's book in Italian, the students are amazed and listen attentively. Stella is no longer seen merely as a Year 1 (CP2) student but as an Italian-speaking child with an Italian-speaking father. Their perception of her father also changes. Through this shared reading experience, the children form connections and build a shared memory.

Integrating and honoring the languages present in the school—such as through the "One Month, One Language" video initiative—invites us into the personal stories of both students and staff. This process fosters a sense of belonging. Valuing everyone's linguistic expertise is a way of recognizing individual identity and striving for social justice. For students, teachers, after-school program leaders, or classroom assistants, acknowledging one's mother tongue contributes to the construction of identity. For others, openness to different languages and backgrounds becomes a source of enrichment, fostering a more nuanced understanding of French cultural diversity.

As a head teacher, my role enables me to guide and encourage initiatives that promote plurilingualism as a pathway to social justice. The first step is to genuinely know the students in our classes. By implementing the "language flower" activity in every classroom, teachers can first identify the linguistic repertoire of their class and then highlight individual students' backgrounds through the creation of these flowers. The foundation for using these plurilingual resources lies in first recognizing them.

Teachers then have the autonomy to decide whether and how to use these resources, depending on the learning context. For instance, when a Year 4 (CM1) student—born and educated in Italy, with Arabic as his mother tongue—joined our school, we placed him in a class with twins who share a similar background. This choice enabled in-class language tutoring, leveraging the linguistic expertise of student peers. These decisions are only possible when we have detailed knowledge of our students' linguistic profiles.

Encouraging plurilingualism in the classroom also means allowing students to think and reflect in their mother tongue. During a writing lesson focused on the lexical field of fear, Armela chose to write her text in Albanian. Her ability to express fear in her native language became an essential part of the learning process. Plurilingualism is not something that can be taught—it must be lived.

AEA PRIMERA reflective break:
Teachers' understanding of their practices leads them to produce new knowledge about these practices. However, the co-produced professional knowledge is just as valuable as the scientific knowledge that teachers have accessed to take a reflective look at their practices. This effect can be explained by one of the postulates of collaborative research, which views teachers as responsible, autonomous, and projective actors and partners in research with whom researchers examine practices and study them reflectively together.[162] One of the consequences of this is apparent in Aurore's declarations: a shift in posture that has resulted in "a dimension of being a devoted advocate," with a concern for social justice. These reflections show the extent to which Aurore no longer hesitates to equate linguistic and cultural issues with political, educational, and school ideologies. She also appears to systematically place students' linguistic and cultural identities at the heart of pedagogical reflections while incorporating strong societal and family anchoring.

Concluding remarks

A community of practice

---

[162] See Desgagné *et al.*, 2001.

At the start of the research, the researchers were able to observe moments of explicit practice by the teachers as they dealt with the day-to-day problems encountered in immersion teaching situations and to reconstruct moments implicit in the research. In this sense, the teachers formed a community of practice, as defined by Wenger (1998), insofar as they collaborated on addressing professional situations arising in shared conditions of practice. The chapter suggests that a boundary may have existed between research and teaching practices, particularly given the distinct formal structures in which researchers and teachers operate. The overriding challenge, therefore, was to create a space conducive to collective learning, the creation of meaning in this shared search, and the development of the identity of a Researcher-Teacher Collective. In this space, the PRIMERA Collective successfully negotiated the meaning of the practices of both researchers and teachers through the implementation of a methodological approach that mobilized language and facilitated exchanges among all members. Focal points were chosen, including teamwork, teachers in English, and teachers in French, taking into account the languages present to learn and develop one's identity, for example. This enabled the Collective to participate actively in the process of raising awareness about immersion practices and their effects on students as well as parents. The mutual commitment of the researchers and the teaching team to negotiated actions is what defines the Collective as a community of practice.

Critical awareness

Committed to collaborative research,[163] the Collective distanced itself from action, developed critical reflexivity on its practices, and confronted frames of reference, including training in Utah, ministerial prescriptions, academic injunctions, and scientific literature. Each of the original communities of practice became involved in each other's professional repertoires, shared resources, and went beyond individual skills to put them in service of the Collective. Whether in Aurore's, Damien's, or Delphine's discourse, it becomes apparent that awareness played a fundamental role in the

---

[163] See Vinatier *et al.*, 2012.

space for expression and reflection created by their shared quest. Collective members became aware of each other's practices, their diversity, the beliefs and myths that guided them, and the constraints they faced. The Collective took charge of addressing the questions and problems encountered and negotiated solutions to be implemented in the classroom. The construction of collaboratively negotiated collective knowledge[164] on immersion teaching has led to a deeper understanding of practices, critical questioning of the program, its societal implications, and learning, particularly for students who are struggling or those arriving mid-course. However, many challenges remain. The Collective has yet to create spaces where, as a community of practice, it can initiate changes that more effectively support the success of all students and foster professional development.

---

[164] See Mottier-Lopez, 2015.

3.2. "Difference is Always There, of course; the Question is How You Deal With It." Experiences from a German-Italian Primary School Project in Frankfurt Am Main, Germany

Gabriele Budach and Ulrike Dreher

Introduction

This text is the result of conversations between Ulrike Dreher, a primary school teacher in Germany since 1990 who has been active in a bilingual German-Italian project at an elementary school in Frankfurt am Main since 2003, and Gabriele Budach, a sociolinguist who has been involved in research in the field of multilingual education and multimodal education for 25 years. The two have a long history of collaboration and friendship dating back to the pilot phase of this bilingual project (2003–2007), in which Ulrike Dreher was involved as a teacher and Gabriele Budach as a researcher advising on the project. Both met again for this article and exchanged ideas that will hopefully be useful for readers, teachers, and the broader interested public.

The text primarily addresses the role of difference and explains how differences were and are dealt with in the project. It talks about differences in children's linguistic repertoires, in national curricula and their respective characteristics; and it looks into the socialization and teaching experience of German and Italian teachers involved in the project. The text also explains what pedagogical approaches were adopted to deal with difference to either bridge or maintain it, while highlighting its potential as a learning resource for bilingual teaching appropriately. The text discusses both challenges and advantages of the project. Let's get closer and listen in on the conversation:

Gabi: In many school systems and curricula, the image of an idealized, homogeneous student body still seems to prevail. In this project, how did you deal with the heterogeneity of the children, language differences, and difference in general?

Ulrike: Of course, difference is always there, even if you have a supposedly monolingual class and a supposedly monolingual curriculum. The question of how to deal with difference, therefore, exists in all classes, both bilingual and standard. The challenge is always to ensure that all children benefit and that the teachers focus on the learning level of each child.

In the bilingual project, we placed a particular emphasis on the children and their capacity to learn from and with each other. This implied that children had to work together, help each other and find ways of solving problems together. To start from there has always proved to be a great advantage.

Gabi: That was certainly not easy. Did you create particular structures? It surely requires specific approaches and a learning culture that encourages children to exchange ideas. It's not a given that children experience that their knowledge is valued and that it counts as much as the knowledge of their teachers. How did you manage that?

Ulrike: Yes, that is interesting from a pedagogical point of view. Some colleagues formed mixed language pairs, that is, German-Italian tandems. The children then had to sit next to each other in pairs and work together. I didn't do it that way, but I organized table groups with four children. At each table, there would always be one child competent in Italian able to help and assist others if support with the Italian language was needed. And that worked really well.

We then designed tasks that made working in groups both possible and necessary. That was also when I discovered and developed the weekly plan as a suitable system for the class and for myself. It was a good fit for me. I've always enjoyed drawing up plans with different tasks from different subjects, some monolingual, some bilingual. Some of the tasks were to be done alone, others together. Some could only be done with an Italian partner child, some in a mixed-language group. Other teachers used similar forms of cooperative learning, such as learning tables or stations where students move through to engage with different activities and resources related to a specific topic and where they can work in both languages. There are many different systems.

Gabi: Such forms of teamwork and diversification also exist in standard lessons. What is special about bilingual lessons here?

Ulrike: Such approaches to learning exist of course also in standard elementary school lessons. Depending on the teacher, activity- and goal-oriented work is also used in standard classes. It's not just knowledge transfer from teacher to pupil. To say that would not do justice to primary school teaching. But in bilingual lessons there is also this aspect of differentiated language use. In standard lessons, it is evident that the expectation is to work in German. In bilingual lessons, however, work is done in German and Italian. Sometimes the children don't even realize which language they are working in because they are trying to solve a specific problem. It's important, however, to ensure that both languages are used to an appropriate extent. For example, it is important to insist that children write down their results of an experiment in Italian, as German children in particular would not do this by themselves or without encouragement by the teachers. You have to make sure that they get enough writing practice in Italian, as German is the dominant language for them. In the past, German was often the lingua franca among the children. In my current class, however, children actually do speak both languages.

Gabi: An important goal in the early years of elementary school is literacy learning. In your bilingual class, you have developed an interesting approach to teaching literacy in both languages, German and Italian, simultaneously. Would you say that this approach is fundamentally different from monolingual literacy teaching?

Ulrike: It depends on what you mean by fundamentally, but actually, no. I think learning to read in the bilingual class is more or less the same, or at least largely similar. The letters are the same, and children learn how to associate sounds and letters. So, the actual process of learning to read and write is very similar. But of course, it is different if you do it in two languages, instead of only one. The lessons are organized differently, and there are two teachers in class, each of them incorporating different types of exercises.

Gabi: To come back to the question of dealing with difference. How important is it to actively and explicitly compare languages in bilingual lessons?

Ulrike: The children in the bilingual project are constantly comparing the languages, also because the teachers actively encourage these comparisons. For example, we use a bilingual phonics table, where letters (and phoneme-grapheme relations) in both alphabets are compared. I worked in an international school in France for several years. I noticed that although there were interferences in spelling between German and French, the children never actually made this connection. To be honest, this surprised me, especially after my experience in the bilingual project, where the children constantly compared the languages by themselves, and they commented on differences without any prompting.

Gabi: So, comparing languages is an important pedagogical approach in the bilingual project?

Ulrike: Yes, and not just in terms of language, but also with regard to cultural differences, such as different arithmetic systems, ways of calculating, for example in written arithmetic, how and where to write down the carry forward (in written addition). Or with regard to spelling systems, we are constantly asking: How is this taught in Italy and how is it taught here?

Gabi: How do you ensure that the children have fun and also gain independence in dealing with (systematic) comparisons?

Ulrike: We don't just work with language. We also include a lot of objects that children bring from home, for instance, during literacy lessons. This encourages language and cultural comparison and is very stimulating.

Gabi: Would you say that personal objects help involve the children's home environment and that children are encouraged to discuss it in class?

Ulrike: Yes, of course, it was always exciting to see what the children brought with them and what ideas they had. Sometimes they were also inspired by inventing imaginary words or sentences with words that always had to start with the same letter. Made-up language games in different languages, and all the things they come up with— that is also a lot of fun. Things like that are stimulating, but to be honest, they are also stimulating in standard lessons.

Gabi: Did you find it challenging to combine contents from the German and the Italian curricula? And how did you do that?

Ulrike: We had things like the abacus or the geoboard. These came more from the Italian curriculum. Since they were a useful addition to the German lessons and the children enjoyed making and working with them, we included them.

Children always especially enjoyed carrying out experiments on a given subject. They loved to work on something in both languages and to then present the results. Some of their tasks were in Italian, others in German. This meant that language learning was not just an end in itself, but that the task was a means to an end in order to find out something. To achieve this goal both of the languages had to be used. Children, in general, love exploring things and reflecting on them. If the task is set in a child-oriented way and languages can be used for discovery that has no pre-designed path, children tend to be very open and love it.

Gabi: Is there anything to be learned from this for standard lessons?

Ulrike: I think the focus in standard lessons is very often mainly on language. Perhaps less so in elementary school than later on. In our project, we try to not primarily focus on language or on language alone, but to always put content first. Language then follows along.

Gabi: An important point we should also address is team teaching. Since the beginning of the project, you have always been working together with an Italian colleague, either in the same classroom or in separate lessons. How did you experience this collaboration? How did your Italian colleagues respond to the project?

Ulrike: Bilingual teaching was new to all Italian colleagues. No one had any previous experience. This was a big challenge. You are asking of your Italian colleagues to jump right into an entirely new school system, to learn its ropes and, at the same time, adapt your own ways of teaching. And of course, working in this way, also creates more lively, noisier classrooms, where children talk while working together, rather than sitting quietly and working alone.

Gabi: What prerequisites should you have for tandem lessons? What is important for it to succeed?

Ulrike: You need, of course, a basic structure. And I think it's an advantage for me that I've been teaching for so long now. I have internalized this basic structure. I know it inside out. I no longer need to worry about it. What content is covered in which school year and so on. You can then easily integrate all sorts of other things into this basic structure.

With regard to tandem teaching, I think that at least one of the two tandem teachers should already have some experience, otherwise you are very insecure. With professional experience, you feel more confident to just try things out. You learn your trade and can then confidently present what you do to others, especially to parents, who will then feel more reassured.

In the beginning, it is more challenging to work with another colleague or to integrate new content, because you're still busy learning how to structure your own lessons properly. It's only with time that you gain a certain level of confidence, also with literacy teaching.

To this day, I have 25 years of experience teaching children how to read and write. So far, I have succeeded with all of them and parents can rest assured that their child will leave school with these skills.

Gabi: Would you say that the project is suitable for all children, or are there also children who are overwhelmed?

Ulrike: Some children were pushed to their limits, especially children who already find learning difficult. Children who are already struggling to learn to read and write will find it an additional burden if they have to do it in two languages. For the German children, you should then consider whether the project makes sense so that they don't have a harder time than they should at school. But no child has really failed in the 16 years that I have taught in the bilingual project. There have been children who did not cope with certain aspects of school, but this was generally not due to the bilingual lessons, but to the school situation as a whole.

In these cases, it would be easier for everyone involved if there was a way out of a class, so to speak, without losing face and looking like a failure. But that doesn't just apply to the bilingual project.

The children who had difficulties tended to come from the Italian community. But they all ultimately benefited from being bilingual and from the fact that Italian was available to them as a school language.

For some German children with a low tolerance for frustration, it was initially difficult to cope with multilingualism in the classroom and they could not cope so well with not understanding anything or not understanding everything at first.

Gabi: After all these years in the bilingual project, would you choose to teach in it again?

Ulrike: Definitely, because you are constantly learning as a teacher. With every new colleague anyway, but also with the same ones. That's exactly why I would like to do it again and again.

Gabi: Thank you very much and I wish you continued success and joy in bilingual teaching, with the children and your colleagues.

3.3. Building Up Bilingual Practice in Rural India: Current Efforts of Language and Learning Foundation
Cynthia Groff and Dhir Jhingran

Introduction: Indian multilingualism and education

With its vast diversity of languages and peoples, India provides an exceptional context for exploring the use of multiple languages in educational contexts. The People's Linguistic Survey of India has documented 780 spoken languages.[165] While 22 languages have received official recognition in the Indian Constitution, the Census of India (2011) lists 270 mother tongues, which are classified into 121 language groups. Although language policy in India acknowledges some of this diversity, many non-dominant languages and varieties are made invisible.[166] Within education, only 36 of those languages are currently used as an official language of instruction in Indian schools, meaning that approximately 60% of Indian children receive primary education in a language other than their home language, and about 35% face a moderate to severe learning disadvantage as a result.[167] The complexity of the language context in India encompasses remote communities where children are familiar only with their home language, multiple home languages in the same region, the prevalence of language variants, and widespread adult multilingualism, in which some languages are more dominant than others. Educational inequalities are further perpetuated by a system in which higher-quality education is accessible primarily to families who can afford non-government schools, many of which use English as the language of instruction. Conscious efforts to incorporate non-dominant languages into education have taken various forms in India over the years and have faced multiple challenges.[168] The importance

---

[165] See Devy, 2014.
[166] See Groff, 2017.
[167] See Jhingran, 2005.
[168] See Mohanty, 2006.

of building on children's existing linguistics resources has been gaining attention internationally. Multilingual education programs that emphasize the use of the mother tongue aim to counter educational inequalities by incorporating unrecognized and minoritized languages and varieties while still providing access to the languages of power in society.

Bilingual education for Wagdi children

Language and Learning Foundation (LLF) is a non-profit organization working in eight states in India to improve children's foundational learning in primary grades, with a focus on areas where children's home or primary languages are not used as the mediums of instruction and where children have limited understanding of the official medium of instruction. Using an interview format, we describe below the current efforts of the foundation to develop a high-quality bilingual education program within the government school system, which provides children with the language support they need in the early years of education and is replicable across contexts.

Cynthia: Tell me about the program you have been working on in Rajasthan. How and when did it start?

Dhir: In 2017, we initiated a bilingual education program in approximately 30 schools in Rajasthan with the support of UNICEF. This initiative initially targeted non-formal schools located in remote tribal areas, which were managed by the Tribal Affairs Department—regions where regular government schools were not available. These schools were known as *Mabadi* centers.

We chose these centers because introducing children's home languages into the mainstream government school system posed significant challenges. Our approach was to pilot a bilingual model in the *Mabadi* centers and then advocate for its adoption in formal schools under the Education Department.

For two years, we implemented the program in 30 *Mabadi* centers. Wagdi—a language belonging to the Bhili language group in Central and Western India—was the home language of nearly all the children, and all the teachers were native speakers of Wagdi. The learning outcomes among these children were deeply concerning;

most were not acquiring even basic literacy in Hindi, the official medium of instruction.

Our core question was: How can we ensure that these children learn effectively, that Wagdi is developed as an oral language, that higher-order comprehension happens in Wagdi, and that Wagdi is maintained in the classroom—while also ensuring proficiency in Hindi, as demanded by the system?

We worked within that system for two years. Fortunately, the government then agreed to shift from the informal to the formal school system—positive news for us. However, it coincided with the discontinuation of funding for the *Mabadi* schools. UNICEF also reoriented its focus toward regular government schools.

During that phase, a key achievement was the development of numerous "big books" and other Wagdi-language materials, including children's poems, posters, and folktales. We also conducted a situational analysis to understand the children's initial grasp of Hindi upon entering school. We found that their exposure to Hindi was minimal and that standard Hindi was not spoken in their immediate environment. Most children acquired some conversational Hindi only by Grade 3, and the textbooks were far too advanced for their level.

This was the context in which we launched a bilingual program for Grades 1–3 in the non-formal schools.

In 2019, just one year before the COVID-19 pandemic, we transitioned to working in 40 government schools, focusing on Grades 1 and 2 in similarly Wagdi-speaking regions. We adapted lessons from the earlier program in several ways. Like the *Mabadi* centers, these government schools typically had just one teacher covering Grades 1 and 2, creating a pervasive multigrade teaching environment.

In collaboration with the Education Department, we defined specific learning outcomes in Hindi for the end of Grades 2 and 3. We accepted accountability for ensuring that the majority of students met these goals. We selected schools where teachers (often just one) for Grades 1 to 3 were Wagdi-speaking members of the local community—making it possible to implement a strong first-language-based education program.

We initially conducted extensive consultations with the community, administrators, and teachers. There was no real objection to introducing Wagdi, provided that by the end of Grade 3, children would be learning an adequate level of Hindi. During implementation, there was no significant pressure on us (LLF) to achieve high levels of proficiency in Hindi, as the baseline learning levels were already relatively low. However, learning outcomes were still to be measured in Hindi, which was the children's L2.

As a result, we opted for an imperfect model—not a mother-tongue-based multilingual education (MLE) program, but rather a bilingual one that is not even an early-exit model. It is a program where the L1 is used extensively, primarily in the oral domain, and to some extent in reading and writing—mainly through workbooks that include Wagdi words and sentences. However, official exams and the formal medium of instruction continued to be in Hindi. That said, this policy is mainly symbolic, as it is widely understood that the children do not know Hindi.

We developed an instructional design, which was a week-by-week plan for the first year. We had a full year of teaching and learning before the COVID-19 pandemic began in 2020. So, you have a design, and you follow what is called a balanced approach to teaching literacy. We talk about four blocks: Oral language development, which is the most important. Decoding, reading, and writing. They all go together, also. We developed an instructional design for each week, helping teachers think through how to allocate time between Grades 1 and 2, and combining groups for oral language development using storybooks, conversation, and big books.[169] The focus was on listening comprehension, especially using higher-order questions.

Cynthia: What is the current phase of the project?

Dhir: The current phase is as follows: We have completed three years—two of which were during the COVID-19 pandemic. For the last four to six months, schools have been open. So, I would say 1 year, 9 months of school closure. However, we continued a community-based learning program for children throughout, except

---

[169] Big books are enlarged texts used for shared reading in the classroom.

for the worst part of the second wave, with local volunteers continuing. So, I would say three years, with two years being very different from what happens in a classroom.

Cynthia: I'd like to revisit something you mentioned about an "imperfect model." You said what you developed is an "imperfect model." Why would you call it imperfect?

Dhir: If you can use children's home or familiar language as the medium of instruction for as many years as possible, that's ideal for their learning. Research indicates that this approach yields the most effective results. In that sense, the late-exit model—or continuing with the first language for as long as possible—should be considered the gold standard. By that yardstick, what we implemented was a compromise.

Children were expected to acquire formal literacy in Hindi, though we incorporated many Wagdi words. Phonological awareness activities, the introduction of the Devanagari script, and initial decoding work were all conducted using Wagdi vocabulary. However, Hindi remained the formal medium of instruction, which limited the potential benefits of extended literacy development in Wagdi.

In terms of oral use, we secured agreement from the government that until Grade 5, teachers and children could continue to use Wagdi to support comprehension in Hindi—particularly when introducing new topics or encouraging children to express themselves. Still, Wagdi remained primarily confined to oral use. It appeared in "big books" and was used for informal expression, reading, and writing, but it was not officially recognized as a medium of instruction.

We continued to explore the best way to implement this bilingual approach, and we are now also researching to understand how using a child's first language supports confidence and social adjustment during the first two or three years of school. We ask: What benefits does this bring? How does incorporating orality into the classroom help children participate more naturally?

There are benefits. However, this remains an imperfect model—one that does not use children's languages for long enough or in literacy development to the extent we would prefer.

Cynthia: Yes. Ok. But it is going much further than what was happening before.

Dhir: Yes. These classrooms have become so vibrant. I do not know what the results will show, but children talk, they speak. You see, they want to participate, unlike the other silent classrooms, even in the next block.

Cynthia: Yes, so even that is one of the main differences between your bilingual treatment schools and the other schools.

Dhir: Yes.

Ideological and implementational challenges

If a program like the one described above were easy to initiate and implement, we would likely see many more like it. In reality, challenges often arise in both ideological and implementational domains. Ideologically, a multilingual program may conflict with local or national beliefs about the role of language in education. From an implementational standpoint, policy constraints and logistical realities often limit program effectiveness.

The historical and societal acceptance of the languages used in a program is crucial for its legitimacy in educational settings. Equally important are language policies at local, regional, and national levels, as well as how educational decision-makers interpret and apply them. At the school level, practical barriers—such as administrative constraints and financial limitations—can also hinder implementation.

In the Wagdi context, the perceived importance of learning Hindi in schools could potentially lead to ideological resistance, particularly if a monolingual mindset prevails—that is, the belief that using the mother tongue might reduce exposure to Hindi and, therefore, hinder its acquisition. However, in this case, community support was strong. Parents were persuaded that mother-tongue instruction would enhance, not diminish, their children's learning of Hindi. As Jhingran explained, "We haven't faced any major challenges on that account."

From an implementation perspective, teacher training and classroom monitoring were among the most pressing concerns, compounded by a shortage of qualified teachers and limited instructional time. Considerable effort was dedicated to designing an effective instructional model and training teachers in its application. Another challenge was adapting the program to the diverse varieties of minority languages and varying sociolinguistic contexts.

We continue the interview:

Cynthia: Let us talk some more about the program itself. What are the difficulties and challenges that you were confronted with, maybe in ideology and policy, and implementation?

Dhir: What worked from a policy perspective came later. Initially, there was little formal support; however, today, we have the National Education Policy (NEP) 2020, which is notably supportive of integrating children's home languages into schooling. It makes a practical recommendation: wherever possible, mother tongue instruction should continue through Grade 8 across the country.

The Foundational Learning Mission, launched in 2021, also emphasizes the importance of using children's languages in early education—but our work began two years before that. We implemented the program in a remote area, largely unnoticed by policymakers. For government officials based in the capital, it did not raise concerns at the time.

Fortunately, there was a key administrator—the then Secretary of Education—who genuinely valued children's languages. We were able to meet with him, and his support made a significant difference. Ultimately, much depends on individuals in positions of influence who are willing to enable and support such initiatives.

Dhir: In contexts where students have a stronger understanding of Hindi, implementation has proven challenging, as the instructional design assumes minimal prior knowledge of the language. Adapting the program to schools where Hindi is more prevalent—or where some students are familiar with Hindi while others are not—has required careful adjustments. We are addressing these challenges through targeted teacher training and ongoing instructional support.[170]

---

[170] Working in classrooms where students have mixed language abilities requires some extra thought and planning.

Cynthia: Ok. So, you said resistance has not been too challenging, and then that flexibility is needed in implementation and adapting to different contexts. And then, of course, before that, working with the government is a challenge in itself.

Dhir: If we were to scale this initiative, we would face greater challenges. For instance, while we have developed a substantial amount of material in Wagdi, questions remain about sustainability at scale. Although the government does not object—they permit us to use supplemental materials alongside the official Hindi textbooks—they are uncertain whether the state will fund the production and distribution of these resources across all schools in the district.

As the program expands, the issue of varying sociolinguistic contexts across schools—particularly differences in students' understanding of Hindi and other languages—will become even more complex. This diversity, manageable across our current network of forty schools, would likely be far greater across a whole district or region.

Another complication is linguistic variation within Wagdi itself. Even in a relatively small geographic area, Wagdi includes three dialectal variations. This raised the question: Which variety of Wagdi should we use? Although the differences were relatively minor—mainly in vocabulary, such as nouns—we still had to make a decision and adopt one form of the language for instructional materials. These dialectal differences pose an additional challenge when considering broader implementation.

Cynthia: So, how did the teachers respond to that? Were they also having difficulties with which variety would be valued above the other?

Dhir: Languages—and even variations within a single language—are valued differently. There is often a dominant or "powerful" variety. For example, Wagdi is widely spoken across Rajasthan, parts of Haryana, and northern Gujarat. However, within this region, the dialect spoken in the district headquarters is generally regarded as the standard form of the Wagdi language.

As a result, some schools located in peripheral areas felt that the language used in instructional materials differed slightly from their local variety. To address this, we included guidance in the teacher's manual, encouraging teachers to substitute local words as needed when reading from big books, poetry posters, or storybooks. This flexible approach enabled us to manage variations effectively.

Cynthia: So, you permitted them to use their own local words.

Dhir: Yes, the problem came when—if you introduce a letter and say this word is used with a picture to introduce that letter, and that has some other name in another dialect—then you are stuck because you can't use that. But that was rare. That happened in only one case, I think. If they had differences in pronunciation or slightly different spelling, the starting letter would be the same. Otherwise, they could improvise... For big books, we said, stick a small piece of paper over that word. It was very few words where this was the case.

Cynthia: So, you could replace that word with another word in that book. So, you are training them to embrace that diversity and work with it. It is challenging and fun! Maybe, stepping back a bit—knowing all the challenges that you would face—why did you do this work? What makes it worthwhile?

Dhir: When we were set up as a foundation—Language and Learning Foundation—if you look, it was one of our four core beliefs: that we work to improve children's foundational learning. We believe that one of the most effective ways to achieve this is to incorporate their first languages. The second is that we were very keen to collaborate with marginalized communities with low literacy, and this was an opportunity for us. The third, I think, was that we wanted to demonstrate how the use of children's languages leads to better learning, and this was our first demonstration program... That is the reason we did this: we approached the government. However, we worked small because we knew that obtaining permissions would be easier if we started small—so that is how we bypassed the need for big approvals.

Program effectiveness and monitoring

An essential step in gaining support for a bilingual program and implementing it on a larger scale is demonstrating the program's effectiveness, as well as monitoring the quality of its implementation. Besides building capacity within the entire education ecosystem and supporting states through systemic reforms, a central task of Language and Learning Foundation is to create proof-of-concepts through school-level demonstration. This is accomplished through both internal and external monitoring and evaluation.

Cynthia: Is there scientific monitoring for the program? And have you mostly done that yourself?

Dhir: So, we do two kinds of things. (1) We have four staff members who provide monitoring and academic support. They visit schools regularly, and we have developed a monitoring instrument, a classroom observation tool, to observe what the teachers are doing. How closely is the teacher following the expected standards? What are the patterns of language use? That is internal monitoring. The data gets analyzed, and then we have reflection sessions on it and draw up a follow-up plan for the next month's visit. That is one part of it. (2) We also have an external evaluation conducted by a third-party contractor, who is funded separately by a donor. They conducted the baseline and are now conducting the end-line.[171] This is only for student assessments at the baseline and end-line, with control schools and treatment schools. However, as I have mentioned, we have conducted fairly extensive documentation of this program, given that we were completing three years. This documentation includes the processes, challenges, and lessons learned. As I mentioned, we are now conducting research in our fourth year. Although it was delayed due to COVID-19, it was initially planned for the third year. Independent researchers will observe schools and classroom teaching and learning processes, including the use of Hindi and Wagdi, as well as teachers' beliefs and attitudes. So, that is the monitoring, evaluation, and research component. Research is just beginning, while internal monitoring is ongoing.

Cynthia: That seems like a lot of evaluation and monitoring, actually, for a very young program.

---

[171] Since the time of the interview in May 2022, the external evaluation report has been completed and has shown excellent results for student learning improvement over the baseline in the project schools compared with control schools.

Dhir: The reason we are doing this is that, typically, they work at a larger scale in other programs. In this case, we have treated the three-year program with government schools as a research and learning initiative—one aimed at generating insights to influence policy across Rajasthan. Our goal is to present the findings from this research and evaluation. We are also engaged in developing and implementing short courses on multilingual education for administrators and teachers. In Rajasthan, we are currently developing a comprehensive program for the entire education system, starting at the state level, based on the lessons learned here. The objective is not only to show results for these forty schools but also to influence the broader system in Rajasthan and, potentially, beyond. That is our aim.

Cynthia: That is the bigger goal. I am curious: How do you envision this adapting for more multilingual schools, specifically those with a variety of different languages?

Dhir: It's not easy. We've had the advantage of teachers who speak Wagdi, and all materials are available in both Wagdi and Hindi. So, I think what is important, what will come out, is the fact that it's very important to give adequate time for developing the core language of children. To support higher-order comprehension orally, do not just start doing... decoding work straight away. To be able to give time for children to express themselves, even if it takes time, to express themselves in their own language. Do not focus on or pressurize production initially. Also, I think what we've tried to establish is, you know, what Krashen calls comprehensible input.[172] We don't say that, but essentially, it means: Make everything simple. You know, when you are using an unfamiliar language, stories should be simple, and there should be a picture that supports it— some of these learnings. And the last thing, I think, is mixed language use. We don't call it translanguaging or anything like that. We say: Encourage children to use whatever language pattern works best for them.[173] Internally, we refer to it as the use of 'mixed' language.

---

[172] See Krashen, 1981, 2003.
[173] On natural multilingualism in India, see, e.g., Agnihotri, 1995, 2007; Khubchandani, 1978, 1997, 2003; Mohanty, 2006, 2018; Pattanayak, 1990, 2003.

A sentence pattern of Wagdi with Hindi words, or later a Hindi pattern with Wagdi words thrown in, or saying one sentence in Wagdi, one in Hindi. And do that yourself – that is for the teacher. So, these are four or five things that will help us, even in situations where there are multiple languages. However, we have not yet formulated a teaching model for a multilingual, multiple-home-language situation.

Oral language, mixed language, and higher-order thinking

Cynthia: I was thinking about translanguaging as a significant trend in our field, prevalent around the world—the latest and greatest.[174] But I was thinking about the informal multilingualism of India – that there is just lots of this kind of practice going on. And then, I assume, also in the classroom, that even outside of any formal multilingual program, the teachers are using Kumauni, for example. I heard from the girls there that the teachers "resort" to Kumauni. It is an informal, unofficial activity that they engage in undercover.[175] What would you say about that?

Dhir: Yes, obviously. However, when we conducted a situational analysis in these areas for these schools, we found that while most teachers do use the children's home language, some do not. Those who do not tend to rely heavily on Hindi. However, even among those who use their home language, there is often no precise method or strategy in place. For instance, in some cases, they read a story in Hindi and then switch everything else to the local language. There is little strategic thinking about how to utilize the children's language to support their transition into learning Hindi. That is the first issue.

The second issue is that not every teacher consistently does this. Another challenge is the lack of emphasis on oral language development. In many classrooms—language classrooms and even math classrooms to some extent—teaching often begins with abstract concepts and letter recognition. As a result, little oral work is happening. Even when teachers use the home language, the focus tends to be on teaching the alphabet from the outset, and this limits opportunities for oral language use in the classroom.

---

[174] See García, 2009; García & Lin, 2017.
[175] See Groff, 2018a, b.

Cynthia: Yes, so can you give some practical examples of what it looks like in the classroom? The strategic use of bilingual practice. How do you teach it?

Dhir: We don't recommend a specific formula—for example, using a defined percentage distribution of Wagdi and Hindi during the first six months. Instead, we assume that, before school, children have had little to no systematic exposure to literacy or even structured oral language development. With that in mind, we treat school entry as the starting point. What we emphasize is that, during the first eight weeks, teachers should focus on telling stories in Wagdi, reading big books in Wagdi, and encouraging children to express themselves orally in higher-order discussions. Hindi exposure during this phase is limited mainly to what is called Total Physical Response—explicit teaching of nouns and verbs through rhymes and action songs at designated times of the day. As the program progresses, the use of big books in Wagdi continues. These sessions feature rich discussions in the local language, enabling children to make predictions, respond to questions, and express themselves freely. Later, the same book is revisited in a Hindi translation using the same pictures and structure. During this stage, teachers tell the story in Hindi and ask mostly literal questions, whereas higher-order questions remain in Wagdi.

The suggested approach for the first 6–8 months is as follows: for simple yes/no or one-word responses (e.g., identifying a noun or naming a picture), if children have already learned the Hindi word, they can respond in Hindi. However, for all higher-order comprehension work, both teachers and children should use Wagdi to allow for fuller, more expressive communication.

We encourage what we call "mixed language," which emerges naturally and serves a pedagogical purpose. The purposive element involves prompting higher-order responses and allowing children to respond in the language with which they are most comfortable. If they use a mix of Hindi and Wagdi, that is not only acceptable—it is encouraged. Teachers are advised not to correct this mixing heavily. The natural part involves letting children speak however they usually would. Over time, especially by the end of the first year, teachers may begin to expect children to incorporate more Hindi words into their conversations. This progression continues into the second year. Our training focuses on several key dimensions—distinguishing lower- and higher-order work, using big books in both Wagdi and Hindi, and allowing children to speak in a mixed language. It is a flexible, stage-based approach rather than a rigid formula.

Cynthia: This lower-order and higher-order distinction, I think, is interesting because, in some ways, it is the opposite of what has happened in traditional bilingual classrooms. Often, all the simple requests are made in the "low" language, and then they switch to the formal, academic language for other things. It is the opposite of a diglossic situation, I guess.

Dhir: Yes, it seemed the correct thing to do for us. You can see that with the Grade 1 kids, the level of discussion increases if you allow them to speak in their native language. Of course, the teacher uses a mix of methods. Where she feels that they will understand some things, they will use a mix of approaches. That is left to the teacher to decide. But, yes, that is a distinction we draw very clearly.

Cynthia: So, it feels like you are flipping the power dynamics, which makes me think of the continua of biliteracy—consciously giving more power to one less powerful side.[176] It is a nice concrete example of that. Just flip it over: Give power and a place of higher-order thinking for the home language.

Dhir: Yes. This also stems from our belief that classrooms—especially language classrooms—often operate with low expectations of children. This is a widespread issue nationwide. Frequently, teachers read aloud from a text, pose a question, and then either answer it themselves or simplify it to the point where students can respond only with "yes," "no," or a choral reply. To counter this, we actively promote the use of open-ended questions and encourage open-ended discussions. The most effective way to achieve this is by allowing children to speak freely and by supporting teachers in creating an environment that fosters this expression.

Cynthia: Great! I am excited about what you're doing and what you're going to do! Is there anything else you would like to ensure teachers are aware of regarding this bilingual practice?

---

[176] See Hornberger, 1989; Hornberger & Skilton-Sylvester, 2000.

Dhir: I think one of the key considerations is determining how much of each language to use, when to use it, and in what manner. This needs to remain flexible, depending on the local context—and even within a single classroom, it may vary for different children. Of course, this is not easy to implement. But if teachers understand what is working for their students at any given moment—and are able to assess that formally or informally—then that becomes an excellent guide for making decisions about how to use languages in combination. What we have emphasized is this: Wagdi and Hindi can and should be used together, not in isolation. Teachers should not think in terms of rigid time blocks, such as "this is pure Hindi time" and "this is pure Wagdi time." Yes, there will be moments when you want children to use standard Hindi—such as during reading practice—but that does not mean excluding Wagdi altogether.

In India, there is still a widespread belief that using the local language will "corrupt" children's Hindi, especially when the two languages are somewhat similar. One of our key goals is to raise awareness and sensitize educators to the fact that children's first language supports their learning in many ways and should be used as long as needed. That is the mindset shift we aim to cultivate.

Multilingual spaces in the language policy context

Cynthia: So, would you say India has been ahead in multilingual practice? I am reviewing publications on multilingualism in India and multilingual classroom practices.[177] Is this something you would say India has been ahead on, at least as far as scholarship and thinking? Or not?

Dhir: I would say that, in some ways, we have regressed. In the early 2000s, there was a push in states like Odisha and Andhra Pradesh to implement multilingual education at the state level. One of those efforts has since been abandoned, while the other has been scaled back to a boutique program—currently operating in approximately 1,500 schools across 20 languages in Odisha. So, it still exists, but on a much smaller scale.

---

[177] See, e.g., Agnihotri, 1995, 2007; Jhingran, 2005, 2009; Khubchandani 1978, 1997, 2003; Mohanty, 2006, 2018; Pattanayak, 1990, 2003.

At present, there is no state where non-dominant languages are formally used as a consistent medium of instruction, except in parts of northeastern India—such as Assam—where, due to identity politics and community demand, several languages are officially recognized as mediums of instruction. However, this is often only on paper. In practice, textbooks are not printed for every grade, and teachers qualified in those languages are often not available in many schools.

Multilingual education programs at scale have not progressed beyond the achievements of the late 1990s. This remains a significant challenge. That said, there is a silver lining: current national policy and the foundational literacy and numeracy mission both emphasize the importance of using children's home languages in education.

At the same time, the Government of India has launched the "Schools of Excellence" initiative, which many states are interpreting as a mandate to introduce English-medium instruction from the pre-primary level. So, there is a parallel push toward English that complicates the picture. Still, it is worth noting that today, terms like "multilingual education" or "mother tongue instruction" are no longer viewed as problematic—unlike in the early 1990s. These concepts now have a place in policy, which marks a significant step forward.

Cynthia: So that is a good step.

Dhir: So, it is indeed a significant step forward that the new policy promotes the use of local languages. However, the general interpretation of "local languages" tends to prioritize the promotion of the state's dominant official languages—such as Marathi, Tamil, and Hindi. There is a lack of awareness about the existence of many non-dominant languages and the support they require.

The government appears to favor expanding the use of dominant Indian languages—like Hindi, Marathi, Tamil, and even Sanskrit—as mediums of instruction, potentially up to the level of engineering education. While this may be framed as a way to promote Indian languages, the critical issue that often gets overlooked is that, for a large number of children in the country, these dominant languages are second languages—not their mother tongues.

Cynthia: Yes. So, the policies are multilingual to an extent, but they do not acknowledge all the other forms of diversity beyond that.

Conclusion

The program being developed among Wagdi speakers by Language and Learning Foundation illustrates best practices for multilingual education in the Indian context, as well as the challenges and rewards of strategically incorporating children's home languages into early education. Key takeaways include the importance of developing higher-order thinking through the home language, building communication skills from oral language foundations, and maintaining flexibility in response to mixed-language use and linguistic variation. While home languages are often used informally in rural Indian schools—outside the official medium of instruction— this program demonstrates the value of a conscious and strategic bilingual approach in the classroom. The use of children's home languages enhances their self-confidence and self-esteem, supports socio-emotional adjustment to school, and facilitates early learning. Even when limited to oral use, familiar languages transform classroom dynamics, making teaching and learning more interactive and vibrant. Such classrooms enable richer, higher-order comprehension and extended dialogue, unlike many classrooms that use only the official language, where choral repetition and rote memorization often prevail.

The key ingredient is the teacher's balanced and purposeful use of both languages while encouraging children to express themselves using a mix of languages—at the word or sentence level—in ways that help them communicate most effectively. No rigid formula can define the ideal balance between L1 and L2; however, it is generally accepted that most instruction in Grade 1 should occur in children's L1, alongside effective strategies for gradually introducing L2.

Another important insight from this program is that introducing children's home languages must be accompanied by a structured early literacy design. This includes oral language development, systematic instruction in decoding, and diverse reading strategies such as read-alouds, shared reading, guided reading, independent reading, and writing composition.

3.4. The Role of Key Actors and an Innovative Biliteracy Program in Bringing National Languages into Primary Education in Senegal

Erina Iwasaki and Carol Benson

Introduction

As scholars and practitioners, we, the authors of this chapter, believe that regardless of where bi- or multilingual education is practiced, we can all learn from and be inspired by one another. We aim to inspire readers by describing an innovative approach implemented from 2009 to 2018 in the two national languages of Senegal, Wolof and Pulaar. We also analyze the influence of key activists on national policy in Senegal, aiming to promote the use of national languages alongside French in formal education. Our chapter addresses these research questions:

- How did the simultaneous bilingualism/biliteracy approach work in Senegalese schools, and what were the results?
- What has been the role of the key activists in bringing national languages into the education system in Senegal?
- What are the implications of Senegal's experiences for language-in-education policy and practice in other multilingual contexts?

The "simultaneous bilingualism" approach, like previous bilingual experiments in Senegal, was designed to address the barriers to learning caused by the use of a foreign language as a medium of instruction. Since its Independence in 1960, Senegal has conducted all formal education in French, even though Senegalese people speak one or more home languages (L1s) from the Atlantic-Congo or Mande language families.[178] The Constitution of 2001 granted six languages—Wolof, Pulaar, Seereer, Soninke, Mandinka, and

---

[178] See Eberhard *et al.*, 2022.

Diola—the status of *langues nationales* (national languages) based on their level of corpus and orthography development. Since then, eight more *langues nationales* have been recognized (personal communication with Fary Ka, President of the Senegalese Academy of Languages, January 2019), and 11 others are in development.[179] These Senegalese languages have long been used for adult literacy, and some have been used for piloting bilingual primary and pre-primary programs.[180] The two languages chosen for the "simultaneous" program are the most widely spoken in the country: Wolof, with an estimated five million L1 and L2 speakers as of 2015,[181] and Pulaar, spoken by an estimated 3.5 million in Senegal and millions more across West Africa in a range of varieties.[182]

L1 speakers of French in Senegal comprise less than 1% of the population.[183] Even with government investment in education amounting to over 21 percent of GDP in 2017, only 60 percent of enrolled students complete their studies. Enrolled students represent less than 50 percent of those who should be in school.[184] Likely, the high dropout, failure, and repetition rates during the six years of primary education can be attributed to the mismatch between learners' languages and the language of the school.

To improve school quality, Senegal has experimented with bilingual education in its national languages since gaining independence from France in 1960. Diouf (2019) identifies three phases of experimentation in formal education. The first phase, from 1977 to 1984, and the second phase, from 2002 to 2008, were government-led efforts. The third phase, from 2008 to the present, has mainly been led by civil society and NGOs. The latest and most influential program to date was known as the "simultaneous bilingualism" approach. It was implemented from 2009 to 2018 by the Senegalese NGO known as ARED, or Association in Research and Education for Development, in collaboration with the National

---

[179] See also Diagne, 2017.
[180] See DPLN, 2002.
[181] See Eberhard *et al.*, 2022.
[182] See Eberhard *et al.*, 2022.
[183] See Eberhard *et al.*, 2022.
[184] See UIS, 2019.

Ministry of Education (MEN). The original project utilized Wolof or Pulaar in conjunction with French as an after-school intervention during the 2009-2010 school year. Still, it was successfully integrated into public classrooms the following year, where bilingual classes soon outperformed traditional ones.[185] The next round of financing allowed ARED to scale up the model to 98 schools and 101 classes in three regions of Senegal from 2014 to 2018. The evaluative data we share in this chapter come from the 2018-2019 external evaluation that Benson and Iwasaki conducted with their colleague, Mbacké Diagne, in the field for the donor through an educational consulting firm.[186] The analysis of stakeholders who consider themselves militants or advocates for national languages in education in Senegal is based on virtual and field research conducted by Iwasaki for her doctoral dissertation.[187]

In the next section, we describe ARED's program and discuss the findings of our evaluation. Next, we examine the role of key actors in developing ARED's approach and their motivations for participating in this endeavor. Finally, we describe the progress that has taken place in terms of language-in-education policy change and what this may mean for Senegal and the world.

ARED's "simultaneous" bilingual approach and its implementation

ARED (2014) refers to its approach as "bilingualism in real time" due to the simultaneous teaching of literacy and other curricular content in both a national language (ideally but not always the learner's L1) and French (known as the L2 here because it is a new language for virtually all learners). Benson (2022) has also referred to the approach as "simultaneous biliteracy" because one of its most salient features is the teaching of initial literacy in both L1 and L2, beginning on the first day of school. Overall, ARED's approach must be seen as an effort to address social justice and equity in education by providing education in languages students understand rather than by reproducing and strengthening elite education in French, a language that learners or teachers do not widely speak at home.

---

[185] See Dalberg, 2014.
[186] See MWAI, 2019.
[187] See Iwasaki, 2022.

Practically speaking, the simultaneous aspect means that instruction is completely bilingual from the first to fourth years of schooling (corresponding to levels CI to CE2 in the Senegalese system), followed by the study of the national language as a subject in years 5 and 6 (CM1 and CM2). For example, a literacy lesson focuses on a phoneme that is common to both L1 and L2. During the first 30 minutes of the lesson, that phoneme (for example, the letter/sound A) is taught using keywords in Wolof or Pulaar. During the next 30 minutes, the same phoneme is taught in French using French keywords in the same context. According to teachers, trainers, and model designers, this approach offered numerous benefits. Because many phonemes are shared between the languages, only part of the second 30-minute period is needed to consolidate the phoneme in French, representing a "*gain de temps*" or time saved that can be spent working on new vocabulary or reinforcement activities.

The teaching of the other two major areas of the curriculum, mathematics and *Éducation à la science et à la vie sociale* (ESVS), is also conducted in a split-lesson format. At the same time, stakeholders reported gains. For example, a lesson on photosynthesis taught in the L1 does not need to be repeated in French; instead, content already taught can be reviewed and consolidated using French vocabulary. Model designers and trainers developed the concept of *niveau d'ancrage* to help teachers plan lessons based on the level at which concepts can be "anchored," using the transfer of knowledge learned in the L1 to express that knowledge in French.

The ARED program was designed to follow the national curriculum and timetable, where each subject area was split between L1 and French, ensuring no disruption to learning from preschool or if learners transferred midway through their primary education to a non-bilingual school.[188] Wherever possible, two cohorts were chosen in each school, one that would follow the bilingual model and one that would receive traditional (all-French) instruction, both following the national curriculum. Key elements of the program included: (1) teacher professional development; (2) the development of teaching and learning materials (in Pulaar and Wolof, also in French) and

---

[188] See ARED, 2014.

teachers' guides; (3) awareness-raising among communities, focusing on parent involvement in school management committees (SMCs); and (4) a system of monitoring and evaluation. The external evaluation conducted in 2018-2019 examined these elements in conjunction with student achievement, as reported below.

Outcomes of ARED's "simultaneous" bilingual approach

The external evaluation was a large-scale mixed-methods study designed to determine the degree to which and in what ways the program was successful, as well as how the approach might influence a change in Senegal's language-in-education policy.[189] The field data involved 21 days of intensive travel. Although time and resources did not permit the selection of a representative sample of the 98 schools and 101 classrooms that implemented the approach, we identified a range of contexts from the four *Inspections d'Académie* (IAs), taking into consideration rurality, school size, and level of implementation. We interviewed bilingual focal points and other school inspectors from nine of the ten Inspection de l'Éducation et de la Formation (IEF) offices and visited schools in eight of them. We visited a total of 15 schools, conducting interviews or focus group discussions in the appropriate languages with community representatives, School Management Committee members, school directors, bilingual teachers, and bilingually educated learners. At ten schools (six Wolof and four Pulaar), we conducted our own L1 writing assessment with bilingually and non-bilingually educated learners (a total of 386) who were completing CM1 or year 5 of primary schooling.

Across all stakeholders, the results were consistently positive regarding the bilingual approach in terms of stakeholder satisfaction, learner achievement, and even unintended outcomes. Support for the program was unprecedented; we heard the same positive comments from regional and district school inspectors, including the bilingual focal points/trainers, school directors, community members, parents, CGE members, bilingual and traditional teachers, bilingual and traditional learners, and even two high-ranking officials at the

---

[189] See MWAI, 2019.

Ministry of Education in Dakar.[190] The main findings of the evaluation, along with our sources of evidence, were the following:

- The superior performance of students in the bilingual program in comparison to their peers in traditional (all-French) classes, as evidenced by yearly district-wide assessments, our writing assessment, the national primary school leaving examination (CFEE), and data on student promotion to secondary schools;
- Active engagement of stakeholders at all levels, according to interviews and focus groups;
- Stakeholders' conviction that ARED's bilingual approach compares favorably to other models due to its progressive, systematic, and coherent approach, according to all reports;
- "Exhaustive" engagement by ARED in the implementation process, as evidenced by support to training and follow-up, and provision of textbooks on time and in appropriate quantities;
- A nearly universal call for generalization or system-wide implementation of ARED's bilingual model, including expansion into additional languages.[191]

The overarching goal of the program was that bilingually educated learners would demonstrate higher learning achievement than those in the traditional, all-French system. Educators at all levels described bilingual learners as joyous and motivated to learn. They also reported widespread success in reading and passing the national examination (CFEE) to progress to secondary school.

> ARED est venu à un point nommé pour adresser le problème crucial de la lecture. Si on regarde la première génération, on a des résultats très satisfaisants des CM2- presque 90% de réussite. Ces enfants sont plus forts. Ces élèves savent décoder et décortiquer les textes. (2018.11.28 School director, Wolof)

---

[190] See Benson, 2022.
[191] See MWAI, 2019.

[Translation: *ARED came at just the right time to address the crucial problem of reading. Examining the first generation, we have achieved very satisfactory results from CM2, with an almost 90% success rate. These children are stronger. They know how to decode and deconstruct texts.*]

Tu as des enfants extraordinaires ; tous les élèves sont passés. Il y a eu un taux de réussite de 100%. Tous les élèves qui ont fait ARED dans mon école sont partis ! Mais ils ont réussi en masse. (2018.11.26 School director, Wolof)

[Translation: *You have extraordinary children; all the students passed. There was a 100% success rate. All the students who did ARED in my school have gone on! But they succeeded in droves.*]

The results of our writing assessment revealed that bilingual students (273 of 386 from the sample) scored significantly higher than the 97 traditionally taught students on written self-expression in both L1 (Pulaar/Wolof) and L2 (French).

The bilingual program's three sub-goals were: (1) for teachers, school directors, and inspectors to demonstrate mastery of ARED's bilingual teaching and learning strategies, (2) to develop and distribute high-quality bilingual materials that facilitate the use of the bilingual approach, and (3) for MEN policymakers, primary school inspectors, teachers, and community members to gain confidence in and support the bilingual model. Regarding ARED's bilingual approach, stakeholders highlighted:

- Its simultaneous approach to beginning literacy in both the national language and French;
- Its systematic, progressive approach to teaching curricular content in an understandable manner and;
- Its coherence with the national curriculum.[192]

Effectivement, aussi sur le niveau des acquis et de l'apprentissage, lorsque nous décrochons de la langue locale vers la langue française, on avait plus d'activités en langue française parce que les enfants avaient déjà des acquis en langue locale. Dans ma classe, on pouvait faire 5 à 6 activités

---

[192] See MWAI, 2019.

> et ça ne peut que renforcer la qualité de l'apprentissage. (2018.11.28 Bilingual teacher, Wolof)
>
> [Translation: *Indeed, also on the level of learning outcomes and learning. When we moved from the local language to French, we had more activities in French because the children had already learned in the local language. In my class, we can do five to six activities that reinforce the quality of learning.*]

Both the model and the materials received high praise from inspectors, school directors, and teachers. We coded a total of 71 unsolicited comments from stakeholders at all levels, mentioning the richness of the materials, their *pertinence* to the learners, and the fact that every learner received materials (which seemed to be unusual in these schools).

> Ce sont des textes adaptés au milieu. C'était très fort ici. Les élèves s'intéressaient. Ces textes parlent du vécu de l'enfant. (2018.11.23 School director, Pulaar)
>
> [Translation: *These are texts adapted to the environment. They were very meaningful here. The students were interested, as these texts speak of the child's reality.*]
>
> Ce sont des manuels riches. Même cette année, même s'il n'y a pas d'expérimentation, on continue à utiliser ces manuels. Même hier, il y a un enseignant de CE2 qui est venu me demander ces manuels et je donne à chaque élève ces manuels. Parce que vraiment ces manuels sont bien faits, des textes très riches et en phase avec le curriculum. Donc même les enseignants les utilisent pour l'enseignement apprentissage. (2018.11.30 School director, Wolof)
>
> [Translation: *These are rich textbooks. Even this year, despite the absence of experimentation, these manuals are still being used. Even yesterday, a third-grade teacher came to ask me for these textbooks, and I provided each student with one. These textbooks are exceptionally well done, rich in content, and aligned with the curriculum. So even [non-bilingual] teachers use them for teaching and learning.*]

The impact of the program was apparent in the comments of parents and CGE members, even those who were critics at the beginning:

Il y avait un parent d'enfant qui venait ici, et elle ne voulait pas le pulaar parce qu'ils parlaient le pulaar à la maison. Elle pensait que ce n'était pas la peine. Mais après, elle a compris que c'était par le pulaar que l'enfant pouvait acquérir [des connaissances]. Maintenant l'élève était excellent et avait des résultats les plus hauts et la maman est venue s'excuser. Ce qu'elle nous a dit c'est qu'elle n'avait pas bien compris le programme. On l'a même emmenée chez l'inspecteur pour s'excuser. (2018.11.23 Bilingual teacher, Podor, Pulaar)

[Translation: *There was a parent of a child who attended here, and she didn't want Pulaar because they spoke Pulaar at home. She thought it wasn't necessary. But then she realized that it was through Pulaar that the child could acquire [knowledge]. Later, the student performed excellently and achieved the highest results, and the mother came to apologize. What she told us was that she had not fully understood the program. We even took her to the inspector's house to apologize.*]

Nous sommes conscients de l'utilité de la langue maternelle, nous souhaitons que cela soit introduit dans toutes les étapes même au secondaire. On ne doit pas l'arrêter ; les enfants viennent à la maison nous montrer comment on lit le wolof et comment on nomme les choses et nous rectifient. On entend du wolof riche et de niveau élevé avec les enfants. (2018.11.27 Parent leader, Wolof)

[Translation: *We are aware of the usefulness of the mother tongue. We want it to be introduced at all stages, including secondary school. We must not stop it; the children come to the house to show us how to read Wolof and how to name things, and they correct us. We hear rich, high-level Wolof with the children.*]

Ce programme est utile parce qu'il permet de sauvegarder notre patrimoine linguistique, qui n'est pas, d'ailleurs, à l'écrit. (2019.01.08 Parent, Pulaar)

[Translation: *This program is helpful because it helps to preserve our linguistic heritage, which is not, moreover, in writing.*]

The structures for training and professional development developed by ARED were a two-tier cascade model for training and pedagogical circles for bilingual teacher support, promoting collaboration between teachers, school directors, and inspectors. As of May 2017, ARED reported that 90% of inspectors, 80% of teachers, and 72.5% of school directors had mastered the bilingual teaching model, while 86% of teachers and 93.9% of students were using the materials (ARED, 2017).

Positive spillover effects were evident throughout the program. Bilingual students taught their peers to read and write in the L1, and bilingual teachers shared their L1 knowledge and bilingual teaching strategies with their colleagues working in non-bilingual classrooms. Some of the latter teachers sought permission and were allowed to convert to bilingual teaching, basically eliminating the experimental "control" cohorts at their schools. Bilingual students taught their siblings, grandparents, and extended family members how to read and write in Wolof or Pulaar, and family members reported helping children with their homework. A raised awareness of the importance of Senegalese national languages was articulated at all levels – not only for those whose own languages were Wolof or Pulaar but also for those with other mother tongues, who discovered that bringing Wolof and Pulaar into formal education made their languages more visible and valuable.

When a Bainouk parent in one region was asked why he allowed his children to be in a Wolof-French bilingual class, he responded eloquently:

> C'est que j'ai constaté que si les enfants viennent à la maison et si je les aide à mieux comprendre leurs leçons j'emploie ma langue maternelle, le baynouk, et ils comprennent plus vite. C'est à travers cela que j'ai compris que s'ils apprennent par le wolof qui est une langue qu'ils parlent bien mieux que leurs parents, et le français, ils pourront mieux comprendre. Les parents aussi y gagnent parce qu'on apprend le wolof mieux aussi. (2018.11.27 Parent, Wolof)
>
> [Translation: *It is because I have found that if the children come home and I help them to understand their lessons better, I use my mother tongue, Bainouk, and they understand faster. Through this, I have come to understand that if they learn through Wolof, which is a language they speak more fluently than their parents, and*

> French, they will be able to understand better. Parents also benefit because we learn Wolof better, too.]

Overall, educators considered ARED's bilingual model superior to other forms of primary education due to its progressive, systematic, curriculum-based, and coherent approach. Nearly all stakeholders interviewed called for generalization (expansion throughout the country) of ARED's bilingual model, including expansion into additional languages (MWAI, 2019). The following section discusses the key advocates for national languages in education and how ARED's program and other efforts contributed to the development of the latest policy.

Bilingual education advocacy key actors and their reasons for advocacy

Since our involvement with ARED and bilingual education in Senegal from 2018 to 2019, it became increasingly apparent that momentum was building for a shift in Senegal's education policy away from monolingual French-medium education and toward bilingual education using Senegalese national languages. This momentum has been generated by bilingual education advocates and actors who refer to themselves as *"militants des langues nationales,"* meaning people working in the defense and promotion of national languages in education. Over the past four years (2019-2022), alongside investigating ARED's "simultaneous" bilingual and biliterate model, we realized how widespread the *militants* and *militantisme des langues nationales* are in Senegal. We examined the identities of these militants and their motivations for advocating for national languages in education more closely. Iwasaki designed her 2021-2022 doctoral fieldwork to answer the following question:

> How and why have self-proclaimed militants advocated for the use of national languages in the Senegalese educational system since the 1950s, and what are their current contributions at this critical moment in possible language-in-education policy change?

Iwasaki (2022) looked at the *militants'* lived experiences with national languages and education, the extent of their multi-generational work and network, and their influence in shaping the language-in-education policy landscape as the country adopts a national bilingual education policy, which states that students will learn both national languages and French starting at primary school.

Iwasaki's (2022) qualitative case study drew on 40 in-depth interviews with 36 people working in the defense and promotion of national languages in education who strongly self-identified as *militants*. She began by identifying some of the key actors involved in implementing the simultaneous approach and then used snowball sampling to identify others. Almost half were university professors ($n = 15$), while the others included NGO representatives ($n = 7$) and bilingual teachers in ARED's program ($n = 5$). The remaining *militants* ($n = 9$) were from the national language literature and media community or organizations working with national languages. All reported having been confronted at some point in their lives with the shortcomings of French-medium education in addressing the needs of the Senegalese population. As most interviewed *militants* were between 40 and 70 years old, many had experienced trauma from corporal punishment growing up in a colonial education system that suppressed their use of their languages. They experienced a "retournement fondamental dans [leur] manière de penser"[193] when they rediscovered the richness of their languages in adulthood, and they questioned the injustice of not having learned in their languages:

> J'étais *traumatisé* par la manière dont on nous a instruits à l'école, avec le symbole. On nous a *imposé* le français qu'on ne parlait pas, avec le symbole, alors que notre langue de socialisation partout en dehors de l'école c'était le fulfulde, le pulaar. Alors qu'arriver à l'école, on nous interdisait de la parler et de parler les autres langues. Donc on se taisait presque tout le temps. On n'avait pas encore une maîtrise du français qui nous permettait même de jouer en français. C'était pas possible. Or, c'était *interdit* même de parler autre chose que le français dans la cour de l'école. C'était *extrêmement* traumatisant. (2021.08.26 Fulfulde linguist and professor)

---

[193] "fundamental shift in mindset."

[Translation: *There is also the fact that I was traumatized by the way we were taught at school, with the symbol [e.g., any degrading marker that a student would have to wear for having spoken their language]. French, which we did not speak, was imposed on us, with the symbol, when our language of socialization everywhere outside of school was Fulfude, Pulaar. As soon as we arrived at school, we were forbidden to speak [our languages] and to speak other languages [French]. So, we said almost nothing almost all the time. We did not yet have a mastery of French that would allow us to play in French. It was not possible. Yet it was forbidden to speak anything other than French in the schoolyard. It was incredibly traumatizing.*]

Tu te dis mais comment on n'a pas pu enseigner cette langue [wolof]? C'est simplement énorme. [Pause] [...] Et surtout une beauté. Et c'est vrai. Mais même cette beauté de la langue, elle est capable de faire des rimes. Nous on pensait que la poésie ça n'existait qu'en français. Alors qu'en wolof... Parce que nous, on nous a enseigné la poésie en français. Donc moi je découvre la poésie du wolof à travers des publications, à travers les proverbes, à travers mes rencontres avec les gens. Et puis, tu découvres la sagesse, tu découvres la culture. Tu découvres pleins de choses. (2021.09.01 Wolof linguist and retired professor)

[Translation: *You tell yourself, but how is it that we were not able to teach this language? It is simply outrageous. [Pause] [...] And above all [there is] a beauty. And it is true. But even the beauty of this language is capable of rhyming. We always thought that poetry only existed in French. That in Wolof... Because we were taught poetry in French. I discovered the poetry of Wolof through publications, proverbs, and my encounters with people. And then, you discover wisdom, you discover the culture. You discover lots of things.*]

Bilingual education in this context is a means to integrate and value students' Senegalese L1s for better comprehension of the content thus learning. It is connected to the country's process of decolonization:

On est dans un mouvement irréversible vers l'introduction des langues nationales à l'école parce qu'on a atteint un point où on se rend compte qu'on ne peut plus aller loin avec le français. C'est même pas pour des raisons politiques, patriotisme... C'est que le système d'enseignement en langue française s'est complètement effondré. (2021.12.10 Writer)

[Translation: *We are in an irreversible movement toward the introduction of national languages in school because we have reached a point where we realize that we cannot go further with French. It is not even for political reasons, patriotism... It is just that the teaching system in French has completely collapsed.*]

All *militants* interviewed participated in various advocacy actions related to national language education. They ranged from national language literacy classes, media and literature development in national languages, and policy change advocacy. They all insisted that their advocacy was rooted in concrete actions aimed at normalizing the use of national languages in institutions and schools as a language of instruction. Their language activism consisted of delivering adult literacy classes in national languages to promote reading and writing in these languages, developing authorship in national languages and publishing it, and translating well-known literature from French and other languages into national languages, allowing people to read in their native languages. Finally, in terms of policy change advocacy, these *militants* have held many roles throughout their careers that participated in bringing the national languages agenda to the forefront in many national discussions and forums, some as early as at the États Généraux de l'Éducation et de la Formation held in 1981, where the national language issue in education was publicly discussed as an essential element of educational reform.[194]

Most of the *militants* were educators in the past, either in formal or non-formal education, and many of these policy entrepreneurs wear different hats. It was not uncommon to find militants who were university professors and served as Ministry officials, having also previously served as consultants on projects and initiatives related to national languages. There were retired professors who are now consultants, and there were Ministry officials on leave working for an NGO or an international consulting firm implementing donor-

---

[194] See MEN, 1981; Iwasaki, 2022.

funded programs. It was not uncommon for me to interview a *militant* who had been involved as a consultant in previous programs that utilized national languages and who also served as an acting advisor to the Ministry of Education, participating in various working groups that led up to the present events. Others held multiple memberships in language-affiliated organizations, whether at the national, Pan-African, Francophone Africa, or UNESCO levels, some of which led them to participate in global-level policy discussions as well as draft regional and international policy documents. They all viewed bilingual education as an act of self-determination and sovereignty, enabling them to move away from inherited and internalized patterns of colonial education, particularly by leveraging the dynamics of international aid and development in education to fund programs and actions based on national languages.

The effects of militant activism and the simultaneous bilingual program

As ARED submitted its final reports on the simultaneous bilingual program, its leaders and other *militants* became catalysts in the development of the national bilingual education policy, known as the Modèle Harmonisé de l'Éducation Bilingue au Sénégal (MOHEBS).[195] The process of developing MOHEBS involved gathering representatives from MEN, Senegalese language specialists, and development partners to assess prior programs, synthesize their models, and clearly define the State's vision for the use of national languages in bilingual education.

The MOHEBS, validated in April 2021 by MEN, roots Senegal's national bilingual education model in three levels of "cadre référentiel": the international discourse on bilingual education, the West African sub-regional discourse, and finally, the national policy plan. Surprisingly, despite support for ARED's simultaneous approach, the harmonized model recommends that national languages be the sole medium of instruction in the first two years of school, with French taught orally. After this, national languages and French are to be used in parallel. It is worth noting that while the

---

[195] See MEN, 2019.

MOHEBS promotes a "late-exit" model, keeping national languages in the system throughout the six elementary years, there are contradictions in the document. One example is: "Pour l'enseignement moyen, la langue nationale sera uniquement objet d'enseignement,"[196] which implies that by third and fourth grade, the national language will only be taught as a subject. According to informal conversations with members of the planning committee, the details will need to be worked out. Still, they foresee opportunities to bring in lessons learned from the simultaneous approach as the policy is implemented.

MOHEBS does provide a detailed progressive plan for "generalizing" bilingual education throughout Senegal starting in 2023. It also elaborates on the eligibility criteria for a national language to be used in education, stating that the program will initially focus on the six original codified languages.[197]

Since the 2021 validation of MOHEBS, the MEN has taken further steps toward generalization by appointing Professor Mbacké Diagne, our colleague on the earlier evaluation of ARED's simultaneous biliteracy program, as Inspector General of Education and Training with a focus on Bilingual Education at the Ministry of National Education—a first in Senegal's educational history[198] and the adoption of a national bilingual education policy within the Ministry of National Education in May 2021.[199] MEN planned to implement bilingual education for the 2023-2024 school year in 9 different regions in Senegal.[200] This is the third national initiative in Senegalese history to integrate national languages as languages of instruction into the national curriculum as more people become aware of the importance of national languages in Senegal.[201] This is why we find that Senegal is now at a critical juncture in its language-in-education policy.

---

[196] See MEN, 2019: 26.
[197] See MEN, 2019: 26.
[198] See Ndiaye, 2021.
[199] See SIL LEAD, 2021.
[200] See SIL LEAD, 2021.
[201] See Iwasaki, 2022.

Implications and conclusions

As we show with our descriptions of ARED's simultaneous bilingual education program and the Senegalese *militants* working on behalf of national languages in education, it appears that these, along with previous efforts, have had a positive effect on language-in-education policy change in Senegal. A kind of synergy has been created among members of national language communities, particularly family and community members involved in implementing the simultaneous approach, educators at all levels who have implemented the program or learned about it, organizations that have supported bilingual programs of all kinds, and MEN policymakers. Moving the policy agenda forward will arguably require stakeholders at all levels to commit to implementing national languages in bilingual education nationwide. The primary commitment must be to respecting learners' linguistic and educational rights and supporting literacy and learning across the curriculum; this must be accompanied by the technical and financial resources to implement the plan.

We hope that readers agree that the case of Senegal is inspiring because of the work of the self-proclaimed *militants* and the implementation of the innovative simultaneous approach. We imagine that readers can relate many of their own experiences to those of the stakeholders we have described and can draw some inspiration from the evidence of success we have provided. Many of the stakeholder quotes demonstrate their enthusiasm for a program that utilizes and values their languages while enhancing teaching and learning for elementary students.

Whatever direction language-in-education policy takes in Senegal, the simultaneous bilingual approach offers a refreshing perspective on how to adapt a national curriculum—once based on a single dominant language—to incorporate home languages and support quality education for young learners. Many features of the approach—giving each language approximately the same attention each day, initiating literacy by using letters and sounds that the L1 and L2 have in common, and teaching the differences between languages—draw on established international theories of bilingual education, including interdependence, common underlying proficiency,[202] and interlinguistic transfer.[203] Side-by-side treatment of both languages fosters metalinguistic awareness, a feature already prevalent in bi- and multilingual societies, such as Senegal's, and the approach supports learner-centered pedagogy and the development of critical thinking skills.[204] These are precisely the skills needed to question the historical dominance of foreign languages of instruction and open people's eyes to the potential of their languages in educational policy and practice in multilingual countries.

---

[202] See Cummins, 2009.
[203] See Bialystok, 2001.
[204] See Benson, 2022.

3.5. The Parity School in Ladinia: How a Language Minority Preserves its Own Language(s) as well as Italian and German

Stephanie Risse

Italian and German schools in South Tyrol

Three languages, three language groups, and three school systems in one European nation-state. For decades, the Autonomous Province of Bozen-Bolzano, commonly known as "South Tyrol," has boasted a legal system that is as idiosyncratic as it is overly complex in legal terms and its structure unusual in Europe. This autonomy came about after the Second World War as a result of an ongoing—sometimes violent—conflict between the German- and Italian-speaking populations. The area that is now South Tyrol was awarded to the Kingdom of Italy after the end of the First World War. Between Italian Fascism and German National Socialism, the German and Italian languages became equally politicized in the following decades.

Ladin-speaking peoples, who are geographically situated between two large national language groups, have continuously inhabited the area around the Sella massif. This area extends across present-day Switzerland and Italy. The Ladin population in South Tyrol, which can be linguistically divided into two idioms—Ladin in Val Badia and Ladin in Val Gardena—comprises less than 5% of the more than half a million inhabitants of South Tyrol.

The conflict between the two large language groups, which had been escalating in violence for decades, was resolved through a complex constitutional law instrument. Moreover, the resulting "Statute of Autonomy" is enshrined in international law. The official declaration of the settlement of the dispute was submitted to the United Nations in 1992.[205] This legal instrument is primarily based on the division of the population into three officially recognized

---

[205] See Clementi & Woelk, 2003; Marko *et al.*, 2005.

language groups—Italian, German, and Ladin—whereby the Ladin group unites politically the two Ladin idioms, those of Val Gardena and Val Badia. All "speakers of other languages," especially migrants, can declare themselves as belonging to one of the language groups if they are citizens of the European Union. Otherwise, they are "languageless." This means that their languages have no political or legal relevance.

The declaration of belonging to one of the three language groups has far-reaching consequences for the individual. It can determine their job, the allocation of housing, or even the opportunity to be politically active. To transform the conflict into what can today be described as a "balanced, if not always conflict-free coexistence,"[206] further measures appeared necessary, which are reflected in particular in education and culture.

The Statute of Autonomy is first interpreted in accordance with the fundamental idea that "the more we separate, the better we understand each other."[207] In cultural, linguistic, and, therefore, above all educational matters, the respective language groups decide for themselves; financial resources are distributed to the language groups according to their affiliation. Every ten years, a census is conducted to determine the population's language affiliation, resulting in a percentage distribution that has remained relatively constant for years. Around two-thirds of the population declare themselves to belong to the German language group, slightly less than a third to the Italian language group, and the proportion of Ladins in the population is just under 5%.

Accordingly, there are also three school administrations and three different school systems, all of which are, of course, subject to Italian national school legislation. Italian schools in the Autonomous Province of Bozen-Bolzano are organized in the same way as in the rest of Italy, with one crucial exception: German is taught as a second language from the first year of elementary school right through graduation from upper secondary school. German-speaking teaching staff have also been working in Italian kindergartens for around two decades. German-language schools, where Italian is taught as a

---

[206] See Holtzmann, 2000: 3.
[207] See Risse, 2013: 15f.

second language throughout, have a similar approach. There are significant differences, however, compared to Italian schools because the national Italian guidelines for all curricula must be translated into German, as it is the language of instruction.

In many subjects, teaching materials and concepts are imported from other German-speaking countries, such as Germany, Austria, and Switzerland, and then adapted to meet curricular requirements. For culturally sensitive subjects, such as German history and geography, on the other hand, separate teaching materials must be developed for regional topics. Furthermore, the increasing dominance of dialectal speech is an additional factor that contributes to the complexity of the language situation in South Tyrol: while the Italian spoken in South Tyrol can be described as near-standard Italian, with borrowings from German due to decades of language contact, the mother tongue for South Tyroleans, who conceptualize themselves as a minority, has always been "the dialect." By this, the speakers usually mean the dialect of their hometown, even if it is very confined in terms of its spatial extent. The South Tyrolean dialects belong to the large family of Bavarian dialects, specifically Southern Bavarian, which is primarily spoken in the inner and southern Alpine region.[208]

This situation has consequences in every respect and for all language groups. Teaching native German at school, for example, requires an awareness of the two registers—standard German and the dialects—in a way that enables children and young people to use both competently. Teaching the dialects is also essential for learning German as a second language because dialects dominate everyday (language) life in South Tyrol. Without at least passive knowledge of the local dialect, essential areas of everyday life cannot be managed linguistically. This "inner multilingualism" has been a topic of

---

[208] Hannes Scheutz (2016: 25ff) points out that the Bavarian dialects encompassed most of Austria (with the exception of Vorarlberg) and the eastern part of the Free State of Bavaria. The dialectological term "bairisch" must be separated from the geopolitical term "Bayrisch." The latter refers exclusively to the Free State of Bavaria, although the majority of "Bairisch" speakers live outside the Free State.

discussion in schools since at least the 1980s and has partly found its way into the development of teaching materials.[209]

According to recent observations, the language skills of young Germans and Italians (in other languages) have been declining since the beginning of the 2020s. This is evident in the number of students who have not achieved the required language levels, as measured by the CEFR (the Common European Framework of Reference for Languages), in recent years. To be admitted to a degree program at the Free University of Bozen-Bolzano, the language requirements for the respective degree program must be met. The language levels specified are based on the Common European Framework of Reference for Languages (CEFR) and can be verified by internationally recognized language certificates. It was previously assumed that native students, in particular, would be able to demonstrate the required language skills in German and Italian without any problems. After all, after 13 years of continuous language education, you should be able to achieve at least a B2 level in the respective second language. Reality, however, demonstrates that native students, in particular, have not reached this level in recent years.[210]

The at times unsatisfactory language situation in the country's German and Italian schools must be interpreted against the historical background of a strict language separation. The aim of this was not to educate bilingual individuals. Instead, the Statute of Autonomy was implemented politically to protect the South Tyrolean linguistic minority in a monolingual nation-state. The fact that bilingualism and multilingualism are seen as educational goals worth striving for is a more recent phenomenon. Multilingualism gained political visibility within the European Union through the development of the Common European Framework of Reference for Languages (CEFR)

---

[209] Gurschler & Tscholl (2015) is representative of a range of materials and is referenced on one of the most recent handouts.
[210] By decision of the Faculty Council of the School of Education at the Free University of Bozen-Bolzano in May 2022, the language requirements for the second language in the largest degree program "Educational Sciences for Primary Education" were lowered to level B1.

and the establishment of a separate department for multilingualism within the European Commission.

The difficulty of implementing multilingualism within the Union, however, is evident in almost all member states, albeit to varying degrees. Countries are still broadly conceived as nation-states and are based on the idea of "one nation that speaks only one language." In the monolingual classroom, this idea has been institutionalized. The Autonomous Province of Bolzano is no exception. Although bilingualism and trilingualism must be guaranteed in institutions, this does not mean that individuals are expected to be multilingual. On the contrary, the protection of languages stipulates that a citizen should be able to move about in everyday life within the Autonomous Province of Bozen-Bolzano in the "habitus of monolingualism." This is an enforceable right.

Despite the criticisms that can be leveled at South Tyrolean autonomy, it is important to acknowledge that this legal framework has brought stability and fostered both bilingualism and multilingualism among the region's inhabitants. In relation to the two major languages, Italian and German, all studies identify stable language forms characteristic of language contact situations. Put simply, the two languages coexist within a historically evolved, balanced system that is actively supported by the local population.

The Ladin parity schools (1): Two idioms and three languages

In the shadow of the large language blocks, the Ladins have developed their very own school system, the "parity" school, which can justifiably serve as a model for other regions. Parity means that school lessons are held in Italian and German with the same number of hours. The minority language, Ladin, is only present in a few lessons and serves as a "bridge language" in the five-year elementary school. Teachers are not only allowed to switch to Ladin, but they are also expected to do so if the children have problems understanding in class. Even in the subsequent grades, the three-year middle school, after which compulsory schooling is completed, only a few lessons are reserved for Ladin; depending on the valley, it is either the Val Gardena idiom or the Val Badia idiom. Italian and German are also taught equally in middle school, with each language receiving a 50% allocation of class time.

The South Tyrolean secondary school system holds a special position in the Italian education system and is regularly presented as exemplary by government representatives in Rome. This also has an ethnopolitical-linguistic background. Due to the country's traditionally strong economy, which is now primarily based on tourism, as well as agriculture and skilled trades, vocational secondary schools were quickly established after the Second World War, and they were also attended mainly by German speakers. In the absence of an Italian model, these South Tyrolean vocational schools were increasingly oriented toward the Austrian and German vocational school systems, gaining a certain prestige. This resulted in a wide range of vocational schools, some of which are leading in their fields in Italy, such as the agricultural schools and artisan high schools in Val Badia and Val Gardena. These, in turn, are rooted in the centuries-old artisan tradition of the Ladins, whose woodcarving art dates back to the 17th century. At that time, people made a virtue of necessity: to secure an income during the harsh winter months, they began crafting wooden figures for both sacred and secular purposes. Students from other language groups are also now attending the Ladin secondary artisan schools, which provide them with a distinguishing characteristic.

Many students from the Ladin villages remain in their hometowns during their compulsory schooling. They then transfer to German- or Italian-speaking areas and thus to Italian or German secondary schools if they do not decide to pursue a local artisan education. As a result, continuous trilingual language learning recedes into the background to some extent; nevertheless, the Ladins manage to maintain and sometimes improve their trilingualism.

Removed from the politically heated conflict between South Tyroleans and Italians, the Ladins have ultimately not done much other than continue the centuries-old multilingualism of the region and, to a certain extent, also the quite successful efforts of the imperial monarchy. Boaglio emphasizes that the German language, in particular, has been very present in everyday life and the school system in many (now) Italian regions since the 17th century, which largely went unnoticed to the extent that nationalism as a concept was successful.²¹¹ Moreover, at the time, some of these regions were not part of today's nation-state of Italy.

Although the Ladin language is historically the oldest documented language in today's South Tyrol, it has had a weaker position because a standardized written language never developed. Although the passage of time had forced a growing awareness of a collective identity, this did not turn into linguistic chauvinism. The "critical mass" was lacking.

> The current population of Ladinia is around 38,000 people, of which around 32,000 are native Ladin speakers. Before the First World War, the region had approximately 23,000 inhabitants, and by around 1800, the population had decreased to around 21,000. These figures make it understandable why the Ladins were not precisely at the center of interest in the Habsburg Monarchy.²¹²

This makes it understandable why German and Italian were always accepted as the dominant written languages. Remarkably, the Ladin idioms were nevertheless able to survive for so long. In the 1990s, efforts were made to standardize and unify the two idioms, partly to strengthen their position in language policy. The "Ladin Dolomitan" project, initiated by local researchers and financially supported by European funds, ultimately failed due to the population's veto in the valleys. Because the Statute of Autonomy stipulates that all linguistic, cultural, and educational policy matters can only be decided by the language group concerned, the "Ladin Dolomitan" was put to a vote by the population at the turn of the millennium. The idea failed, with the majority of the population rejecting a standardized Ladin language. Accordingly, since 2003, the respective Ladin Valley language has been used in addition to German and Italian. Furthermore, it is a political guideline to ensure the equal presence of both idioms in public life.²¹³

---

[211] 2018: 183.
[212] See Videsott P., 2018: 223.
[213] See resolution of the South Tyrolean provincial government n° 210 of 27.02.2003.

The Ladin parity schools (2): Trilingual teachers and a universal language concept plus English

It should, therefore, be noted that the already "small" minority language, Ladin, is additionally split into two idioms. Furthermore, it is crucial to promote the "major" languages, Italian and German. Since the 2001/2002 school year, English has also been taught as a foreign language in secondary schools and, since the 2007/2008 school year, in elementary schools from the fourth grade onward. At first glance, this educational approach appears to be highly ambitious. It should have become clear, however, that this is not an education available only to a small, motivated elite. The success of the parity schools rests mainly on the following foundation: the local population has managed to develop and maintain a collective Ladin identity over the past few centuries despite the relatively weak linguistic and political anchoring of Ladin as a non-unified standard language. Due to the strong presence of Italian and German among the local neighbors and tourists, who mainly come from these language groups, these two languages have a high prestige. They are not perceived as "threatening." On the contrary, the added value of multilingualism is so self-evident for the people of Val Gardena and Val Badia that the introduction of English as a foreign language was also supported. Franceschini[214] showed that although the population in the valleys is also concerned about preserving their mother tongue, they are oriented toward multilingualism.

A well-thought-out educational policy and methodical, didactic decisions also support this system. For example, kindergarten teachers and elementary school teachers are trained in a separate five-year course at the School of Education at the Free University of Bozen-Bolzano.[215] It is a political requirement that students and future teachers must be trilingual. It should also be emphasized that work in preschool education in Italy has experienced a significant revaluation since the mid-1990s, which has been highly acclaimed in Europe. As part of the education reform known as the "Ruberti

---

[214] 2013: 57f.
[215] Analogous to the three-tier school system, teacher training for the local schools is also divided into three sections: it takes place in the Ladin, German, and Italian departments.

Law," it was envisioned that kindergarten teachers, like schoolteachers, would need a university degree. This, in turn, provides for special language support in the Autonomous Province of Bozen-Bolzano. This means that Ladin children—if they complete the prescribed educational course from kindergarten to high school graduation (Abitur/A-levels)—have continuous trilingual instruction from the age of three until the 13th grade. If they only complete compulsory schooling, they still have trilingual instruction for at least eight years of school. This is supplemented by English and possibly other foreign languages.

A specific methodological, didactic feature runs through all Ladin educational institutions. Language acquisition has a uniform concept, especially in kindergarten and elementary school, which the following example can illustrate. All three languages are assigned a color right from the start: Ladin (both idioms) is green, Italian is yellow, German is red, and English is blue. When a child enters kindergarten, it is already signaled at the entrance to the room which languages are spoken on that day, or in which lesson or activity, which language is mainly used.

In elementary school, literacy is systematically taught in three languages simultaneously; children learn to write in all three languages from the start, typically using the assigned colors. The newly revised teaching materials are also based on the principle of parallel literacy. Grammar is taught exclusively in a comparative and contrastive way,[216] which, in turn, requires teachers to be proficient in three languages. Since 2018, a complete set of teaching materials has been available for the first to fifth years of elementary school in both Val Gardena and Val Badia.[217]

---

[216] See Videsott R., 2021a and 2021b.
[217] See the 12-volume series "Junde!" (Val Badia) and "Jonde!" (Val Gardena), which have been published successively since 2018 and have recently been made available in full. "Auf, auf, los geht's!" is the German translation of the title. The authors—Ruth Videsott, Veronica Rubatscher, and Daria Valentin—have thus produced the first textbook for teaching Ladin grammar in elementary school. The focus is on trilingual literacy and the English language is also taken into consideration. The textbook is also suitable for use in Montessori schools.

The parity schools in Ladinia (3): A model for monolingual German and Italian schools in South Tyrol and beyond?

Large-scale studies have proven the success of this school model. For example, the transversal study "Ladinia," conducted from 2008 to 2013 on behalf of the Ladin School Board of the Autonomous Province of Bolzano by the Competence Center for Languages at the Free University of Bozen-Bolzano, demonstrated the good to very good written language skills of trilingual students.[218] This study is significant to the extent that it can provide statistically reliable results: in total, a comprehensive text corpus of 1,500 texts was collected from the last grades before transferring to the next school level, that is, from the fifth grade of elementary school, the eighth grade of middle school, and the final year of high school.

These, in turn, were compared with texts from monolingual control groups from German and Italian schools. The results show that the respective Ladin idiom remains the dominant language. The written language skills in Italian and German are balanced and do not differ significantly from those of the native-speaker control groups.

The results of qualitative post-analyses of the texts are also remarkable. Here, the Ladin students show, at least in German—analogous analyses are still pending for Italian—that they have an even richer vocabulary than their monolingual peers. In two qualitative analyses, conjunctions and prepositions were examined as indicators of text quality. These results support the findings of the quantitative studies, indicating that language acquisition does not proceed at the same speed in all three languages simultaneously. However, at the end of their school career, Ladin students write texts just as well as their monolingual German peers in terms of grammatical and stylistic correctness.[219]

From the teachers' perspective, another finding is of considerable importance. It is well known that there are "good" and "bad" mistakes in language acquisition. "Good" mistakes are those that

---

[218] The results were published in four volumes by the Ladin School Board between 2009 and 2013 and can be ordered there on request. They are cited in this article as "Comitê": 2009, 2010, 2013.

[219] See Risse, 2014; Risse & Franceschini, 2016.

indicate to the teacher whether the learners have made an error but which also demonstrate that they have understood the underlying grammatical principle. A prime example of such errors is the overgeneralizations that can be observed in many studies on children's language acquisition. "Bad" errors, on the other hand, are those that indicate an actual need for remedial work.[220]

According to Bredel, Ehlich, and Reich (2008), when examining the dynamics of the language acquisition process from a teaching perspective, the following strategies can be distinguished among learners: exploration, compensation, avoidance, and neutralization. Ladin writers almost exclusively use strategies of exploration and compensation, both of which equally indicate that language acquisition is dynamic and solution-oriented. A compensation strategy means that a learner actively registers a "vocabulary gap" and "fills" it with a word, even if this turns out to be "wrong" on the linguistic surface. The exploration strategy refers to the search for a linguistic alternative, which multilingual learners often rely on when they fall back on their multilingual repertoire. These strategies can be seen as positive, as they demonstrate an actively progressive learning process.

On the other hand, students who attempt to "muddle through" language lessons by using neutralization and avoidance strategies require additional support. If, for example, only standard solutions are used, such as a series of main clauses in German to cover up weaknesses in the knowledge of verb order, which usually come to light with more complex subordinate clauses, then this should give the teacher more food for thought than if a German learner at least exposes himself to the risk of error in order to produce a more complex and possibly more precise syntactic structure. Neutralization strategies can also indicate a need for support in consolidation, such as unclear articulation and writing, for example, to conceal a lack of knowledge of inflectional rules in German. These strategies are hardly noticeable in the multilingual learners from the Ladin valleys in the studies.

---

[220] See Bredel, Ehlich & Reich, 2008.

Finally, it is worth noting that the investigation of English skills in Ladin Elementary School further substantiates the results of the transversal study. But aren't four languages too many? Franceschini and Irsara[221] answer this question as follows:

> In this regard, it should be noted that the English language is progressing, and—as can also be seen from the qualitative review—in a sustained and satisfactory manner. If this were asking too much, the curves would flatten, stagnate, or even decline. This is demonstrably not the case: English continues to progress from one level to the next. The fact that these children are literate in three languages from the first grade makes them little language experts who know almost intuitively how to acquire a fourth language.

In addition, comparative language analyses following "Ladinia" show that students who learn competently in a cross-language teaching model can gain advantages for the "weak" minority language Ladin.[222] Overall, therefore, balanced teaching conducted by multilingual teachers appears to be beneficial, as the languages complement each other.[223]

In everyday life, many Ladin people feel exposed to the prejudice from the German- and Italian-speaking population that they are multilingual but do not speak any of the languages "properly and well." The Ladinia study was commissioned in part to counter this prejudice. The results of the Ladin schools are not surprising, given that multilingual education around the world is observed to result in languages mutually "boosting" each other and also in the transfer of knowledge (transknowledging).[224]

Because the "Ladin" approach has been so successful, the author and her teaching team have also been using an adapted form for their

---

[221] See Comitê, 2013: 40.
[222] See Irsara, 2017, 2020.
[223] See Risse & Franceschini, 2016.
[224] In multilingualism research, studies of the "Southern Initiative" (here as an example: Heugh, 2017), which take a comparative look at areas with traditional, autochthonous multilingual education systems worldwide, are particularly relevant. These are very suitable as a comparison for European models, as long-established forms of multilingualism can also be found here. This is particularly true of the African continent and India.

"Language acquisition and didactics of the mother tongue" courses at the Free University of Bozen-Bolzano for several years in the monolingual-oriented teacher training program for the German language group in South Tyrol. The parallel use of picture books, for example, which are available in different languages, can be put to practical use here. For example, schools in the two major national languages in South Tyrol are now beginning to investigate the advantages of simultaneous, coordinated literacy teaching in German and Italian. Of course, this is also taking place against the background that the "monolingual habitus" of the school systems does not correspond to the plurilingual reality of the classrooms.

Passarella (2011) demonstrated that parallel literacy training has positive effects on phonological awareness, which in turn supports the acquisition of written language. As bilingually literate children can draw from a larger reservoir, they can recognize phoneme-grapheme correlations more quickly. This results in a measurable "time gain" compared to traditional second-language teaching. Against this background, Salzmann (2022) presents initial didactic recommendations for parallel Italian-German literacy training for kindergarten children in South Tyrol.

Paradoxically, yet logically, the Ladin school model is now slowly gaining recognition in South Tyrol. With its language concept, it is becoming a model for the schools of the two major national languages, Italian and German. The multilingual habitus of the Ladins[225] has gained greater local appreciation due to the general appreciation of plurilingualism. It will probably become a model for multilingual education in Europe and beyond in the coming decades.

---

[225] See Franceschini, 2010.

3.6. Pomeranian-Portuguese Literacy in Brazil: Experiences from the Genesis of a Multilingual Project
Peter Rosenberg, Mônica Savedra and Reseda Streb

This chapter describes the genesis of a multilingual project based in Brazil that focuses on Pomeranian and Portuguese literacy and then aims to use Pomeranian as a bridge language due to its linguistic relatedness for learning Standard German and English. Two aspects of the project will be dealt with here, based on information provided in Chapter 1:
1. The conceptual challenges: to date, there have been few projects involving bilingual literacy that include a language that is used almost exclusively orally (Ch. 2).
2. The practical challenges of implementing such a project in schools in a country with a strong monolingual tradition (Ch. 3).

1. *Educação plurilíngue*: A multilingual education project in rural communities in Brazil

1.1. Origin and background of the project

Minority languages have been allowed to be taught at schools in Brazil for a number of years. This applies to indigenous languages as well as so-called immigrant languages, including German and Italian varieties. Brazil has 274 languages—in addition to the predominant Portuguese—including 180 indigenous languages, 56 immigrant languages[226] as well as Afro-Brazilian languages, Creole languages, and the Brazilian sign language LIBRAS. Since 2002, some of the indigenous languages, and since 2007, also some of the immigrant languages, have been "co-officialized" at the municipal level, meaning they can be used in schools and administrations.

---

[226] See IBGE, 2012; IPOL, 2016.

For Brazil, this is a turning point in a language policy whose significance can hardly be overstated: minority languages had been neglected, negated, and some even banned for more than 60 years. The 1988 constitution introduced a gradual recognition of cultural and linguistic diversity in Brazil. In 2007, under Lula's first government, some minorities were recognized as *Povos Tradicionais*, traditional peoples of Brazil, and since 2010, some languages have been inventoried and promoted as part of Brazil's national cultural heritage and linguistic diversity,[227] with Pomeranian becoming the fourth language in 2022.

These languages, however, are often not used by their speakers in a standardized form but in a variety that is usually only spoken, not written, and which they often do not know exactly how to write. These include varieties spoken by immigrants from Germany, Pomeranian, and Hunsrückisch; immigrants from Italy use Talian, a Venetian variety. Pomeranian is still in the early stages of standardization and transcription. It was part of the Low German diasystem, which enjoyed supra-regional prestige in the Middle Ages with the written language of the Hanseatic League in Lübeck. But Low German was subject to a dialect-like development with the advance of High German, from which it is clearly structurally distanced:

> But we have other *abstand* languages which fate has also largely relegated to dialect-like primary group functions and which the speakers [...] feel to be mere dialects of an all-powerful literary language.[228]

Pomeranian thus faces a doubly difficult situation of "diglossia"[229]: it is historically regarded as a substandard of German and currently as an informal, non-public variety that is also not suitable for official use under the umbrella of Portuguese.

Co-officialization is taking place mostly in rural communities with a particularly high proportion of immigrants and a lively speech community, even if the younger speakers are sometimes stronger in the national language due to the dominance of Portuguese. For

---

[227] See Decreto 7.387/2010 - Política de Diversidade Linguística.
[228] See Kloss, 1967: 35.
[229] See Ferguson, 1959; Lüdi, 1989.

Pomeranian, whose speakers have settled in Rio Grande do Sul (RS) since 1858, in Espírito Santo (ES) since 1859, and in Santa Catarina since 1861. Over time have founded further settlements in the interior of Rondônia (from 1970), co-officialization has taken place in nine municipalities to date: Pancas (2007), Laranja da Terra (2008), Santa Maria de Jetibá (2009), Vila Pavão (2009), Canguçu (2010), Domingos Martins (2011), Itarana (2016), all ES; Pomerode, SC (2017); Espigão do Oeste, RO (2023). A bilingual literacy project is currently being prepared in Santa Maria de Jetibá and Domingos Martins (ES) and Canguçu (RS) as well as in two other locations (Arroio do Padre and Turuçu, RS).

1.2. The project idea Educação plurilíngue[230]

Co-officialization makes it possible to teach the languages at school, which is a courageous undertaking given the lack of curriculum planning and materials to date. The project now aims to organize school lessons in the following way:

1. In the first two years of elementary school (Ensino fundamental), bilingual literacy is to be taught in Portuguese and Pomeranian (Pom.). The initial phase is based on the translanguaging approach, which takes the pupils' bilingual abilities as a starting point, allows for both languages depending on the pupils' strengths, and actively mobilizes them, gradually introducing periods of monolingual instruction.

2. Standard German (SG) is to be introduced in the third grade. This is based on the concept of intercomprehension, which uses Pomeranian as a bridge language (*língua ponte*) to teach the related language, Standard German.

---

[230] The study is part of the CNPq Productivity Project by Monica Savedra entitled: Bilingual/Multilingual Education in the Context of Germanic Immigration (2023-2026) and the project "Scientists of Our State" (Cientistas do nosso estado) by the same author: "Comprehensibility between Germanic Languages for Multilingual Education" (2021-2024). Both projects are part of the research group LABPEC - UFF and PRInt UFF for Multilingualism, which works in partnership with the Borders in Motion research group at the European University Viadrina.

    3. English (Engl.) is to be taught from the fifth grade onward. This is also in line with the idea of intercomprehensive language learning of closely related Germanic languages.

The project developers believe that this approach can make use of the opportunities created by co-officialization in a way that is both realistic and ambitious. Realistic because it accepts the pupils as they are: they are respected and supported in their bilingualism, that is, in their ability, and not seen as deficient. The concept of the bridge language is also realistic in that it can show families in which Pomeranian was no longer practiced that it is worth learning Pomeranian as the language of the local community and as a bridge to the world.

The guiding principle behind a school-based promotion of the minority language is the idea of transculturalization and not a renaissance of the autonomy of the minority, which would be illusory in Brazil's modern and mobile society. The project aims to pave the way into the 21st century, not back to the 19th century.

1.3. The phases of the project

Currently in the preparatory phase, the idea for the project *Educação plurilíngue* (Portuguese for multilingual education) originated with linguists from the Universidade Federal Fluminense (Mônica Savedra) and the European University Viadrina (Peter Rosenberg) with the initiators/coordinators of the Pomeranian teaching project *Programa de Educação Escolar Pomerana - Proepo* (Ismael Tressmann). Their discussions, underway since 2016, centered on the multilingual embedding of Pomeranian lessons, which had already begun with one- or two-hour lessons a week. This pertained mainly to the municipalities of Santa Maria de Jetibá and Domingos Martins (ES).

Continuing education for teachers and other interested parties began with an online course on "Multilingual Education and Writing Practices" (led by Reseda Streb, Katharina Müller, and Willian Radünz). Another component of the project offered in 2021 was an online Pomeranian language course, which addressed the spelling of Pomeranian and the didactics of teaching it (led by Lilia Stein). In 2022, the idea of bilingual literacy in the sense described above was taught in theory and practical application in an online course (led by Reseda Streb) with 25 participants.

As the project progressed, locations were expanded to include Pomeranian municipalities in the state of Rio Grande do Sul, whereby in 2021, the cooperation was extended to the south of Brazil (Aloi Schneider, Bernardo Limberger, and Gisleia Blank from the Universidade Federal de Pelotas).

2. Conceptual challenges of plurilingual education

2.1. Translanguaging

Translanguaging means building on the multilingual practice of speakers and making it the starting point for language teaching efforts:

> Translanguaging […] means that we start from a place that leverages all the features of the children's repertoire, while also showing them when, with whom, where, and why to use some features of their repertoire and not others, enabling them to also perform according to the social norms of named languages as used in schools.[231]

It goes without saying that this represents a considerable challenge for teachers who, until then, had neither been exposed to the underlying theoretical concepts nor were accustomed to continuing education in which demanding scientific texts were discussed after an evening of strenuous teaching.

The basis for bilingual instruction in the selected locations is that many of the pupils grow up with Pomeranian as their first language and often only come into close contact with Portuguese when they start school. On the other hand, Portuguese is taking hold in families, and it represents the mainstream educational future in Brazil's hitherto monolingual school system. Given the strength of the local Pomeranian language, some children in standard school classrooms fall silent because, on the one hand, they lack the language skills to participate immediately in class and, on the other hand, due to the linguistic prestige-based devaluation of the minority language speakers. Bilingual literacy makes it possible for pupils to participate

---

[231] See García & Kleyn, 2016: 15.

in lessons and learn from each other from the first day of school, regardless of whether their more proficient language is Pomeranian or Portuguese. This would also seem to make it possible to combat the decline in the number of speakers.

The world in which the younger speakers of Pomeranian, in particular, live is multilingual. Nevertheless, only Portuguese has the reputation of being the language of education, the language of the educated, and the speakers of minority languages—all the more so if they have neither a standard nor a written tradition—are considered uneducated, at least if they are not able to switch to formal Portuguese. Language switching and language mixing are seen as deficits, not as an expression of linguistic diversity.

This monolingual habitus is criticized by Blommaert & Rampton[232] as a language ideology that narrows real language practice to the postulate "that there are distinct languages." This, however, is a habitus with very significant consequences in the school context, which a project must not overlook.

Anyone who wants to be successful in this educational context will respect the multilingual language practice that pupils bring with them to school. But the pupils will not leave school with this practice. Kleyn & García,[233] therefore, distinguish between the "process and product" of teaching within the concept of translanguaging: meeting pupils where they are linguistically (process) and leading them to a conscious multilingual practice that includes "distinct" language skills (product).

The authors see multilingual practice as the "norm": "Translanguaging positions bilingual and multilingual practices as the norm."[234] This may correspond to the normality of students' speech, but it certainly cannot be considered the target norm of teaching. School is a normative institution that should prepare students for the highest possible educational and professional goals. This includes a high level of individual language competence. The competence goal must take into account the different linguistic abilities required in the various registers: the formal-public register,

---

[232] 2011: 3-4.
[233] 2019: 75.
[234] See Kleyn & García, 2019: 72.

which is predominantly reserved for Portuguese; the informal-public register, which also provides space for other languages; and the intimate register, which features multilingual family language use.[235] Nevertheless, the aim of this modern concept of multilingualism must be to impart a high level of multilingual competencies, not merely a fluent code-mixing practice.

2.2. Intercomprehension and intelligibility

The use of the minority language Pomeranian as a bridge to the acquisition of related languages (língua ponte) follows the idea of the Intercomprehensive Language Learning approach, or intercomprehension for short. Knowledge of the vocabulary and grammar of Pomeranian should be used to make it easier to learn Standard German and English.

From the third grade onward, Pomeranian is intended to serve as a bridge language for learning German. As both Pomeranian and Standard German are Germanic language varieties, it is assumed that instruction in recognizing the differences and similarities between the two languages can make learning them considerably easier. In this way, the minority language can serve as an important resource for learning other languages, and its linguistic efficiency value can also be recognized. In a similar vein, the project provides a link with English learning from the fifth grade onward, thus aligning itself with the current Brazilian standard school context. This is because Brazil—after a long period of abstinence—has sensibly embraced foreign language teaching.

Today, however, this is largely "English only"—at the expense of all other languages: after a long period of Portuguese monolingualism, a compulsory foreign language was introduced in 1996 (with the legislation Leis de Diretrizes e Bases, LDB) from the fifth grade of elementary school (Ensino Fundamental). The choice of language had to be decided by the school district. Since 2005, Spanish has been compulsory in secondary school (Ensino Médio).[236] The range of languages on offer was reduced in 2017 by making

---

[235] See Maas, 2005: 108.
[236] Lei [law] n° 11.151/2005.

English the only compulsory foreign language.[237] In recent years, there have been several initiatives to increase the diversity of the languages on offer, including the "co-official" Brazilian minority languages. This is, however, contested in the face of traditional Portuguese monolingualism and—because co-officialization takes place at the municipal level—is threatened with every new mayoral election. The intercomprehension approach aims to tackle the modest diversification of foreign language teaching in Brazil and integrate the co-officialization of minority languages into a modern concept of multilingualism.

In line with the idea of intercomprehension, Hufeisen & Marx[238] have formulated "seven sieves"[239] for foreign language learning. These are "strategies for approaching texts from related languages in order to arrive quickly at a global, and thanks to language relatedness, to a detailed understanding directly."[240] Specifically, the first steps consist of the consideration of: (1) internationalisms and common Germanic vocabulary (internationalisms, for example: *Mode* [English: fashion], *Pizza, Laptop, Sushi*; common Germanic vocabulary, for example: Pom. *knai* / SG *Knie* / Engl. *knee*); (2) function words (*ik / ich / I; un/und / and; dit / dies / this*); (3) sound and grapheme correspondences ([i:] => [ai]: *wijd / weit / wide*); (4) spelling and pronunciation (pronunciation: ‹d› => [-t]: *wald / Wald*); (5) syntactic structures (subject - predicate - object: *hai mag (geirn) matematik / er mag Mathe / he likes math*); (6) morphosyntactic structures (compounding by: *-er + as / -er + als / -er + than*); (7) prefixes and suffixes (*for-/ ver- / for-, af- / ab-; -ung / -ung / -ing*).

The concept of the seven sieves, which is used in various European foreign language learning models (e.g., EuroComGerm, EuroComRom, EuroComSlav), is, however, primarily used to quickly build up (receptive) reading competence, so it certainly does

---

[237] Lei [law] n° 13.415/2017.
[238] 2007, 2014.
[239] Using a concept once developed by Horst G. Klein and Tilbert D. Stegmann (Klein & Stegmann, EuroComRom - Die sieben Siebe: Romanische Sprachen sofort lesen können, Aachen: Shaker, 2000).
[240] See Hufeisen & Marx, 2007: 5, own translation.

not do full justice to the aims of teaching languages in a classroom setting.

The theoretical development of the intercomprehension concept can be traced back to the 1970s. Selinker (1972) saw different levels of interlanguage (IL) approximation between the "native language" (NL) and the "target language" (TL). The learner constantly establishes connections between these three varieties, which can be seen in the transfer of language structures and language practice routines, in learning and communication strategies, and overgeneralizations.[241] Selinker's perspective, however, was clearly focused on second language acquisition, which explains his interest in overgeneralization and fossilization in the use of the target language.

An expansion of the scope to include truly multilingual language use, referred to by Blommaert & Rampton[242] as "superdiversity," also requires new models for second and foreign-language didactics. Hufeisen & Jessner[243] speak of "multiple language learning," which requires a departure from the traditional foreign language model of "multiple monolingualism." The decisive difference in learning a third, fourth, etc., language is that the learner possesses prior knowledge (from several languages), which—consciously or unconsciously, accepted or not — will have an impact on the learning process: "It is crucial to take into account the fact that the L3 learner relies on a different set of previous knowledge from that which the L2 learner is equipped with."[244]

Consequently, the use and awareness of this prior knowledge is of great importance: "Multilingual awareness in its forms metalinguistic awareness and language (learning) awareness have been identified as salient in cross-linguistic processes."[245] Awareness of the connections between the languages plays a decisive role in more recent second language acquisition models.[246] This requires the teacher to actively

---

[241] See Selinker, 1972: 215.
[242] 2011: 3-4.
[243] 2019: 66.
[244] See Hufeisen & Jessner, 2019: 67.
[245] See Hufeisen & Jessner, 2019: 73.
[246] See "M-factor" in the DMM model in Herdina & Jessner 2002, "foreign language learning-specific factors" in the factor model in Hufeisen, 2010.

mobilize and use the respective prior knowledge and the resulting assumptions in the classroom.

This teaching strategy seems plausible, as the learner is already forming hypotheses about the new language based on what they have learned so far: "The learner will continually formulate and reformulate hypotheses about the new language, thereby constructing a spontaneous hypothesis learner grammar."[247] According to Meißner (2004), however, the accuracy and thus the usefulness of these hypotheses depend on how closely the languages are related: "This hypothesis-led construction process works especially well when the languages involved are related to each other."[248]

The most closely related previously learned language might assume the role of a bridge language. However, Meißner (2004) and Hufeisen & Jessner (2019) emphasize that successful learning is not automatic, even with related languages. If this is to be successful, three conditions apply: language affinity, language competence, and language teaching:

> There must be an etymological relationship between the languages; the learner needs to be proficient in the bridge language(s); and finally, the learner needs to receive instruction in how to use the knowledge of previously learned languages as bridge languages. Only when these three conditions are met can the spontaneous grammar be established and continue to develop.[249]

There are still large gaps in research, however, especially when it comes to such closely related varieties of a language or within a linguistic diasystem.[250]

Recent studies on West Germanic languages confirm the greater comprehensibility and, thus, the bridging role of closely related languages.[251] Passive language skills can also contribute to this, as

---

[247] See Hufeisen & Jessner, 2019: 82.
[248] See Meißner, 2004: 47.
[249] See Hufeisen & Jessner, 2019: 82.
[250] See Hufeisen & Jessner, 2019: 67.
[251] See most recently Kürschner, 2019 and Gooskens, Kürschner & van Heuven, 2022.

Gooskens/Kürschner[252] showed in the understanding of Low German words among residents living along the Dutch border (with reported Dutch dialect competence).

Phonetic similarity has the greatest influence. For the comprehension of Danish and Swedish by Germans, for example, it was shown "that comprehensibility is higher with a matching consonant structure than with a matching vowel structure."[253]

The genetic relationship between the languages is not, however, a sufficient condition to guarantee comprehension. Kürschner's (2019) study on comprehensibility in vocabulary between West Germanic languages (German, Dutch, and West Frisian) makes the general statement that in studies on intra-Germanic language comprehension, the lexical and phonetic distance (number and phonetic correspondence of cognates) determines comprehensibility (although this general tendency could not be confirmed in the study).[254]

Cognates, that is, words related in form and content, are the focus of most studies, as it is assumed that word comprehension (above a certain threshold) is the key to text comprehension: "The underlying assumption when testing isolated words is that word recognition is the key to text understanding."[255]

The comprehension of related words is reduced, however, in the case of phonetic differences, longer words, similar words with divergent meanings, different numbers of syllables, unknown sounds, rarity of the word, and orthographic differences.[256] Gooskens (2006) also points to extralinguistic factors such as language attitudes—for example, the assumed "difficulty" of languages.

As regards understanding loanwords from related languages, the interaction of phonetic, orthographic, and morphological factors is emphasized:

> To sum up, the intelligibility of certain groups of loanwords can be explained by the degree of phonological and

---

[252] 2009: 292.
[253] See Kürschner, 2014: 46.
[254] See Kürschner, 2019: 136.
[255] See Gooskens, Kürschner & van Heuven, 2022: 6.
[256] See Kürschner, Gooskens & van Bezooijen, 2009: 83.

orthographical similarities between the source and target languages, the degree of integration, and the point of time when the words entered the language.[257]

Gooskens, Kürschner & van Heuven (2022) conclude that loanwords from other Germanic languages that exist in both languages only facilitate understanding if they are not so old that they have participated in language change, that is, if they do not deviate too far, especially phonetically (and usually also orthographically). Medieval borrowings from Low German are phonologically similar to Danish heritage vocabulary (e.g., Low German *schapp*, Danish *skab*, Swedish *skåp*, SG *Schrank* 'wardrobe,' or Low German *teller*, Danish *tallerken*, Swedish *tallrik*, SG *Teller* 'plate'). They are then difficult for Swedes to decipher—more difficult than, for example, loanwords from English (e.g., *team*) or French (e.g., *miljø*, French *milieu* 'environment'). Of course, even this does not diminish their value in facilitating understanding compared to completely foreign vocabulary.

Especially with closely related languages, it is evident that speakers use their whole language knowledge: in a study on the translation strategies of German listeners to Dutch words, Kürschner[258] observed that related English words were used as an aid (although not always with the correct result), even if a similar German word had been available—a clear indication of the use of the speakers' entire linguistic repertoire:[259]

> We can conclude from such observations that a relation between a stimulus in a foreign (but closely related) language is not solely established with words in the mother tongue, but that the available knowledge of all languages is used.[260]

In Brazil, Karen Pupp Spinassé[261] investigated the comprehensibility of (oral) Standard German for Hunsrückisch speakers: it was found that, given "this language's very close relationship with Standard

---

[257] See Gooskens, Kürschner & van Heuven, 2021: 23.
[258] 2013.
[259] See Hufeisen, 2018.
[260] See Kürschner, 2013: 176.
[261] 2020.

German [...] the number of misunderstood elements was low."[262] The study evaluated comprehension difficulties in the translation of High German sentences into Hunsrück German (so-called Wenker sentences traditionally used in dialect research, which are also used by the ALMA-H dialect atlas project in Brazil). Of the 40 sentences tested, which were translated into Hunsrückisch by an average of 4 test subjects in 12 locations in Rio Grande do Sul, comprehension problems only occurred in 20.6% of the total of 1,680 sentences,[263] although in some cases with several words. Pupp Spinassé & Salgado[264] interpret this as "uma alta inteligibilidade entre o Hunsrückisch e o alemão standard" (a high level of comprehensibility between Hunsrückisch and Standard German, own transl.). Almost three-quarters of these difficulties affected younger speakers (under 35 years of age), which indicates the long absence of German lessons at school; among those over 55 years of age, the figure was only 6%.[265] The elements that were not understood or misunderstood mainly concerned the word level (61%), primarily nouns, then verbs.[266]

This study also aims to raise the status of the minority language and to use it as a bridge language for the acquisition of Standard German:

> Contudo, o desprestígio e o status negativo de língua minoritária de imigração não deixa o Hunsrückisch se valer do possível bônus que essa proximidade poderia trazer (...). Em ambiente escolar, por exemplo, raras são as vezes em que professores permitem ou proporcionam que falantes de Hunsrückisch façam relações entre sua língua materna e a variedade standard que aprendem em sala de aula. (...) Com isso, objetivamos dar nossa contribuição para caracterizar o status linguístico do Hunsrückisch e, consequentemente,

---

[262] See Pupp Spinassé & Salgado, 2020: 9 (own transl.).
[263] See Pupp Spinassé & Salgado, 2020: 18.
[264] 2020: 18.
[265] See Pupp Spinassé & Salgado, 2020: 19.
[266] See Pupp Spinassé & Salgado, 2020: 21-22.

também para legitimar seu uso como língua-ponte para se acessar ou para se chegar ao alemão standard.²⁶⁷

[Translation: *The discrediting and negative status of a minority language of immigration, however, does not allow Hunsrückisch to benefit from the potential bonus that such proximity could bring (...). In school, for example, teachers rarely allow or enable Hunsrückisch speakers to make connections between their mother tongue and the standard variety they learn in class (...) In this way, we want to contribute to characterizing the linguistic status of Hunsrückisch and thus also to legitimize its use as a bridge language for access to or acquisition of standard German.* Own transl.]

The historical relationship between languages is a matter of diachrony—that is a historical fact. However, this is not necessarily significant for synchrony, the current use of language, linguistic competence, and the language attitudes of speakers. It, therefore, makes sense—as is done in the studies mentioned above—to separate these two levels analytically and to ascertain which elements of the related languages are currently understood or not or misunderstood by the speakers and to what extent.

The similarity of words in Hunsrückisch and Standard German has been calculated in several studies, including Pupp Spinassé & Salgado (2020), using the Levenshtein distance,²⁶⁸ which counts the necessary alternations (substitution, insertion, deletion) of sounds/letters that are necessary to get from one word to the other. Of course, this is a fairly simple method and only related to lexis, but it is suitable as a first approximation.

An example from the study by Pupp Spinassé & Salgado (2020) for Hunsrückisch is *Kerich*, SG *Kirche* 'church,' with three necessary changes: substitution of *i* instead of *e* in the first syllable, omission of *i* and addition of *e* in the second syllable. To measure (relative) intelligibility—regardless of the length of the words—Kürschner²⁶⁹ calculates the number of necessary changes as a proportion of the total number of sounds in the word. For *Kerich-Kirche*, this would be

---

²⁶⁷ See Pupp Spinassé & Salgado, 2020: 10.
²⁶⁸ After Nerbonne & Heeringa, 2010.
²⁶⁹ 2014: 47.

3/5, or 60% of the sounds (‹ch› is counted as one sound) or 3/6 of the letters (i.e., 50%), which Pupp Spinassé & Salgado[270] count.

In Pomeranian, the change would generally be somewhat greater than in Hunsrückisch: Pomeranian (like all Low German-based varieties) has not undergone the High German sound shift and has therefore retained *p, t, k*, which have changed in High German (as in all Upper German and to varying degrees in the Central German dialects) to *f/pf, s/*[ts] (‹z›), and ‹ch› (as palatal sound [ç] with a palatal preceding and the velar sound [x] with a velar preceding).

Examples from Pomeranian for the missing sound change from *p* to *f* or *pf* are: Pom. *åp* – SG *Affe* 'monkey (ape)' or Pom. *përd* – SG *Pferd* 'horse'; from *t* to *s* or [ts] (‹z›): Pom. *eete* – SG *essen* 'eat' or Pom. *tau* – SG *zu* 'to'; from *k* to [ç, x] (‹ch›): Pom. *ik*, – SG *ich* 'I', Pom. *måke* – SG *machen* 'make' (Tressmann in prep.: 43, 721, 209, 961, 431, 619). In addition, Low German has *u* and *o* (written ‹oo› [ou]) as well as *i* and *e* (written ‹ë› [εi]), where *au* and *ei* [ai] appear in High German: Pom. *huus* – SG *Haus* 'house', Pom. *loope* – SG *laufen* 'walk (lope)'; Pom. *mijn* – SG *mein* 'my', Pom. *arbëd* – SG *Arbeit* 'work'.[271] Of course, this is already a greater distance from Standard German than exists in Hunsrückisch, which has a Central German origin. If we compare Pomeranian *åp* with Hunsrückisch *Aff* with regard to the phonetic distance from Standard German *Affe*, it is 3/3 (100 %) for Pomeranian and 1/3 (33 %) for Hunsrückisch.

But there are also counterexamples such as the Pomeranian *kirch* – SG *Kirche* 'church' recorded by Tressmann,[272] which has a gap of only 20% (1/5) compared to the Hunsrückisch *Kerich* mentioned above with 60% (*kirch*, however, is probably of High German origin, which may have been conveyed by High German pastors in the past, Low German would originally have been *kerk* or *kark* with a value of 3/5, i.e. also 60%, cf. Sass 2016: 375).

Another example mentioned by Pupp Spinassé & Salgado[273] is the Standard German *gekommen* 'come (past participle),' which corresponds to the Hunsrückisch base dialectal *komm*. The distance

---

[270] 2020: 21.
[271] See Tressmann in prep.: 422, 606, 647, 649.
[272] 2006: 250.
[273] 2020: 21.

would be 4/7 (57%) phonetically and 4/8 (50%) in spelling. The Pomeranian *kåme* (Tressmann in prep.:478) would have a distance of 3/7 (43 %) in phonetic terms and 5/8 (62.5 %) in spelling from the Standard German *gekommen*, whereby the letter ⟨å⟩, which is foreign to both German and Portuguese, presents a particular difficulty. Tressmann's spelling (reinforced in the new edition Tressmann in prep.), which contains several graphemes that do not exist in either German or Portuguese (⟨å⟩ for velar [ɑ], ⟨ë⟩ for [ɛi], ⟨ij⟩ for long [i:]), is intended to reflect the independence of Pomeranian. These graphemes, however, pose an additional difficulty when it comes to learning Standard German (and English). Of course, the phonetic or graphemic distance is only one basis for assessing comprehensibility. There are also phonetic and prosodic differences in pronunciation. Furthermore, the differences are not all of equal weight. For example, grammatical divergences (in word formation, for example, in the case of plural endings or the word order in the sentence) can make comprehension more difficult than purely phonetic or graphemic differences. Conversely, grammatical similarities undoubtedly help: the one who knows *apel - äpel* [274] will easily learn the Standard German plural umlaut *Apfel - Äpfel* (and, anyway, the English *apple - apples*).

But the similarity of all varieties spoken by German immigrants to Standard German—regardless of their somewhat greater or lesser phonetic, lexical, and grammatical proximity in detail—is, in any case, a great help in learning Standard German (and also English).

The *língua ponte* aspect of the second and third phases of our project focuses precisely on this function of facilitating comprehension. It aims to use prior knowledge of Pomeranian as a bridge language for the acquisition of Standard German and English by activating language awareness in the learners. Similarity is the basis of comprehensibility, but the phonetic differences, which in Pomeranian regularly deviate from High German, require systematic linguistic comparison and recognition. But even where there are differences, their regularity also makes this recognition possible.

---

[274] See Tressmann, 2006: 25.

We believe that Pomeranian-Portuguese bilingual literacy, which builds on the language practice of translanguaging, prepares for this awareness because the primary phase also raises the children's bilingual language practice above the threshold of consciousness, a bilingual practice that had previously remained unconscious or at least unelaborated.

The challenge for the teaching task now lies in developing a didactic approach to intercomprehension, not a threefold monolingual language teaching approach. The advantage is precisely that the students' prior knowledge can and should be mobilized.

2.3. Written form

To raise the status of minority languages, their domains of application must be expanded, and proof must be provided that they are languages capable of wholly valid communication. If they are to be taught at school, this generally includes their use as a written medium—and this, in turn, requires standardization.

Anna Maria Escobar (2013) has put this into words for the minority languages in Latin America: "The development of a written tradition is essential in promoting the revitalization of indigenous (and other minority) languages."[275]

On the other hand, Hobsbawm rightly warns that this does not leave languages and their community-building function untouched: Any language that moves from the purely oral to the realm of reading and writing, [...] any language that becomes a medium for school teaching or official use, changes its character. It has to be standardized in grammar, spelling, vocabulary, and perhaps pronunciation.[276]

This effect is familiar to anyone who has ever observed that speakers who diligently learn a foreign language but still make some mistakes can count on a certain amount of goodwill from native speakers. If the same phenomenon occurs with dialects or other group languages, the learner's effortful but error-prone way of speaking is easily regarded as an inappropriate and illegitimate attempt at ingratiation that is better avoided. This has primarily to do

---

[275] See Escobar, 2013: 742.
[276] See Hobsbawm, 1996: 1072.

with the boundary-marking, not purely communication-oriented function of these varieties, which is defended against outsiders. The character of the varieties changes with the objectifying role that writing plays. According to Maas (2010), the written variety is a specific linguistic variety that is *situationally* characterized by the formal-public reference, *cognitively* serves the task of not only expressing thoughts but also making them the object of processing, *communicatively* characterized by decontextualized communication. *Structurally*, as slowed-down language production, written language focuses on the linguistic form, resulting in greater complexity, elaboration, and differentiation of the linguistic form, and *medially*, it is characterized by symbolic representation as written characters and by their analytical-abstracting reference to language.[277]

It is, therefore, not surprising that the spelling, the type of phoneme-grapheme relationships, and the introduction of special characters and diacritics attract particular attention in the community of speakers, even assuming a proxy function in questions of status and regional claims to validity.

3. Practical challenges: What could modern multilingual didactics look like in Brazilian rural communities?

3.1. Organizational challenges of implementation

Selection of municipalities

Online courses, several WhatsApp groups, a tour by the project leaders through the locations interested in participating, and discussions with mayors, education administrators, school principals, and teachers served as organizational preparation for the launch of the project.

Although the municipalities are primarily made up of places where Pomeranian is already a co-official language, the project has also found favor in other municipalities.

Finding and training teachers, selecting schools, and raising awareness among the local language communities

The participants in the above-mentioned preparatory course for bilingual literacy were selected and registered by the municipalities.

---

[277] See Rosenberg & Schroeder, 2016: v.

Of the 25 participants, however, not all were actually active teachers, but some were members of the education administration. Some of the teachers were working in upper grades, making them unavailable for the initial lessons. And of those who remained, several became pregnant. The number of teachers trained and active in the initial stage was, therefore, lower than expected.

On the other hand, a number of other teachers were motivated to take part, but some had not completed any training in bilingual literacy. In contrast, others felt insecure about spelling Pomeranian. Obviously, longer preparation times had to be expected. The selection of schools was based on the willingness of teaching staff on the one hand, while on the other hand, the school management and local administration, and finally, the parents themselves had to be committed to the project. Since the communities identify strongly with the Pomeranian language, this was not initially a major hurdle.

Raising awareness among parents requires special attention, however, as Pomeranian is not spoken in all families, and the Pomeranian language community must be seen as an oral community that needs to be convinced of the value of Pomeranian as a written language and as an educational tool, suitable for a (co)official register. A survey to ascertain the attitudes of parents will, therefore, be part of the project. The involvement of families—parents and grandparents—in the school curriculum will also be supported by a "contemporary witness" project: parents or grandparents should speak in Pomeranian at school about cultural practices, professional activities, experiences during the time of marginalization of minorities, or simply report on what their lives were like at the time when they were the same age as today's pupils.

This approach has pedagogical links with Paulo Freire's ideas of a "pedagogy of the oppressed," anchoring education in the real world.[278] This is of particular importance for rural Brazil: Brazil is one of the countries with the most pronounced social inequality in the world.[279] Social inequality is clearly reflected in the contrast between the public education system (80% of students) and the

---

[278] See Freire, 1993.
[279] In the Gini coefficient of global income inequality, Brazil ranked 136th out of 145 countries in 2021, see The World Bank, 2023.

private education system (20% of students). This applies in particular to rural education, the reform of which is being called for under the motto "Educação do campo" (education in/for the countryside).[280]

Curriculum and other official requirements
Even when local stakeholders were in favor of the project, official requirements still had to be met: the lessons must comply with the overarching Brazilian educational structure, the Base Nacional Comum Curricular (BNCC), the number of lessons must be accounted for in the teaching plans, and the Department of Education (Secretaria de Educação) must give its approval at the federal and municipal level. To clarify the accountabilities for those involved in the project, a cooperation agreement was drawn up that defined what the project offers and what the municipality has pledged to do. The proposed number of teaching hours—previously only one to two hours per week in the context of co-officialization—was set at five hours per week, which are to be drawn from time reserved for regional topics and regular Portuguese lessons, which are (at least partially) included in the bilingual lessons.

3.2. Didactic challenges to implementation

Creating didactic material and the challenge of writing
The project group is still in the initial phase of creating bilingual didactic material. Part of the online course was the formation of working groups of teachers who devised didactic materials. Examples include the first exercises, games, songs, rhymes, and quizzes that the participating teachers created using online resources (freeware): *Mit dai A fängt dat an: Ameis - Apel - Ananas* (It starts with the A: Ant - Apple - Pineapple. The letter A bilingual); *Wile wij as leese?* (Shall we read? The letter F bilingual); *O corpo - Dai körper* (The body); *Dai numers bet 10 - Os números até 10* (The numbers up to 10); *Qual é o animal que está escondido?* (Which animal is hidden here? Initials of animal names [A, I, O] and vocabulary); *Jogo da memória* (Memory game): *im - abelha* [bee], *Jaguar - onça, åp - macaco* [monkey]); *Dai Fische - Os Peixinhos* (The fishes, song); *Dai tëgen ulsche* (The ten old ones, quiz on the lyrics of the song).

---

[280] See Foerste, Schütz-Foerste & Merler, 2015.

As can be seen from all these examples, the conceptual basis of the bilingual exercises consists of the above-mentioned awareness of the practice of translanguaging already practiced by the bilinguals. Both of the children's languages are accepted and are even activated and exposed to language comparison.

The way in which teachers approach the instruction of bilingual literacy depends on their resources, capacities, and preferences. If both languages are not sufficiently mastered (e.g., also written Pomeranian), there are two teachers as co-teachers for the two languages, Pomeranian and Portuguese. In other cases, one bilingual teacher will be able to encompass all aspects.

The literature occasionally concedes that teachers do not need to know both languages,[281] which in this case could only apply to Pomeranian. In the context of this project, however, this would not be successful. On the contrary, it will be necessary to determine exactly what the balance should be between multilingual phases (in which translanguaging is permitted and activated) and monolingual phases (in which the focus is on developing individual language skills). The goal remains to shape the process from "mixed" language use (translanguaging and code-mixing) to functional multilingualism (register-dependent language choice and code-switching).

The postcolonial objective described by Kleyn & García[282] as a "strong" version of translanguaging "to break down nation-state-imposed hierarchies around named languages that reproduce inequalities" seems unrealistic to us—at least for the Brazilian school system. Rather, the project will have to focus on developing multilingual skills, not just fluent translanguaging, which would risk losing the support of parents.

When creating didactic materials, it was originally planned that the teachers who took part in the bilingual literacy training, and especially those who will take over the pilot classes, would create the teaching materials and be supported by the project group in an advisory capacity. However, it became apparent that this bottom-up planning was asking too much of the teachers.

---

[281] See Kleyn & García, 2019: 76.
[282] 2019: 75.

In November 2023, two project days were therefore held in a school in Domingos Martins (ES) to show teachers, school management, pupils, and interested parents what such a project could look like in practice.

In project planning, it might make sense to first develop a curriculum and didactic material for the first year top-down. It would be useful to base initial bilingual lessons on a Portuguese textbook and to orient bilingual teaching thematically on this.

3.3. Challenges of standardization and codification status

Orthography

An important issue that came up time and again with the majority of participating teachers was their uncertainty regarding the first steps in implementing the project. This included the feeling of a lack of knowledge of Pomeranian orthography.

The spelling previously used in the federal state of Espírito Santo, which was developed by Ismael Tressmann (2006) and is currently being revised in a new edition of his Pomeranian-Portuguese dictionary, is sometimes repudiated in Rio Grande do Sul, partly due to regional pronunciation differences and partly due to inconsistencies in the spelling. For example, Tressmann generally marks long vowels with double vowels, except for the long i, which is marked with ‹ij›, to emphasize the independence of Pomeranian from German through a—phonetically incorrect—echo of Dutch. Conversely, there are reasonable reservations in Espírito Santo about the use of Low German spellings that are based in general on Standard German.[283]

Pomeranian speakers in Brazil are rarely proficient in Standard German. A recent pilot study by Gisleia Blank (2023) showed, however, that there were almost no differences in the reading comprehension of Pomeranian speakers (tested in terms of accuracy and reading speed) between the spelling based on Tressmann[284] and an alternative spelling based on Standard German. This was true for

---

[283] See Sass, 2016: 16, rule 1: "Only characters that are also used in High German are used"; similarly, Herrmann-Winter, 2017.
[284] According to the Schneider 2019 dictionary.

texts as well as for isolated words (although the accuracy rate was quite low at just under 60%).

Regional variation

Pomeranian's regional variation also presents a further difficulty. Due to the lack of standardization of Pomeranian, teachers are unsure which standard they should follow. For example, Kaufmann/Duran (2023) have shown that the pronunciation habits of Pomeranian speakers in Rio Grande do Sul (RS) differ considerably from those in Espírito Santo (ES) and Rondônia (RO), for example, in different preferences in the alternative *Ik häf grote hunger* (in RS) vs. *Ik hä grote hunger* (in ES and RO) – SG Ich habe großen Hunger 'I am very hungry'. The variation that occurs in the oral language also prevents speakers from RS from seeing themselves represented in the orthographic proposal from ES. In our view, allowing regional alternatives should not contradict an agreement on a consensus on spelling.

The oral tradition of the community as an attitudinal problem

Due to the historical discrimination against Pomeranian (like all varieties of the so-called immigrant languages) starting with the 1937 nationalization policy of the "Estado Novo" under President Getúlio Vargas, the language has suffered a considerable loss of prestige,[285] which has in part led to the affected generation of parents not passing on their knowledge of Pomeranian to their children, some of whom therefore only have passive knowledge or no knowledge of Pomeranian at all. Some also do not see the preservation of the language as a benefit for the next generation.[286] The project also aims to highlight the advantages of knowing Pomeranian for learning other languages. In the background is the assumption that in an emerging country like Brazil, the time seems to be over when minorities persist due to the mere remoteness of their settlement areas. Minority language and culture can only be preserved within the framework of multilingualism and transculturality.

---

[285] See Rosenberg, 2018: 221.
[286] See Rosenberg, 2023: 44.

3.4. Next steps

The project is currently in the preparatory phase. This also means that any shortcomings are becoming more apparent as those pedagogues involved are asking for resources. The project finds more favorable conditions in Espírito Santo, where the teachers and school administration already have a certain amount of experience with Pomeranian lessons through the Proepo program. In the southern state of Rio Grande do Sul, practical experience in teaching Pomeranian is being gained first. In some locations, introductory activities (such as days of bilingual Pomeranian lessons) will be used to demonstrate in concrete terms what multilingual education could look like. Parents and grandparents are also invited to the schools for this purpose.

On-site advice and supervision are provided to accompany the first practical steps of implementation. For those who still need further conceptual training, a new edition of the online course on bilingual literacy will be made available as a podcast series. Where there is still a lack of knowledge about Pomeranian itself, a course on the history and linguistic description of Pomeranian will be organized. At the same time, a working group will deal with the creation of a framework curriculum and didactic material for the first year. The challenge here is to systematize existing but scattered material and to integrate it into a progressive course. In all of these tasks—as with all development initiatives—it is crucial that local stakeholders play the central role.

4. Conclusion: Integrating local, national, and transnational interests in language teaching

This project pursues the goal of multilingual education. The minority language, Pomeranian, is to be taught in bilingual literacy classes. In doing so, the common practice of translanguaging in bilingual lessons is accepted and activated. The aim is to develop skills in the two languages of instruction, Pomeranian and Portuguese. To this end, bilingual and monolingual teaching phases alternate. The language lessons are thus anchored in the real world on the one hand and, on the other, meet the requirements of the Brazilian national education system.

From the third grade onward, German, and from the fifth grade onward, English are taught as closely related languages in line with the didactics of intercomprehension. Previous knowledge of vocabulary and structure is incorporated; comparing the similarities and differences between the languages is intended to give learners an awareness of their multilingual skills. Pomeranian thus gains in status and acts as a bridge to the acquisition of other (internationally usable) languages. This is also attractive for families in which Pomeranian is no longer their mother tongue.

Difficulties must be taken into account that result from the fact that standardization and transcription have only just begun, as well as from regional differences and the disregard for a hitherto oral community of speakers.

Because the language policy goal of counteracting marginalization due to widespread language nationalism applies to many minorities within and outside Brazil, the perspective is extended beyond the regional benefits to other contexts in an exemplary manner. The model—the "transcultural" idea—is to promote minority languages and, at the same time, to understand the multiple belongings of their speaker groups as a minority community, as part of the national language community, and as actors in transnational relationships. The perspective is, therefore, the way into the globalized 21st century, not back to the self-sufficiency of the 19th century.

3.7. Bilingual Co-teaching of Writing Genres in Quebec
Joël Thibeault and Marie-Hélène Forget

Introduction

On a pedagogical level, bilingual education raises questions about how to integrate the languages being taught and what parameters should be considered when doing so. Indeed, at a time when the language education research community recognizes the relevance of linking languages that appear in the same curriculum,[287] little work seems to describe the modalities through which it is possible, or even preferable, to get learners to build bridges between languages taught at school.

With this in mind, we conducted a research project in which we collaborated with two Grade 6 teachers in a Quebec elementary school's Intensive English program.[288] In particular, we developed and tested teaching units for integrated writing instruction based on textual genres in French and English. Additionally, the teachers were asked to work in tandem in a bilingual co-teaching environment to implement the units.

This chapter will, therefore, allow us to highlight the theoretical foundations on which our project is based and the development of one of the units we have designed—the one focusing on the written recommendation of a narrative work. We will conclude this chapter by presenting some of the data we collected to document our project; more specifically, we will showcase results coming from a series of individual interviews conducted with each of the teachers following the teaching unit.

Intensive English in Quebec

As mentioned earlier, our research took place in a school offering the Intensive English program in Quebec. This program, introduced in a growing number of Quebec schools where French is the language of

---

[287] See Ballinger *et al.*, 2020; De Pietro, 2020.
[288] In Quebec, in Grade 6, students are approximately 11 years old.

instruction (FL1),[289] takes place over one school year and is offered at the end of the elementary level; it relies primarily on increasing and intensifying the time allocated to teaching English as a second language (ESL) (Ministère de l'Éducation et de l'Enseignement supérieur [MEES], 2017). In Intensive English, therefore, half the school year is devoted to ESL instruction. That being said, this does not mean that non-linguistic school subjects, such as mathematics and the arts, are taught in the second language, as is the case in many bilingual education programs. Indeed, in Quebec, the Charter of the French Language stipulates that French is the sole language of instruction in French-language schools. As a result, the time devoted to ESL in Intensive English, although concentrated, is limited to content related to this discipline. The rest of the curriculum must be taught in French in a condensed manner.

Several models can guide the operation of an Intensive English program.[290] The most common model used in schools is the successive model, where five months of the school year are dedicated to ESL, while the other five months are devoted to various subjects, all taught in French. Other models are based on alternating languages throughout the school year: for example, some schools adopt a model where one week's teaching is in French and the following week's is in English. Other schools opt for a day-to-day alternation.

This last model is the one adopted at the school of the two teachers we worked with for this study. We found this mode of operation particularly interesting due to its organizational structure, which fosters close collaboration between the main classroom teacher and the ESL teacher. To this end, the MEES (2019) has developed an official document for Intensive English that promotes collaboration between the classroom teacher and the ESL teacher. It recommends, among other things, planning interdisciplinary projects, participating in joint in-service training, and implementing similar teaching practices.

Given this context, we suggested that our two collaborating teachers—the first a classroom teacher and the second an ESL

---

[289] See Dezutter *et al.*, 2017.
[290] See MEES, 2018.

teacher – participate in a study on the bilingual co-teaching of writing genres. Before introducing one of the teaching units that we developed during this project, along with some of the elements of the methodology that enabled us to report on it empirically and the results that emerged, we will examine the theoretical framework that underlies the overall project.

Theoretical framework

First and foremost, this study focuses on integrated language teaching. Recognized as one of the four approaches in the Framework of Reference for Pluralistic Approaches to Languages and Cultures,[291] integrated language teaching aims to help learners make connections between the different languages they study at school.[292] Its primary objective is to lead learners in forging links between the languages they are taught at school.[293] In doing so, they can more easily make cross-linguistic transfers and mobilize the knowledge and skills they have in one language when learning the other.[294] On the teacher's side, this integrated teaching is likely to save them time and energy[295] because they can draw on the students' existing knowledge when teaching new curricular content. For teachers working with students enrolled in the Intensive English program, this potential benefit of integrated teaching is significant because, while the English teacher is given considerable time over the school year, it is at the expense of time allocated to other school subjects. The most significant benefit of such integration would be that it would enable the teacher to leverage the knowledge taught in the ESL course.

In Quebec, however, such an integrated approach has been slow to take hold, especially in Intensive English.[296] Nonetheless, the few studies in which French and English teachers have collaborated offer

---

[291] See Candelier *et al.*, 2012.
[292] The other three are: language awareness, intercomprehension between related languages, and intercultural education.
[293] See Gajo, 2008.
[294] See Candelier, 2016; Wokush, 2008.
[295] See Cavalli, 2008.
[296] See Horst *et al.*, 2010.

fascinating insights into the benefits of this type of collaboration. Mainella (2012) explored the joint work undertaken by a French teacher and an ESL teacher at a Quebec high school, who met weekly to identify similarities between their respective curricula for writing. Through this collaboration, they successfully implemented coordinated instruction in both languages. Results show, among other things, that successful language integration is possible when teachers receive adequate support and support each other—even if one of them has limited metalinguistic knowledge of the other language. Moreover, to ensure the success of such integration, it is crucial to allocate quality planning time to the teachers.

In this study, language integration occurred while activities were being prepared; the participants were alone in their classrooms while they were teaching. In our case, we chose to focus on another modality for language integration: that of co-teaching. While co-teaching has traditionally referred to the collaboration of a classroom teacher and a teacher who focuses on special needs students, it is now more holistically defined as the sharing of classroom space by a minimum of two professionals and their joint management, to varying degrees, of instructional activities.[297]

Currently growing in popularity, co-teaching is associated with several benefits: among others, it promotes the sharing of knowledge and skills between colleagues[298] and facilitates classroom management.[299] Needless to say, as with planning sessions leading to coordinated instruction, it requires significant preparation time; however, for students, it would lead to better academic performance,[300] especially in writing.[301] In contexts where co-teaching is proposed from a biliteracy perspective, and collaboration between professionals aims at the joint construction of knowledge related to two different languages,[302] it is vital for the colleagues involved to have chemistry and share a vision of the education they

---

[297] See Tremblay, 2020.
[298] See Saillot & Malmaison, 2018; Tasdemir & Yildirim, 2017.
[299] See Austin, 2001.
[300] See Boland *et al.*, 2019.
[301] See Tremblay, 2013.
[302] See Dillon & Gallagher, 2019; Fialais, 2019/2021.

provide. Additionally, they should consider how to integrate the languages they use in the classroom so that students can learn both languages simultaneously.

The last conceptual pillar on which we based our teaching units for this study is the teaching of writing through genres. Indeed, in the field of French education[303] as well as in that of ESL,[304] the value of teaching writing through the study of these genres is recognized. Genres, or categories of written language productions that, "in a given culture, possess common characteristics" that may be "communicative, textual, semantic, grammatical, graphic, or visual,"[305] would thus benefit from being the pivotal point around which the teaching of writing takes place. Some examples of these genres include blog posts, recipes, and recommendations of narrative works.

To date, the use of genres in writing instruction has been studied primarily from a monolingual perspective, with texts used as examples and learners' productions written in a single language. Some authors[306] recognize, however, that this work on genres in writing can also be done by integrating several languages. From this perspective, Gentil (2011) suggests that the same genre can be applied similarly across several languages if the cultures associated with the languages involved share specific common characteristics. It is, therefore, often likely that the bilingual or plurilingual learner, in one of the languages in their linguistic repertoire, has at least some knowledge related to the genre under study or some of its underlying traits. The integrated teaching of genres will thus allow for the mobilization of this prior knowledge. It will lead the learner to trace the similarities and cross-linguistic distinctions that exist between texts of the same genre.

In light of the theoretical framework we have just outlined, we, therefore, set out to create and assess teaching units based on the integrated co-teaching of writing genres in French and English. The

---

[303] See Dolz & Gagnon, 2008; Forget & Thibeault, 2022a.
[304] See Hyland, 2004; Kessler, 2021.
[305] See Chartrand *et al.*, 2015: 3.
[306] See Balsiger *et al.*, 2012; Sommer-Farias, 2020.

following section outlines the research methodology employed in this study and describes how we developed a specific unit.

Methodology

The project at the heart of this study took place during the 2020-2021 school year in a French-language elementary school in the northern suburbs of Montreal. During our research at this school, 56 students (from two class groups) were in Grade 6, all of whom were enrolled in the Intensive English program. The two teachers who collaborated in our study, therefore, accompanied all these students throughout their 6th year. On Mondays and Tuesdays, one of the classes is with Éliane and covers, in French, the entire school curriculum, except for what concerns ESL. The other class is with Clara; their days are spent in English and revolve around the content of the ESL program. On Wednesdays and Thursdays, the two groups switch, alternating every week of the school year. On Fridays, the groups are brought together, and the teachers work in a co-teaching environment on various school projects that they plan together. This synergy between the groups is made possible by the presence of a movable wall that separates Éliane's and Clara's classrooms, which is raised during co-teaching.

Since Éliane and Clara were already used to co-teaching but had never done so before to integrate the teaching of curricular content related to French and English, we invited them to help us create teaching units on the writing of two genres: the recommendation of a narrative work and the opinion letter. In this chapter, we will focus on the first unit, which was taught in December 2020. Before its implementation in the classroom, the research team met to determine the process and design materials that would facilitate its rollout to students.

The unit, inspired by work on teaching writing through genres[307] and explicitly based on Barth's (2013) social-cognitive mediation model,[308] was spread out over three full 120-minute classes. The first

---

[307] See Dolz & Gagnon, 2008; Hyland, 2004.
[308] In general, this model is divided into three phases. First, the teacher proposes, with the help of examples and counter-examples, a phase of

class was where the bilingual co-teaching took place. During this class, the two teachers first co-facilitated a plenary discussion, during which students analyzed examples and counterexamples of film recommendations. Three recommendations were discussed: one example was in English, one example was in French, and one counter-example was in French. Students, as they ranked the texts, were also asked to justify their position, which allowed for the emergence of the characteristics expected when recommending a film. Éliane and Clara then distributed six recommendation texts to the students, some of which were written in French and some in English. As a practice exercise, students were asked to determine whether each of the texts referred to examples or counterexamples and to justify their decision. During a group discussion, teachers and students were able to identify the structural characteristics of a recommendation based on the analysis of the examples and counter-examples and to insert them into two posters, one in French and the other in English. This class concluded with an exercise in which the students, divided into small groups, had to rewrite two counterexamples, one for each language. They had to identify the elements of the texts that made them counterexamples and rewrite them so that they resembled the previously discussed examples in class. The bilingual nature of the class was also critical: Éliane, the French teacher, spoke primarily in French, and Clara, the English teacher, spoke English. The students, on the other hand, could speak in the language of their choice.

The other two classes of the unit were devoted to writing. In the second class, which Éliane led, students were asked to write a recommendation for a movie they had seen in French. In the third class, Clara took over and asked them to write a recommendation for an English comic book.

---

exploration and observation allowing the fundamental characteristics of the concept studied to be brought to light. This is followed by a clarification and validation phase, during which the teacher must ensure that the students understand these characteristics by inviting them to reinvest them through the analysis of another series of examples and counter-examples. The final phase is one of abstraction, during which the teacher supports the students in synthesizing the knowledge they have built up and helps them prepare for how they could potentially be applied to different contexts.

Throughout the project, to document it empirically, we employed a methodological design that enabled the collection of qualitative data. The preparation meetings and classroom sessions were filmed, and following the implementation of each unit, we conducted individual interviews with each of the two teachers. We also retrieved the texts produced by the students at the end of the unit on recommendations, which allowed us to describe their knowledge of this genre in both languages.[309]

In this chapter, we present some of the results from individual interviews conducted after the bilingual co-teaching of a narrative work recommendation. To construct the interview guide, we drew on the work of Renaud (2020). The researcher, who is interested in reading education, invited teachers to implement a unit that she had designed. Following the initial implementation of the unit, she interviewed them to identify the various criteria that the researcher must consider to perfect it. Each of the 15 criteria (e.g., the teacher's workload in comparison with their usual workload, their observations of student interest, and the relevance of the objectives pursued) was, therefore, the subject of interview questions, which we formulated to focus specifically on the bilingual co-teaching of recommendations.

After transcribing the interviews verbatim, we analyzed the data in two stages. First, we conducted a deductive analysis based on codes that we initially determined using the 15 criteria proposed by Renaud (2020). Since our object of study differs from hers, some of the topics were only briefly discussed by our participants. At the same time, certain direct quotes that seemed interesting to us could not be analyzed using this initial grid. We, therefore, eliminated from our grid the criteria that were not discussed in our interviews.

Furthermore, to include the passages that our initial grid did not allow us to analyze, we inductively generated additional codes. When the set of codes was finalized, we grouped them into three broad categories: teachers' views on the parameters of the integrated units, students' experiences as perceived by the teachers, and teachers'

---

[309] See Forget & Thibeault, 2022b.

experiences of language integration in a co-teaching context. We then started the coding from the beginning, using the final analysis grid.

Results

To present the results, we will look sequentially at the three main categories of themes that emerged from our analyses. Regarding the parameters of the integrated unit, the teachers primarily discussed the nature of the tasks that comprise it. They agreed, among other things, on the merits of presenting examples and counter-examples simultaneously in both languages. For Éliane, this approach has made it possible to break down the barriers that often exist between the languages taught in school.

> What I liked [...] was the fact that we presented "yes" and "no" texts in both languages. It made it so that there was no barrier between the two. They really saw that it's the same thing at the same time.

Refining her reflection further, she also recalls the creation of the class reference posters and the notes taken by students as they were creating them with their teachers. These reference posters, which contain elements derived from the analysis of examples and counterexamples, were first created in French and then in English. According to Éliane, the creation of two separate posters made the students' work more cumbersome:

> The note sheet that we had them take was in French. After that, [Clara] translated it for when we did the activity in English. But in their notes, it's in French. It's funny because she talks about English terms. But what they have on their sheet is in French. I wondered if the note sheet shouldn't have been bilingual from the start.

Another parameter of the unit that the teachers discussed refers to the order of the tasks. In this regard, Clara points out that she felt it was beneficial for the students first to write a recommendation in French, the language most of them know best:

> [T]wo days prior, they had exactly the same thing but in French. They knew exactly what to expect, they had examples, they did one on their own too. Knowing that, they knew exactly what to expect. [...] We wanted to do

French first, precisely to help with English, because we know that English is a little more difficult for most people.

Éliane, for her part, adds nuance to Clara's statements. In her opinion, it would have been helpful to give the students more time to write texts in French and English. This would have allowed for a more solid construction of knowledge on the genre being studied and for more feedback from the teachers. The transfer of knowledge from one language to another, she argues, would, therefore, have been made much easier for the students:

> I think we did it too close in time – in the sense that, in my mind, it was more complementary. You see, they practice a little in French, and then after that, we go back to working in English so that they continue to improve. But to do it two days apart, there was no progress between the two. We didn't provide any feedback on the French text either before.

If we now turn to what the teachers had to say about the students' experience during the unit, we immediately note a shared enthusiasm. Clara, like her colleague, sees notable progress in English, which she attributes to the integration of languages. In particular, she mentions that the integration of French and English has supported the learning of metalinguistic terms that are related to the genre of recommending a narrative work in English:

> They learned to write recommendation texts in English, something I don't know if they would have eventually done in the English program until grade 11. It's possible, but who knows? To make the connection in terms of vocabulary as well, in both French and English, it allowed them to learn a bit more about it.

Éliane, like Clara, recognizes the importance of language integration for learning ESL. That said, she would have appreciated if the learning in English had also been transferred to French, which she did not observe:

> I get the impression that what we did was perhaps more beneficial for English than for French, because we had already worked a lot in French. So the transfer was made to

English, but not necessarily the other way around, especially since we started with French too.

Finally, the teachers noted that students became more motivated as the unit progressed. For Clara, "[t]he act of teaching something bilingually" helped to "get many students' attention." Éliane added that this integration made them understand that the languages do not have to be separate, but rather that they can be complementary: "[...] they found it interesting to see that it could be both, that it was the same thing in the end for both of them. It opened up something for them."

The last of the categories derived from our analyses, that of the participants' experience with bilingual co-teaching, first allowed us to note that it is essential for co-teachers to get along. However, Éliane pointed out that, in the particular context of bilingual co-teaching, it is also necessary to examine the linguistic dynamics that occur within the classroom. For example, even when the class in question was taught mainly in English, Éliane allowed herself to intervene in French, while Clara did the same with English if the class was aimed at writing a text in French. In the end, however, Éliane recalls that what was most important in the implementation of the unit was that they got along "perfectly well" and knew their respective roles.

Notwithstanding the enthusiasm that both teachers generally expressed during the interviews for bilingual co-teaching, Clara admitted to us that she was insecure about her knowledge of French. As a result, she felt that, at times, she was unfamiliar with specific terms related to the French recommendation genre and had to familiarize herself with concepts that were more familiar to her in English. As she notes in this excerpt, one way she worked around these difficulties was to do additional research outside of her normal work time:

> It was just so that I could feel more comfortable with what we're doing. Not knowing things—it frustrates me. [...] Anything I don't know, I want to go look it up on the Internet or wherever, dig through books to understand what I'm talking about, because I wouldn't be able to teach something I'm not comfortable with. Terms—when I don't

know what they mean—it irritates me. I don't really see it as extra workload. Of course, in a way, it took some time, but it was more for me, because I didn't feel comfortable standing in front of a bunch of students not knowing what I'm talking about.

Conclusion

Although integrated language teaching is based on relevant theoretical foundations[310] and undoubtedly meets the social expectations of bilingualism that students must increasingly satisfy, its implementation remains minimally studied by researchers. However, based on the testing of a unit that integrates narrative work recommendations in French and English at the Quebec elementary level, we were able to identify some of the issues that arose during its implementation. Based on the statements made by the co-teachers with whom we collaborated, we believe that writing genres offer an interesting entry point for students to make connections between school languages.[311] Indeed, it appears that the teachers were able to relatively easily pilot the discovery of common characteristics related to the recommendation by using, among other things, examples and counter-examples in both languages.

Nevertheless, future research will need to clarify how and under what conditions language transfer can be truly reciprocal. In our study, teachers primarily observed progress in students' second language, which raises the need for further investigation into potential gains in the language of instruction. The latter is all the more relevant in the context of the Intensive English program in Quebec, given that the time allocated to teaching academic subjects in French is reduced in favor of that devoted to ESL.

Furthermore, the co-teaching model appears to provide opportunities for integrated language teaching to occur efficiently.[312] As previous research notes, however, such co-teaching only works well if those involved have chemistry and can jointly navigate linguistic dynamics marked by the presence of multiple languages in

---

[310] See Ballinger *et al.*, 2020; De Pietro, 2020.
[311] See Gentil, 2011; Sommer-Farias, 2020.
[312] See Dillon & Gallagher, 2019; Fialais, 2019/2021.

the classroom. One might wonder what would happen if, for example, the teachers had different visions of their profession and of the importance of bilingualism or if, unlike the teachers in our study, one of the co-teachers did not know the language of their colleague. Thus, a promising research agenda is gradually taking shape for those who wish to study teacher collaboration and, more broadly, integrated language teaching.

4. Final considerations

4.1. Afterword. G(l)iding through the Inter-Lived Bilingual Experience: Beyond Guiding and Bridging as Afterword
Ofelia García

This book is simply monumental. It provides us with a vast array of experiences that open up spaces where we perceive divergent theoretical understandings and pedagogical practices in complex relationships with one another. Not only does the book's monumentality stem from the breadth of content and the diversity of theoretical and practical experiences, but its importance also lies in the ways the editors and authors have shaped the writing, allowing readers to experience different lived realities simultaneously. Although the editors initially conceived of writing a guide on bilingual education, this book takes readers on a journey through the many terrains, spaces, times, and voices that comprise divergent bilingual lived and educational experiences. The path is tortuous and never linear, unfolding into endless possibilities. Although the editors initially aimed to provide a bridge between theory and practice, the book ultimately constructs not a bridge but an inter-space and time, where we simultaneously experience a shifting terrain that adjusts to specific encounters with others and different educational policies.

Gliding through these inter-spaces of potentiality, readers are reminded of five of the major threads/dimensions of bilingual education:

- *Views of language*: Language in bilingual education refers not only to the social constructions taught in schools as "languages;" but also to the language practices of people (and students) to interact, that is, to their translanguaging. These language practices always extend beyond established linguistic boundaries because language is always intertwined with complex lived experiences.

- *Process of becoming bilingual*: Becoming bilingual is a bodily/semiotic/emotional experience and not simply a mental process.
- *Purposes of bilingual education*: For nation-state governments, the purpose of bilingual education is primarily the teaching of "named languages," especially a global language like English. However, the purpose of bilingual education cannot simply be the teaching of language but rather the education of students who are, or will become, bilingual. These two purposes are often in conflict with each other.
- *Policies in bilingual education*: In protecting "named languages," governmental bilingual education policies often establish rigid compartmentalization spaces for each language and promote bilingual education models based on monoglossic concepts of bilingualism and languages that are written and standardized. These policy models of bilingual education are not universal. In reality, bilingual education policies are protean, taking on a wide range of forms as they adapt to different sociopolitical contexts.
- *Pedagogical practices in bilingual education*: Bilingual education is not simply about teaching in two languages but about leveraging the students' translanguaging and transculturalities. To achieve this, collaboration among teachers, students, and across language and cultural practices, as well as knowledge systems, is necessary.

Before I discuss how these threads are derived from the content of this book, it is essential to note how the book's writing constructs an *inter-space of possibilities for a protean bilingual education*.

Weaving the threads

One of the innovative aspects of this book is that many of the praxis chapters are written as collaborative duets, forming a polyphonic melody where differences are highlighted. This is particularly evident in the first chapter, where teachers and researchers collaborate on the writing process. This chapter does not simply include an interview, as in the chapters by Groff and Jhingran on bilingual practice in rural India or the one by Budach and Dreher on a German-Italian primary school, although these are also significant. However, in the first chapter, the authors adopt a style of speaking, writing, reflecting, and emoting that demonstrates how collaboration ensues.

Many academic papers discuss joint studies between researchers and teachers yet are written by a senior researcher who then reports on the teachers' perspectives. The first chapter of the *Practice* part is distinct because it not only reports on the collaborative research process but also conveys the experience of researching and writing together. The voices of four researchers and three teachers are interwoven as they negotiate their positions and share their reflections and reactions to the issue of creating an English immersion space, similar to those in Utah, within a French-English bilingual program in France. The teachers all had experience teaching in French immersion programs in Utah and were charged with reproducing this in France. The writing mirrors the conflicted views of the teachers. It begins with theoretical reflections, followed by the teachers' reactions, which are commented upon by others, and concludes with a reflective pause. The teachers recognize what they call "the institutional heritage" of "the exclusive use of the target language for learning a second language" and how inappropriate it is for them to reproduce the immersion model of Utah to teach English in France. "Language is full of feeling," one of the teachers says. And the writing here is full of spaces to breathe, to reflect, to feel. Theoretical perspectives are not limited to the mind or head but encompass the bodily-emotional experiences that teachers hold toward their teaching in different contexts, producing a different bodily experience.

In this first chapter, we weave together the different threads of the principles of bilingual education. The chapter, featuring the researchers' and teachers' reflections and voices, represents the weaving together of different views on language, becoming bilingual, and the purpose, policies, and practices of bilingual education.

The threads in the weave

View of language

The chapters in this book present a range of diverse visions of language and those who engage with it in numerous ways. De Mejía and Cummins, for example, describe how named languages on the lips of influential speakers, such as English speakers with institutional power, are considered more complete and fuller than those spoken by immigrants, refugees, and those without power. Not all named languages are considered equal. Languages like English have been cloaked in prestige and are taught as if they infused English learners with privilege. This is evident, for example, in the efforts to teach intensive English in Quebec. However, Italian, in the German-Italian primary school in Frankfurt, as described by Budach and Dreher, is not as easily taught, as its implications for global economic success do not compete with English or German, for that matter.

In contrast to these powerful European languages, Pomeranian in Brazil, a language spoken in specific communities, is introduced in schools as a *lengua ponte* for intercomprehension for German and English, as well as supporting the acquisition of Portuguese as the school language. Efforts to teach through Wagdi in rural India have met with success, yet they have also encountered significant resistance. And yet, it is not the oral and non-standardized nature of language that decrees that a language is less valued than one that is written and standardized. For example, the chapter by Risse makes clear the critical role of Ladin in schools in Ladinia, a region in Northern Italy with a high degree of multilingualism, where Ladin, lacking a standardized written language, plays an essential role in the identity of its people.

Language practices of people always deviate from an actual or imagined standard, especially from the written language taught in most schools. And yet, divergence from an imagined standard is more tolerated depending on the degree of power that speakers have. This contrast between named languages and the language practices of people, including their translanguaging, and the ways this plays out in bilingual education is well captured in the chapter by Seltzer and Otheguy. The three teachers who comprise these case studies develop students' bilingualism and their proficiency in two named standardized languages, English and Spanish. However, they do so by leveraging the bilingual students' language practices, which are not simply about combining two languages but about enabling students to utilize their full, unitary repertoire of elements considered linguistic, as well as those deemed non-linguistic and multimodal, to engage with texts. This is also the case of Carolina, the Bolivian kindergarten teacher described in the chapter by Espinosa. The chapter provides a panoramic view of Carolina's lived experiences as a student in Bolivia, an immigrant to the United States, and a kindergarten teacher. Based on Carolina's immersion in Descriptive Review Processes, the teacher comes to understand biliteracy as a "complicated, interesting, and active" process "in making meaning of the world and their own [the children's] lives." This understanding of bilingualism and biliteracy as more than a simple addition of two named languages frees speakers from traditional understandings of language and literacy that have constrained a vision of human possibility. As Busch declares, "Network practices beyond traditional affiliations are emerging." In creating these shifting disconnected networks, space has become possible for new emergences and understandings.

The bodily/semiotic/emotional experience of becoming bilingual

This thread is especially pulled into the weave by Brigitta Busch's chapter. Based on Merleau-Ponty's phenomenology, Busch reminds us that "language is first and foremost a way of relating, a projection toward the other." This tight link between emotion and language acquisition is especially evident in the chapters in the Praxis section. The success of all the projects and programs described, whether in the Americas, Asia, Africa, or Europe, rests on how students can integrate the new language being taught into their repertoire of experiences and practices. All bilingual and/or biliterate development rests on how the bodily-affective dimension remains present and available in all speech. Developing a repertoire, as Busch points out, rests on both bodily-emotional experience and taking into account the historical and political dimensions of language.

Purposes of bilingual education

Many of these chapters focus on how nation-states organize bilingual education programs in ways that align with their purposes rather than those of the students. This contrast between what nation-states and government institutions want from bilingual education versus what language-minoritized communities or others wish is evident in many of the chapters. For example, Thibeault and Forget describe the co-teaching of writing genres in an Intensive English program in Quebec. However, these teacher-led efforts respond to the need for negotiating space within a language policy that protects French and is cautious about any language integration between English and French. Integrating the teaching of curricular content related to French and English was viewed with suspicion, and it required considerable effort and support for Eliane and Claire to work together in this way. The reasons for this enormous effort on the part of researchers and teachers to counteract the effect of a monoglossic ideology of bilingualism rest on the Quebecois' purpose for bilingual education. While bilingual education in Quebec is seen as protecting French while promoting English, the community of parents and students involved in these efforts aims to foster bilingualism. Students were able to see, as the teachers report, "that it's the same thing at the same time." This simultaneity is how bilinguals experience their bilingualism, not as the nation-state would want, with separation and barriers that are counterproductive to the development of bilingualism.

Another nation-state's purpose for developing bilingual education programs is to teach the languages of neighboring states. This is the primary purpose of the bilingual German-Italian primary school described by Budach and Dreher. However, this school's extension of bilingual instruction to include English is also evidence of the power of English, the primary language of bilingual instruction worldwide.

In contrast to nation-states, bilingual communities initiating their bilingual education programs do so, recognizing their translanguaging and transculturality. For example, Rosenberg, Savedra, and Streb describe how the Pomeranian-Portuguese community in Brazil is moved "by the idea of transculturalization, and not a renaissance of the autonomy of the minority, which would be illusory in Brazil's modern and mobile society." In contrast, Risse describes the use of Ladin in schools in Ladinia as a way to preserve their own minoritized language, which is essential to their identity. Although not considered in this volume, there are Indigenous communities worldwide that have achieved sufficient institutional power to incorporate an agenda of self-determination into their bilingual education programs.

Regardless of the numerous purposes for developing bilingual education programs, it is clear that the national purposes for bilingual education, as institutionalized by governments, have little to do with the purposes of communities of speakers who have the institutional power to organize themselves to educate their children.

Policies in bilingual education

It is this conflict between the purposes of nation-states in supporting bilingual education programs and those of communities of learners that create absurd policy situations, as described by Groff and Jhingran in rural India. Although India has, on paper, an extensive multilingual education policy, languages other than Hindi and the official regional languages are not used in education, thereby excluding millions of Indian speakers, especially those from tribal regions. An analogous situation is evident in the description of Senegal's language education policy, as described by Iwasaki and Benson. Although Senegalese people are highly multilingual, with 14 languages recognized as national languages, education is currently only offered in French.

In Senegal, the experimental so-called "simultaneous" bilingual education program utilizes the two most widely spoken languages in the country—Wolof and Pulaar. Despite the excellent performance of students in the bilingual program in all types of assessments and more active student engagement, the program remains experimental. Only through the actions of those described as bilingual education "militants" are such programs even recognized.

In rural India, with funding from UNICEF, Language and Learning Foundation established instruction in Wagdi, an oral language in the Rajasthan tribal region, in non-formal schools called mabadi centers. Jhingran explains that they chose these non-formal schools because "it was not easy to begin with the mainstream government system." Jhingran continues saying: "But we worked small because we knew that getting permissions would be easier if we started small, so that's how we bypassed big approvals." The government was seen in this case as "a challenge in itself." The project, according to Jhingran, was "imperfect" in that it needed to balance the needs of both the government and the community to ensure the children's development of Hindi. Thus, Wagdi was used orally for higher-order comprehension, "together" with Hindi. And yet, it is Hindi that is the ultimate object of instruction since it is the language of the official exam.

This tendency to measure students' bilingual development by isolating the language of power is the focus of Ossa-Parra's chapter on equitable assessment practices. Although it is possible to design multilingual assessments that provide a holistic, multilingual perspective of the student, this is not often the case. For programs such as the one described by Groff and Jhingran in rural India or the one by Iwasaki and Benson in Senegal to gain national approval, it would be necessary to delink the design of assessments from the nationalistic purposes of nation-states for developing bilingual education programs.

Pedagogical practices in bilingual education

The pedagogical practices in all the diverse bilingual education programs described in this volume share a commonality. Government policy and the national ideology behind these programs promote the acquisition of two distinct and separate languages by students who are said to maintain a single identity and a particular appreciation for the other. Yet, all the pedagogical practices described here respond to the translanguaging and transculturality of students. It is the leveraging of emergent bilingual students' translanguaging (even when not recognized by this term) and the awareness and pull of students' transculturality that weaves the pedagogical practices into a meaningful network of sense-making.

Jürgen Erfurt's chapter centers on transculturality, which, in combination with the concept of translanguaging so well described in Seltzer and Otheguy's chapter, provides a glimpse of the pedagogical innovations in this book. Acknowledging the past in the present and future, the book puts together earlier traditional theories of bilingualism, such as those described by Jim Cummins, with these more innovative concepts. The readers perceive the traces of past theories and practices in the present. Many do not name either translanguaging or transculturality. Instead, they transition from traditional pedagogical approaches, as Jim Cummins calls them, to more collaborative practices, including co-teaching and developing simultaneous bilingualism and biliteracy. Many of the Praxis chapters do not name either translanguaging or transculturality. However, in practice, the described approaches are moving toward these understandings, although part of not naming them is due to the need to negotiate legitimacy with government educational systems. For example, when Cynthia Groff questions Jhingran about whether translanguaging is used in the programs in rural India, Jhingran replies: "We found that some teachers do it. I would say most teachers do it." But it is not named.

Government policies on bilingual education still raise questions about the concepts of transculturality and translanguaging. Erfurt explains that transculturality differs from multiculturalism because it indexes *entanglements*, which do not always lead to harmony. Transculturality constructs a weave that also acknowledges gaps and spaces for conflicts, inequalities, and differences. And yet, upon perceiving this "imperfect" weave, like the simultaneous bilingual program in Senegal, transformations are also possible. Transculturality differs from interculturalism, which, as Erfurt notes, "propagates the image of mutual exchange, interaction, and dialogue aimed at respecting shared values." Transculturality focuses on the entanglements that often also produce conflicts and insecurity as it zooms into inequalities and differences. However, as the chapters in this book demonstrate, it is in this inter-lived, entangled bilingual space that social transformations are possible. These transformations are based on the concept of "emergence" described by Chilean biologist Francisco Varela (1995), who argues that for new visions and realities to emerge, we must focus on the "loopiness of the thing." Bilingual education is not simply a set of disentangled threads that can be easily identified, described, and copied. Bilingual education programs must be constructed by weaving the "imperfect" interactions, wishes, emotions, bodily experiences, and power dimensions of different people, institutions, and governments.

Afterwording and Making Space

This book makes space. It makes space for the past, the present, and the future. It accommodates both theory and practice. It makes space for teachers and students from the Global South, the Global North, and those in between. It creates space for differences and entanglements, for love and conflict—a space to breathe beyond the language education policies imposed by schools while not losing sight of them; a space to view language as human interaction, whether it is one of love or conflict. It creates space for "imperfections" by questioning whether established models of bilingual education are effective, for whom, and why. It facilitates negotiations and accommodates diverse realities.

In this Afterword, I have attempted to highlight how this space has been constructed—by writing with, from within, without losing sight of society's external realities; by including different actors, some powerless, others not. By opening up this inter-lived space of potentiality, we, as readers, are drawn into a bodily-emotional experience that brings life to language and bilingual experiences, giving students and teachers the agency needed to engage holistically with this monumental manuscript.

4.2. Acknowledgments
Valérie Fialais and Reseda Streb

We begin our acknowledgments with a heartfelt expression of gratitude to everyone who contributed to this book. It was a significant individual effort for us to edit this volume alongside our full-time non-academic employment. Over the course of three years, we invested not only a sizable portion of our free time but also personal financial resources in creating this guide. Due to these time constraints, the publication was completed later than planned. We want to extend our sincere thanks for the trust and patience placed in us and for this successful endeavor.

We extend our gratitude to Fabrice Jaumont, President of the Center for the Advancement of Languages, Education, and Communities (CALEC), for his trust in our book proposal, his support throughout the overall planning process, and his patience with our queries regarding the publication process.

For their support in conceptualizing the guide and for their contact recommendations, we are especially grateful to Carol Benson, Gabriele Budach, Rita Franceschini, Ofelia García, Christine Hélot, Juan Jimenez-Salcedo, and Patrícia Velasco. Through constructive discussions with them, we refined the content direction. Their generous support in connecting us with authors from their networks was also a prerequisite for the realization of this book.

A special thank you goes to Christine Hélot and Ofelia García, who have long accompanied us as academic mentors and whose contributions open and close this volume.

We want to express our sincere gratitude to the authors for their impressive contributions. As editors, it is a privilege to work with such renowned and resolute researchers who have embraced our vision of bridging theory and practice. Your theoretical concepts are groundbreaking in our field, and the presented educational projects serve as models for our target audience. The final product is a testament to the productive and necessary collaboration between the academic and school worlds. We are confident that readers will greatly benefit from your expertise. We also appreciate your patience and professionalism throughout the editorial process.

Thank you to: Carol Benson, Gabriele Budach, Brigitta Busch, Damien Céné, Anne Choffat-Dürr, Jim Cummins, Ulrike Dreher, Jürgen Erfurt, Cecilia M. Espinosa, Valérie Fialais, Marie-Hélène Forget, Ofelia García, Cynthia Groff, Christine Hélot, Aurore Isambert, Erina Iwasaki, Delphine Jeandel, Dhir Jhingran, Véronique Lemoine-Bresson, Latisha Mary, Anne-Marie de Mejía, Marcela Ossa Parra, Ricardo Otheguy, Stephanie Risse, Peter Rosenberg, Mônica Savedra, Kate Seltzer, Reseda Streb, and Joël Thibeault.

We also extend our thanks to those involved in the peer review process. Their professional examination and feedback undoubtedly contribute to the quality of this volume: Ingrid M. Rodrick Beiler, Carla España, Dominique Huck, Georg Kremnitz, Carole Le Hénaff, Marie Leroy, Ulrich Mehlem, and Anna-Christine Weirich.

A special thanks goes to the translators who translated the texts written in German and French into English. We are incredibly pleased that they identified with the content and spared no time or effort: Kaitlin Balthasar, Aimée Ducey-Gessner, and Megan Evans. Many thanks also to the authors who translated their texts.

Finally, our gratitude extends to Hélène Bréant and her colleague Hélène, who are already in the process of translating the contributions written in German and English into French.

5. References

AGNIHOTRI, R. K. (1995). Multilingualism as a classroom resource. In K. Heugh, A. Sieruhn, & P. Pluddemann (Eds.), *Multilingual education for South Africa*. Johannesburg: Heinemann, 3-7.

AGNIHOTRI, R. K. (2007). Towards a pedagogical paradigm rooted in multilinguality. *International Multilingual Research Journal*, *1*(2), 79-88.

ALLMAIER, M. (2022). Soll der deutsche Johannes einfach aufhören, Tacos zu machen? *Die Zeit, Nr. 21, 19. Mai 2022*, 59-60.

ALSACE, T. & ST. JEAN, M. (2021). Combatting Colorism in Bilingual and ENL Education: A Battle Whose Time Has Come. *NYSABE Bilingual Times*, 19-21.

AMERICAN COUNCILS RESEARCH CENTER (2021). 2021 Canvass of dual language and immersion (DLI) programs in us public schools.

ANDROUTSOPOULOS, J. (2018). Gesellschaftliche Mehrsprachigkeit. In E. Neuland & P. Schlobinski (Eds.), *Handbuch Sprache in sozialen Gruppen*. Berlin/Boston: De Gruyter, 193-217.

ARED (2017, Nov 30). *Support project for quality education in mother tongues for primary schools in Senegal: Annual Report Jan 1, 2017 - Nov 30, 2017*. Dakar, Senegal: Associates in Research and Education for Development.

ARED (2014). *Dubai Cares pro-forma proposal outline: Support project for quality education in mother tongues for primary schools in Senegal (Phase III: 2013-2018)*. Dakar, Senegal: ARED.

ASCENZI-MORENO, L., ESPINOSA, C., & LEHNER-QUAM, A. (2022). Move, play, language: A translanguaged multimodal approach to literacies with young emergent bilinguals. In S. Brown & S. Hao (Eds.), *Multimodal Literacies in Young Emergent Bilinguals: Speaking Back to Print-Centric Practices*. Multilingual Matters.

ASCENZI-MORENO, L., & SELTZER, K. (2021). Always at the Bottom: Ideologies in Assessment of Emergent Bilinguals. *Journal of Literacy Research*, *53*(4), 468-490.

ASCENZI-MORENO, L. (2018). Translanguaging and responsive assessment adaptations: Emergent bilingual readers through the lens of possibility. *Language Arts*, *95*(6), 355-369.

AUSTIN, V. L. (2001). Teachers' beliefs about co-teaching. *Remedial and Special Education*, *22*(4), 245-255.

BAKER, C. (2011). *Foundations of Bilingual Education and Bilingualism* (5th Edition). Bristol: Multilingual Matters.

BAKHTIN, M. (1938/2008). *Chronotopos*. Frankfurt/Main: Suhrkamp.

BAKHTIN, M. (1981). Forms of Time and of the Chronotope in the Novel. In M. Bakhtin, *The dialogic imagination* (Ed. by M. Holquist). Austin: University of Texas Press, 84-258.

BAKHTIN, M. (1935/1981). Discourse in the Novel (C. Emerson & M. Holquist, Trans). In M. Bakhtin, *The dialogic imagination.* (ed. by M. Holquist) Austin: University of Texas Press, 259-422.

BAKHTIN, M. (1935/1979). Das Wort im Roman. In R. Grübel (Ed.), *Ästhetik des Wortes*. Frankfurt/Main: Suhrkamp, 154-300.

BALL, S. J., MAGUIRE, M. & BRAUN, A. (2012). *How Schools do Policy - Policy Enactments in Secondary School*. London: Routledge.

BALLINGER, S., LAU, S. M. C. & QUEVILLON LACASSE, C. (2020). Pédagogie interlinguistique : exploiter les transferts en classe. *Revue canadienne des langues vivantes*, *76*(4), 278-292.

BALSIGER, C., BÉTRIX KÖHLER, D. & PANCHOUT-DUBOIS, M. (2012). Le détour par d'autres langues : démarche réflexive utile pour améliorer les capacités métalinguistiques des élèves dans la langue de scolarisation ? In C. Balsiger, D. Bétrix Köhler, J.-F. de Pietro & C. Perregaux (Eds.), *Éveil aux langues et approches plurielles. De la formation des enseignants aux pratiques de classe.* L'Harmattan : 193-228.

BARTH, B.-M. (2013). *Élève chercheur, enseignant médiateur Donner du sens aux savoirs*. Chenelière Éducation.

BAUER, E. B., COLOMER, S. E., & WIEMELT, J. (2020). Biliteracy of African American and Latinx Kindergarten Students in a Dual-Language Program: Understanding Students'

Translanguaging Practices Across Informal Assessments. *Urban Education*, 55(3), 331-361.

BECK, U. (2002). The Cosmopolitan Society and its Enemies. *Theory, Culture & Society,* 19(1–2), 17-44.

BENSON, C. (2020/2022). An innovative 'simultaneous' bilingual approach in Senegal: Promoting interlinguistic transfer while contributing to policy change. *International Journal of Bilingual Education and Bilingualism*, 25(4), 1399-1416.

BERGER, P. A. (2010). Alte und neue Wege der Individualisierung. In P. A. Berger & R. Hitzler (Eds.), *Individualisierungen. Ein Vierteljahrhundert "jenseits von Stand und Klasse"?* Wiesbaden: VS Verlag, 11-25.

BIALYSTOCK, E. (2001). *Bilingualism in Development: Language, Literacy and Cognition*. Cambridge: Cambridge University Press.

BLANK, G. S. D. (2023). *Leitura em língua minoritária: um estudo sobre duas ortografias do pomerano*. Programa de Pós-Graduação em Letras – Mestrado. Pelotas: Universidade Federal de Pelotas.

BLOMMAERT, J. & BACKUS, A. (2013). Superdiverse Repertoires and the Individual. In I. d. Saint-Georges & J.-J. Weber (Eds.), *Multilingualism and Multimodality. Current challenges for Educational Studies*. Rotterdam: Sense, 11-32.

BLOMMAERT, J. & RAMPTON, B. (2011). Language and Superdiversities. *Diversities*, 13(2), 1-20.

BOAGLIO, G. (2018). Die Unterrichtssprache Deutsch in den italophonen Gebieten des Habsburgerreiches. In H. Glück (Ed.): *Die Sprache des Nachbarn. Die Fremdsprache Deutsch bei Italienern und Ladinern vom Mittelalter bis 1918*. Bamberg: University Press, 183-220.

BOLAND, D. E., ALKHALIFA, K. B. & AL-MUTAIRI, M. A. (2019). Co-Teaching in EFL Classroom: The Promising Model. *English Language Teaching*, 12(12), 95-98.

BRICEÑO, A. (2021). Influence of Sequential and Simultaneous Bilingualism on Second Grade Dual Language Students' Use of Syntax in Reading. *Reading Psychology*, 42(2), 150-176. https://doi.org/10.1080/02702711.2021.1888345

BUDACH, G., ERFURT, J. & KUNKEL, M. (Eds.) (2008). *Écoles plurilingues - multilingual schools: Konzepte, Institutionen und Akteure. Internationale Perspektiven.* Frankfurt am Main: Peter Lang.

BUDACH, G., FIALAIS, V., IBARRONDO, L., et al. (2019). *Grenzgänge en zones de contact.* Paris : L'Harmattan.

BUSCH, B. (2021a). *Mehrsprachigkeit. 3. vollständig überarbeitete Auflage.* Wien: utb facultas.

BUSCH, B. (2021b). The Body Image: Taking an Evaluative Stance towards Semiotic Resources. *International Journal of Multilingualism, 18*(2), 190-205.

BUTLER, J. (1997). *The Psychic Life of Power. Theories in Subjection.* Stanford: Stanford University Press.

BUTVILOFSKY, S. A., ESCAMILLA, K., GUMINA, D., & SILVA DIAZ, E. (2021). Beyond Monolingual Reading Assessments for Emerging Bilingual Learners: Expanding the Understanding of Biliteracy Assessment Through Writing. *Reading Research Quarterly, 56*(1), 53-70.

CANDELIER, M. (2016). Activités métalinguistiques pour une didactique intégrée des langues. *Le français aujourd'hui, 192*, 107-116.

CANDELIER, M., CAMILLERI-GRIMA, A., CASTELLOTTI, V., DE PIETRO, J.-F., LŐRINCZ, I., MEIßNER, F.-J., NOGUEROL, A. & SCHRÖDER-SURA, A. (2012). *Le CARAP – Un cadre de référence pour les approches plurielles des langues et cultures.* Éditions du Conseil de l'Europe.

CARINI, P. & HIMLEY, M. with CHRISTINE, C.; ESPINOSA, C., & FOURNIER, J. (2010). *Jenny's Story: Taking the Long View of the Child: Prospect's Philosophy in Action.* New York, NY: Teachers College Press.

CARINI, P. (2001). *Starting Strong: A Different Look at Children, School, and Standards.* New York, NY: Teachers College Press.

CARINI, P. (1986). Building from Children's Strengths. *The Journal of Education, 168*(3), 13-24.

CARINI, P. (1977). Building a Curriculum for Young Children from an Experiential Base. *Young Children*, *32*(3) 14-18.

CAVALLI, M. (2008). Didactiques intégrées et approches plurielles. *Babylonia*, *1*, 15-19.

CENOZ, J., & GORTER, D. (2011). A Holistic Approach to Multilingual Education: Introduction. *The Modern Language Journal*, *95*(3), 339-343.

CHALHOUB-DEVILLE, M. B. (2019). Multilingual Testing Constructs: Theoretical Foundations. *Language Assessment Quarterly*, *16*(4-5), 472-480.

CHARTRAND, S.-G., ÉMERY-BRUNEAU, J. & SÉNÉCHAL, K. (2015). *Caractéristiques de 50 genres pour développer les compétences langagières en français au secondaire québécois*. Didactica.

CLEMENTI, S. & WOELK, J. (Eds.) (2003). *1992: Ende eines Streits. Zehn Jahre Streitbeilegung im Südtirolkonflikt zwischen Italien und Österreich*. Baden-Baden: Nomos.

COMITÊ Y SORVIC PROVINZIAL POR L'EVALUAZIUN DLES SCORES LADINES / ZËNTER DE CUMPETËNZA LINGAC DL'UNIVERSITÀ LIEDIA DE BULSAN (Ed.) (2013). Ergebnisse der Englisch-Sprachkompetenztests. Bozen.

COMITÊ Y SORVIC PROVINZIAL POR L'EVALUAZIUN DLES SCORES LADINES / ZËNTER DE CUMPETËNZA LINGAC DL'UNIVERSITÀ LIEDIA DE BULSAN (Ed.) (2010). Ergebnisse der Sprachkompetenz-Studie, 3. Mittelschulklassen. Bozen.

COMITÊ Y SORVIC PROVINZIAL POR L'EVALUAZIUN DLES SCORES LADINES / ZËNTER DE CUMPETËNZA LINGAC DL'UNIVERSITÀ LIEDIA DE BULSAN (Ed.) (2010). Ergebnisse der Sprachkompetenz-Studie, 5. Oberschulklassen. Bozen.

COMITÊ Y SORVIC PROVINZIAL POR L'EVALUAZIUN DLES SCORES LADINES / ZËNTER DE CUMPETËNZA LINGAC DL'UNIVERSITÀ LIEDIA DE BULSAN (Ed.) (2009). Ergebnisse der Untersuchung der Sprachkompetenzen, 5. Grundschulklassen. Bozen.

COOK, V. (1999). Going beyond the native speaker in language teaching. *TESOL Quarterly, 33*, 185-209.

COSTE, D., MOORE, D. & ZARATE, G. (1997/2009). *Compétence plurilingue et pluriculturelle. Version révisée et enrichie d'un avant-propos et d'une bibliographie complémentaire.* Strasbourg: Conseil de l'Europe. Division des Politiques linguistiques.

CUMMINS, J. (2021). *Rethinking the education of multilingual learners: A critical analysis of theoretical concepts.* Bristol, UK: Multilingual Matters.

CUMMINS, J. (2017). Teaching minoritized students: Are additive approaches legitimate? *Harvard Educational Review, 87*(3), 404-425.

CUMMINS, J., & EARLY, M. (Eds.) (2011). *Identity texts: The collaborative creation of power in multilingual schools.* Stoke-on-Trent, UK: Trentham Books.

CUMMINS, J. (2009). Fundamental Psycholinguistic and Sociological Principles Underlying Educational Success for Linguistic Minority Students. In T. Skutnabb-Kangas, R. Phillipson, A. K. Mohanty, & M. Panda (Eds.), *Social Justice Through Multilingual Education.* Clevedon: Channel View Publications, 19-35.

CUMMINS J. (2008). Teaching for transfer: Challenging the two solitudes assumption in bilingual education. In N. H. Hornberger (Ed.) *Encyclopedia of Language and Education.* Boston, MA.: Springer.

CUMMINS, J. (1979). Cognitive/academic language proficiency, linguistic interdependence, the optimum age question, and some other matters. *Working Papers on Bilingualism, 19*, 121-129.

DALBERG (2014). *Résumé du rapport d'évaluation d'impact du modèle ARED.* Dakar: Dalberg.

DARCHY-KOECHLIN, B. (2022). Un point de vue institutionnel sur le réseau des LéA. In R. Monod-Ansaldi, C. Loisy & B. Gruson (Eds.), *Le réseau des lieux d'éducation associés à l'institut français d'éducation.* PUR, 329-342.

DAVIES, A. (2003). *The native speaker: myth and reality*. Multilingual Matters.

DE HOUWER, A. (2018). Language Choice in Bilingual Interaction. In A. De Houwer & L. Ortega (Eds.) *The Cambridge Handbook of Bilingualism*. Cambridge: Cambridge University Press, 324-348.

DE MEJIA, A.M. (2005). Bilingual education in Colombia: Towards an integrated perspective. In A. M. de Mejia (Ed.) *Bilingual Education in South America*. Clevedon: Multilingual Matters, 48-64.

DE PIETRO, J.-F. (2020). De la didactique intégrée aux approches interlinguistiques : Comment l'école de la Suisse francophone conçoit-elle le plurilinguisme ? In B. Schädlich (Ed.), *Perspektiven auf Mehrsprachigkeit im Fremdsprachenunterricht – Regards croisés sur le plurilinguisme et l'apprentissage des langues*. Stuttgart: J. B. Metzler, 23-52.

DEMMERLING, C. & LANDWEER, H. (2007). *Philosophie der Gefühle. Von Achtung bis Zorn*. Stuttgart: J. B. Metzler.

DEMORGON, J. (2014). Managers et interprètes : fondements anthropologiques de leurs coopérations. *Bulletin du CRATIL, 12*.

DEMORGON, J. (2008). Critique de l'interculturel : code, adaptation, histoire. In D. Röseberg & H. Thoma (Eds.), *Interkulturalität und wissenschaftliche Kanonbildung. Frankreich als Forschungsgegenstand einer interkulturellen Kulturwissenschaft*. Berlin: Logos Verlag, 557-575.

DERVIN, F. (2016). *Interculturality in Education*. Palgrave, MacMillan.

DESGAGNE, S., BEDNARZ, N., LEBUIS, P., POIRIER, L., & COUTURE, C. (2001). L'approche collaborative de recherche en éducation : un rapport nouveau à établir entre recherche et formation. *Revue des sciences de l'éducation, 27*(1), 33-64.

DEVY, G.N. (2014). *The Being of Bhasha: A General Introduction. (The People's Linguistic Survey of India, Volume 1)*. Orient BlackSwan.

DEZUTTER, O., LAMOUREUX, K., THOMAS, L., LAU, S. M. C. & SABATIER, C. (2017). Le rapport à l'écriture d'élèves de sixième année du primaire suivant un apprentissage intensif d'une langue seconde. *Nouveaux c@hiers de la recherche en éducation, 20*(2), 4-22.

DIAGNE, M. (2017). Gouvernance linguistique et émergence socio-économique au Sénégal. Sciences & Techniques du Langage. *Revue du Centre de Linguistique Appliquée de Dakar, 12*, 93-109.

DIAS-CHIARUTTINI, A., COHEN-AZRIA, C. & SOUPLET, C. (2021). *Chercher ensemble.* Presses universitaires de Bordeaux.

DILLON, A. M. & GALLAGHER, K. (2019). The Experience of Co-Teaching for Emergent Arabic-English Literacy. *The Qualitative Report, 24*(7), 1556-1576.

DIOUF, P. B. (2019). Innovations pédagogiques pour l'intégration des langues nationales africaines dans l'éducation : Quel état des lieux au Sénégal. *Anadiss, 1*(27), 137-161.

DOLZ, J. & GAGNON, R. (2008). Le genre du texte, un outil didactique pour développer le langage oral et écrit. *Pratiques, 137-138*, 179-198.

DPLN (2002). Etat des lieux de la recherche en/sur les langues nationales (synthèse). Dakar: Direction de la Promotion des Langues Nationales/Ministère de l'Enseignement Technique, de la Formation Professionelle, de l'Alphabétisation et des Langues Nationales.

DUKE, N. (2000). For the rich it's richer: Print experiences and environments offered to children in very low and very high-socioeconomic status first-grade classrooms. *American Educational Research Journal, 37*(2), 441-478.

EBERHARD, D. M., SIMONS, G. F. & FENNIG, C. D. (Eds.) (2022). *Ethnologue: Languages of the World.* 25th edition. Dallas, Texas: SIL International.

EHLICH, K., BREDEL, U. & REICH, H.-H. (2008). Sprachaneignung – Prozesse und Modelle. In *Referenzrahmen zur altersspezifischen Sprachaneignung, 29*(I). Bonn/Berlin, 9-34.

EDESLKY, C. (1986). *Writing in a bilingual program: Habia una vez.* Praeger.

EDELSKY, C. (1982). Writing in a bilingual program: The Relation of L1 and L2. *TESOL Quarterly*, *16*(2), 211-228.

ERFURT, J. (2021). *Transkulturalität - Prozesse und Perspektiven*. Tübingen: Narr Francke Attempto/utb.

ERFURT, J., & De Knop, S. (2019). Über Konstruktionsgrammatik, sprachliches Lernen und Mehrsprachigkeit. In J. Erfurt & S. De Knop (Eds.). *Konstruktionsgrammatik und Mehrsprachigkeit*. Duisburg: Universitätsverlag Rhein-Ruhr, 7-25.

ERFURT, J. & GESSINGER, J. (2022). Sprachbewegungen – oder was bedeutet es, Sprachgeschichte transkulturell zu modellieren? *OBST. Osnabrücker Beiträge zur Sprachtheorie, 100, online*, 85-132.

ERFURT, J., HÉLOT, C., LEROY, M. & STIERWALD, M. (2022). De la francophonie à la transculturalité en passant par le plurilinguisme : ouverture d'une discussion. In J. Erfurt, M. Leroy, & M. Stierwald (Eds.). *Mehrsprachigkeit und Transkulturalität in frankophonen Räumen: Modelle, Prozesse und Praktiken / Plurilinguisme et transculturalité dans les espaces francophones : des modèles théoriques à la négociation des pratiques*. Tübingen: Narr Francke Attempto, 11-33.

ERFURT, J., LEICHSERING, T. & STREB, R. (Eds.) (2013). *Mehrsprachigkeit und Mehrschriftigkeit: Sprachliches Handeln in der Schule*. Duisburg: Universitätsverlag Rhein-Ruhr.

ERFURT, J., WEIRICH, A.-C. & CAPORAL-EBERSOLD, E. (Eds.) (2018). *Éducation plurilingue et pratiques langagières. Hommage à Christine Hélot*. Berlin: Peter Lang.

ESCOBAR, A. M. (2013). Bilingualism in Latin America. In K.T. Bathia & W.C. Ritchie (Eds.). *The Handbook of Bilingualism and Multilingualism*. 2nd ed. Oxford: Wiley-Blackwell: 725-744.

ESPINOSA, C. & ASCENZI-MORENO, L. (2021). *Rooted in Strength: Using Translanguaging to Grow Multilingual Readers and Writers*. New York: Scholastic.

ESPINOSA, C., ASCENZI-MORENO, L., KLEYN, T. & SÁNCHEZ, M. (2020). Transforming Urban Teacher Education: The City University of New York. In City University of New York-New York State Initiative on Emergent Bilinguals

(Ed). *Translanguaging and Transformative Teaching for Emergent Bilingual Students: Lessons from the CUNY-NYSIEB Project*. Routledge, 257-260.

ESPINOSA C., MOORE, K., & SERNA, I. (1998). Learning environments supportive of young Latinos. In M. L. Gonzales, J. Villamil Tinajero & A. H. Macías (Eds.). *Educating Latino Students: A Guide to Successful Practice*. Lancaster, PA: Technomac Publishing Company, 107-138.

FALTIS, C. & HUDELSON, S. (1997). *Bilingual Education in elementary and secondary communities: Toward understanding and caring*. New York: Pearson.

FERGUSON, C. (1959). Diglossia. In *Word* 15: 325-340.

FERREIRO, E. & TEBEROSKY, A. (1982). *Literacy before schooling*. Heinemann.

FIALAIS, V. (2019/2021). *Le modèle d'immersion réciproque en question : enseigner en classe bilingue à New York et à Francfort / Das Two-Way-Immersion Modell im Fokus: Zweisprachig unterrichten in New York und Frankfurt/Main*. Frankfurt/Main.

FISHMAN, J. (1972). *The Sociology of Language: An Interdisciplinary Social Science Approach to Language in Society*. Rowley, Mass.: Newbury House.

FLORES, N. (2020). From academic language to language architecture: Challenging raciolinguistic ideologies in research and practice. *Theory Into Practice, 59*(1), 22-31.

FLORES, N. & ROSA, J. (2015). Undoing appropriateness: Raciolinguistic ideologies and language diversity in education. *Harvard Educational Review. 85*(2), 149-171.

FOERSTE, E.; SCHÜTZ-FOERSTE, G. M. & MERLER, A. (2015). Educação do campo: uma contribuição para a pedagogia social. In E. Foerste, L.Q. Carvalho & P.S. Chisté (Eds.). *A pedagogia social em diálogo: educação profissional, linguagens e saberes do campo*. São Carlos: Pedro e João, 27-44.

FORGET, M.-H. & THIBEAULT, J. (2022a). Regard sur la mise en œuvre effective d'un dispositif de médiation sociocognitive pour enseigner la recommandation d'une œuvre narrative à l'écrit au primaire 3ᵉ cycle. *Revue Didactique, 3*(2), 71-102.

FORGET, M.-H. & THIBEAULT, J. (2022b). Recommander une œuvre narrative en français et en anglais : analyse de textes d'élèves de 6ᵉ primaire écrits à la suite d'un coenseignement bilingue du genre. *Revue canadienne de linguistique appliquée, 25*(2), 23-46.

FRANCESCHINI, R. (2013). Die Entwicklung dreisprachiger Schreibkompetenzen: Resultate aus den ladinischsprachigen Tälern Südtirols. In J. Erfurt; T. Leichsering & R. Streb (Eds.). *Mehrsprachigkeit und Mehrschriftigkeit.* OBST-Osnabrücker Beiträge zur Sprachtheorie, Heft 83, 57-78.

FRANCESCHINI, R. (2010). Der mehrsprachige Habitus: Das Fallbeispiel eines dreisprachigen Schulmodells in Ladinien. In Krüger-Potratz, M.; Neumann, U. & H.H. Reich (Eds.): *Bei Vielfalt Chancengleichheit: Interkulturelle Pädagogik und Durchgängige Sprachbildung.* Münster: Waxmann, 316-339.

FRANQUIZ, M.E. & ORTIZ, A.A. (2018). Coeditors' introduction: Ensuring the success of dual language programs through alignment of research, policy, and practice. *Bilingual Research Journal, 41*(3), 215-220.

FREEMAN, D., & FREEMAN, Y. (2000). *Teaching Reading in Multilingual Classrooms.* Heinemann.

FREEMAN, Y. (1988). Methodos de lectura en español. Reflejan nuestro conocimiento actual del proceso de lectura. *Lectura y Vida, 9*(5).

FREIRE, P. (1993). A alfabetização como elemento de formação da cidadania, São Paulo/Brasília, maio de 1987. In *Política e Educação: ensaios.* São Paulo: Cortez.

FREIRE, P. (1970, 1993, 2000). *Pedagogy of the Oppressed.* The Continuum International Publishing Group Inc.

GAJO, L. (2008). L'intercompréhension entre didactique intégrée et enseignement bilingue. In V. Conti & F. Grin (Eds.). *S'entendre entre langues voisines : vers l'intercompréhension,* 131-150.

GAMBOA-DIAZ, P., MOLINIÉ, M. & TEJADA-SÁNCHEZ, I. (2019). Former des enseignants de langue étrangère et seconde aux dimensions interculturelles explicites en France et en Colombie : un dialogue théorique et épistémologique. In B. Peña Dix, I. Tejada-Sánchez & A.M. Truscott de Mejía (Eds.) *Interculturalidad de formación de profesores. Perspectivas pedagógicas y multilingües.* Bogotá: Editorial Uniandes, 3-42.

GARCÍA, O. (2021). A grandmother's tale of young children's bilingualism: Stir(l)ring the lings in early childhood education. In M.E. Gómez-Parra & L.M. Martínez Serrano (Eds.). *The Crystallised truth of language. In honorem Richard Johnstone.* Editorial Universidad de Córdoba, 59-70.

GARCÍA, O., & ESPINOSA, C. (2020). Bilingüismo y translanguaging. Consecuencias para la educación. In L. Martín-Rojo & J. Pujolar (Eds.). *Claves para entender el multilingüismo contemporáneo* Zaragoza: Editorial UOC y Universidad de Zaragoza, 31-61.

GARCÍA, O. & KLEIFGEN, J.A. (2019). Translanguaging and literacies. *Reading Research Quarterly, 55*(4).

GARCÍA, O. (2018). Translanguaging, Pedagogy and Creativity. In J. Erfurt, A. Weirich, & E. Caparol-Ebersold (Eds.), *Éducation plurilingue et pratiques langagières. Hommage à Christine Hélot.* Berlin: Peter Lang, 39-56.

GARCÍA, O. & LIN, A. M. (2017). Translanguaging in bilingual education. In García et al. (Eds.). *Encyclopedia of Language and Education, Bilingual and multilingual education.* Springer, 117-130.

GARCÍA, O., JOHNSON, S. & SELTZER, K. (2017). *The translanguaging classroom: Leveraging student bilingualism for learning.* Caslon.

GARCÍA, O. & KLEYN, T. (Eds.) (2016). *Translanguaging with multilingual students: Learning from classroom moments.* New York: Routledge.

GARCÍA, O. & WEI, L. (2014). *Language, Bilingualism and Education.* Springer.

GARCÍA, O. & KLEYN, T. (2013). Teacher education for multilingual education. In C.A. Chapelle (Ed.). *The Encyclopedia of Applied Linguistics.* Blackwell, 5543-5548.

GARCÍA, O. (2009). *Bilingual Education in the 21st Century. A Global Perspective.* Wiley Blackwell.

GARCÍA, E. & FLORES, B. (1986). *Language and Literacy Research in Bilingual Education.* Arizona State University, (Edited Volume).

GENTIL, G. (2011). A biliteracy agenda for genre research. *Journal of Second Language Writing,* 20(1), 6-23.

GOGOLIN, I. & KRÜGER-POTRATZ, M. (2010). *Einführung in die Interkulturelle Pädagogik.* Opladen: Budrich.

GOODMAN, K. & GOODMAN, Y. (2014). *Making sense of learners making sense of written language: The selected works of Kenneth S. Goodman and Yetta Goodman.* Routledge.

GOODMAN, K. (1996). *On Reading.* Portsmouth, NH: Heinemann.

GOODMAN, K. (1990). El lenguaje integral: Un camino fácil para el desarrollo del lenguaje. *Lectura y Vida.* Junio, 5-13.

GOOSKENS, C.; KÜRSCHNER, S. & VAN HEUVEN, V.J. (2022). The role of loanwords in the intelligibility of written Danish among Swedes. *Nordic Journal of Linguistics,* 45, 4-29.

GOOSKENS, C.; KÜRSCHNER, S. & VAN BEZOOIJEN, R. (2012). Intelligibility of Swedish for Danes: loan words compared with inherited words. In H. van der Liet & M. Norde (Eds.). *Language for its own sake: essays on language and literature offered to Harry Perridon.* Amsterdam: Scandinavisch Instituut: 435-455. (= Amsterdam Contributions to Scandinavian Studies 8).

GOOSKENS, C.; KÜRSCHNER, S. & VAN BEZOOIJEN, R. (2011). Intelligibility of Standard German and Low German to speakers of Dutch. *Dialectologia*: revista electrònica. Special issue II, 35-63.

GOOSKENS, C. & KÜRSCHNER, S. (2009). Cross-border intelligibility - on the intelligibility of Low German among speakers of Danish and Dutch. In A.N. Lenz, C. Gooskens & S. Reker, (Eds.): *Low Saxon dialects across borders - Niedersächsische*

Dialekte über Grenzen hinweg. Stuttgart: Steiner, 273-295. (= Zeitschrift für Dialektologie und Linguistik - Beihefte 138).

GOOSKENS, C. (2006). Linguistic and extra-linguistic predictors of Inter-Scandinavian intelligibility. In van de Weijer, J. & B. Los (Eds.): *Linguistics in the Netherlands* 23. Amsterdam: Benjamins, 101-113.

GORT, M. & SEMBIANTE, S.F. (2015). Navigating hybridized language learning spaces through translanguaging pedagogy: Dual language preschool teachers' languaging practices in support of emergent bilingual children's performance of academic discourse. *International Multilingual Research Journal, 9*(1), 7-25.

GROFF, C. (2018a). *The ecology of language in multilingual India: Voices of women and educators in the Himalayan foothills.* London: Palgrave Macmillan / Springer.

GROFF, C. (2018b). Language policy and language ideology: Ecological perspectives on language in the Himalayan foothills. *Anthropology and Education Quarterly, 49*(1): 3-20.

GROFF, C. (2017). Language and language-in-education planning in multilingual India: A minoritized language perspective. *Language Policy, 16*(2), 135-164.

GUMPERZ, J. J. (1964). Linguistic and Social Interaction in Two Communities. *American Anthropologist, 66*(6/2), 137-153.

GURSCHLER, M. & TSCHOLL, E.R. (2015). *DaZUgeHÖREN. Südtiroler Dialekt von Jugendlichen für Jugendliche. Arbeitsmaterialien zum Südtiroler Dialekt.* Bozen: Deutsches Bildungsressort.

HALL, E. T. (1959). *The Silent Language.* Garden City, N.Y.: Doubleday.

HASSOUN, J. (2003). *Schmuggelpfade der Erinnerung.* Frankfurt/Main: Stroemfeld Verlag.

HÉLOT, C. & ERFURT, J. (Eds.) (2016). *L'éducation bilingue en France : Politiques linguistiques, modèles et pratiques.* Limoges : Lambert-Lucas.

HÉLOT, C. (2012). Linguistic diversity and education. In M. Martin-Jones, A. Blackledge & A. Creese (eds.) *The Routledge Handbook of Multilingualism*. London: Routledge, 214-231.

HÉLOT, C. & YOUNG, A. (2005). The notion of diversity in language education: Policy and practice at primary level in France. *Language, Culture and Curriculum, 18*(3), 242-257.

HERRMANN-WINTER, R. (2017). *Neues hochdeutsch-plattdeutsches Wörterbuch*. 4. Auflage. Rostock: Hinstorff.

HEUGH, K., PRINSLOO, C., MAKGAMATHA, M., DIEDERICKS, G. & WINNAAR, L. (2017). Multilingualism(s) and system-wide assessment: a southern perspective. In *Language and Education, 31*(3), 197-216.

HOBSBAWM, E. (1996). Language, Culture, and National Identity. *Social Research, 63*(4), 1065-1080.

HOLTZMANN, R. (2000). *Mehrsprachigkeit und Sprachkompetenz in den ladinischen Tälern Südtirols. Eine ethno- und soziolinguistische Darstellung*. Mannheim: Dissertation.

HORNBERGER, N. H. (2005). Opening and filling up implementational and ideological spaces in heritage language education. *The Modern Language Journal, 89*(4), 605-609.

HORNBERGER, N. H. (1989). Continua of Biliteracy. *Review of Educational Research, 59*(3), 271-96.

HORNBERGER, N. H. & SKILTON-SYLVESTER, E. (2000). Revisiting the Continua of Biliteracy: International and Critical Perspectives. *Language and Education, 14*(2).

HORST, M., WHITE, J. & BELL, P. (2010). First and second language knowledge in the language classroom. *International Journal of Bilingualism, 14*(3), 331-349.

HUDELSON, S. (2008). Phonics in Bilingual Education. In J.M. González (Ed.), *Encyclopedia of Bilingual Education*, 2. Sage Publications, Inc.

HUDELSON, S., FOURNIER, J., ESPINOSA, C. & BACHMAN, R. (1994). Chasing windmills, overcoming obstacles in Spanish literature for children. *Language Arts, 3*(71), 164-171.

HUDELSON, S. (1987). The role of native language literacy in the education of language minority children. *Language Arts, 64*(8), 827-841.

HUDELSON, S. (1984). Kan Yu Ret en Rayt en Ingles: Children Become Literate in English as a Second Language. *TESOL Quarterly, 18*(2), 221-238.

HUDELSON, S. & SERNA, I. (1994). Beginning Literacy in English in a Whole Language Bilingual Program. In A. Flurkey & R. Meyer (Eds.). *Under the Whole Language Umbrella: Many Cultures, Many Voices,* 278-295.

HUFEISEN, B. (2010). Theoretische Fundierung multiplen Sprachenlernens — Faktorenmodell 2.0. In *Jahrbuch Deutsch als Fremdsprache, 36*(1), 200-207.

HUFEISEN, B. (2018). Institutional Education and Multilingualism: PlurCur® as a Prototype of a Multilingual Whole School Policy. *European Journal of Applied Linguistics, 6*(1), 1-32.

HUFEISEN, B. & MARX, N. (2014). *EuroComGerm - Die Sieben Siebe. Germanische Sprachen lesen lernen* (2nd ed.). Aachen: Shaker.

HUFEISEN, B. & MARX, N. (2007). *EuroComGerm - Die Sieben Siebe. Germanische Sprachen lesen lernen.* Aachen: Shaker.

HYLAND, K. (2004). *Genre and second language writing.* University of Michigan Press.

INSTITUTO BRASILEIRO DE GEOGRAFIA E ESTATÍSTICA (IBGE) (2012). *Os indígenas no Censo Demográfico 2010 primeiras considerações com base no quesito cor ou raça.* Rio de Janeiro: IBGE.

INTERNATIONAL AND CRITICAL PERSPECTIVES. *Language and Education: An International Journal, 14*(2), 96-122.

IPOL - Instituto de Investigação e Desenvolvimento em Política Linguística (2016). "Plataforma do Letramento: O Brasil e suas muitas línguas."

IRSARA, M. (2020). Applying typological insights in a minority-language context: Motion event lexicalisations in Ladin, Italian, German and English texts compiled by Ladins. In *Glottodidactica. An International Journal of Applied Linguistics, 47*(1), 23-40.

IRSARA, M. (2017). Promoting cross-linguistic awareness: English motion events in a multilingual teaching model. In *Lingue e Linguaggi, 23*, 121–132.

IWASAKI, E. (2022). *National languages, multilingual education, and the self-proclaimed "militants" for change in Senegal* (Publication No. 29161222) [Doctoral dissertation, Columbia University]. ProQuest Dissertations and Theses Global.

JHINGRAN, D. (2009). Hundreds of home languages in the country and many in most classrooms: Coping with diversity in primary education in India. In *Social justice through multilingual education*. Multilingual Matters, 263-282.

JHINGRAN, D. (2005). *Language disadvantage: The learning challenge in primary education.* APH Publishing.

KASPER, G., & KELLERMAN, E. (1997). *Communicative strategies: Psycholinguistic and sociolinguistic perspectives.* Longman.

KAUFMANN, G. & DURAN, D. (2022). Of *snoidels* and *hofdüütsch*: Some (Standard German) keys to the phonetic variation in Pomerano. In B. Ganswindt, Y. Hettler & I. Schröder (Eds.): *Niederdeutsche Dialektologie*, Stuttgart: Steiner, ZDL-Themenheft; *89*(2-3). 231-282.

KESSLER, M. (2021). The longitudinal development of second language writers' metacognitive genre awareness. *Journal of Second Language Writing, 53*.

KHUBCHANDANI, L.M. (2003). Defining mother tongue education in plurilingual contexts. *Language Policy, 2*(3), 239-254.

KHUBCHANDANI, L.M. (1997). Language policy and education in the Indian subcontinent. *Encyclopedia of Language and Education: Language Policy and Political Issues in Education*, 179-187.

KHUBCHANDANI, L.M. (1978). Languages of instruction in plurilingual India. *International Review of Education, 24*(3), 375-380.

KLEEBERG, B. & LANGENOHL, A. (2011). Kulturalisierung, Dekulturalisierung. *Zeitschrift für Kulturphilosophie, 5. Jahrgang* (Heft 2), 281-302.

KLEYN, T. & GARCÍA, O. (2019). Translanguaging as an Act of Transformation. Restructuring Teaching and Learning for Emergent Bilingual Students. In L.C. de Oliveira (Ed.) *The Handbook of TESOL*. Hoboken, New Jersey: Wiley, 69-82.

KLOSS, H. (1967). 'Abstand Languages' and 'Ausbau Languages'. *Anthropological Linguistics, 9*(7), 29-41.

KRAMSCH, C. & HUFFMASTER, M. (2015). Multilingual practices in foreign language study. In J. Cenoz & D. Gorter (Eds.) *Multilingual Education. Between Language Learning and Translanguaging*. Cambridge University Press, 114-136.

KRAMSCH, C. (2009). Third culture and language education In L. Wei & V. Cook (Eds.). *Contemporary Applied Linguistics: Language Teaching and Learning*. New York, NY: Continuum Press, 233-254.

KRAMSCH, C. (1993). *Context and Culture in Language Teaching.* Oxford: Oxford University Press.

KRASHEN, S.D. (2013). The case for non-targeted, comprehensible input. *Journal of Bilingual Education Research & Instruction, 15*(1), 102-110.

KRASHEN, S.D. (2004). *The Power of Reading: Insights from the Research*. 2nd edition. Portsmouth, NH: Heinemann.

KRASHEN, S.D. (1981). Bilingual education and second language acquisition theory. In *Schooling and language minority students: A theoretical framework*, 51-79.

KRISTEVA, J. (2002). From One Identity to an Other (1975). In *The Portable Kristeva. Updated Edition. Ed. by Kelly Oliver*. New York: Columbia University Press, 93-115.

KÜRSCHNER, S. (2019). Wie gut erkennen Deutschsprachige niederländische und westfriesische Wörter? Zur Verstehbarkeit zwischen westgermanischen Sprachen. In J. Strässler (Ed.): *Sprache(n) für Europa: Mehrsprachigkeit als Chance; Auswahl an Beiträgen des 52. Linguistischen Kolloquiums in Erlagen 2017.* Frankfurt am Main: Lang, 135-147.

KÜRSCHNER, S. (2014). Von *flacher Flagge* und *matter Macht*: Verstehen niederländischer und schwedischer Kognaten durch

Deutschsprachige. In P. Bergmann; K. Birkner; P. Gilles; H. Spiekermann & T. Streck (Eds.): *Sprache im Gebrauch: räumlich, zeitlich, interaktional. Festschrift für Peter Auer.* Heidelberg: Winter, 35-53. (= OraLingua 9)

KÜRSCHNER, S. (2013). Strategies in the recognition of Dutch words by Germans. In C. Gooskens & R. van Bezooijen (Eds.): *Phonetics in Europe: Perception and Production.* Frankfurt am Main: Lang, 159-179.

KÜRSCHNER, S.; GOOSKENS, C. & VAN BEZOOIJEN, R. (2009). Linguistic determinants of the intelligibility of Swedish words among Danes. *International Journal of Humanities and Arts Computing,* 2(1-2), 83-100.

LANGENOHL, A. (2017). Inter- und Transkulturalität. In C. Leggewie & E. Meyer (Eds.). *Global Pop: Das Buch zur Weltmusik.* Stuttgart: J.B. Metzler, 54-59.

LEONI, L., COHEN, S., CUMMINS, J., BISMILLA, V., BAJWA, M., HANIF, S., KHALID, K. & SHAHAR, T. (2011). 'I'm not just a coloring person': Teacher and student perspectives on identity text construction. In J. Cummins & M. Early (Eds.), *Identity texts: The collaborative creation of power in multilingual schools.* Stoke-on-Trent, UK: Trentham Books, 45-57.

LIDDICOAT, A. & SCARINO. A. (2013). *Intercultural Language Teaching and Learning.* John Wiley & Sons.

LINDHOLM-LEARY, K.J. (2001). *Dual Language Education.* Clevedon: Multilingual Matters.

LITTLE, D. & KIRWAN, D. (2019). *Engaging with Linguistic Diversity. A Study of Educational Inclusion in an Irish Primary School.* London: Bloomsbury.

LOPEZ-GOPAR, M. (2016). *Decolonizing Primary English Language Teaching.* Bristol: Multilingual Matters.

LOVE, B. (2020). *We want to do more than survive: Abolitionist teaching and the pursuit of educational freedom.* Beacon Press.

LÜDI, G. (1997). Towards a Better Understanding of Biliteracy. In C. Pontecorvo (Ed.). *Writing Development: an Interdisciplinary View.* Amsterdam; Philadelphia: Benjamins, 206-218.

LÜDI, G. (1989). Situations diglossiques en Catalogne. In G. Holtus; G. Lüdi & M. Metzeltin (Eds.). *La Corona de Aragón y las lenguas románicas. Miscelánea de homenaje para Germán Colón. La Corona d'Aragó i les llengües romàniques. Miscel.lània d'homenatge per a Germà Colon.* Tübingen, 237-265.

LUGONES, M. (2003). *Pilgrimages/Peregrinajes: Theorizing Coalition Against Multiple Oppressions.* Lanham, MD: Rowman & Littlefield Publishers.

MAAS, U. (2010). Literat und orat. Grundbegriffe der Analyse geschriebener und gesprochener Sprache. *Grazer Linguistische Studien, 73*, 21-150.

MAAS, U. (2005). Sprache und Sprachen in der Migration im Einwanderungsland Deutschland. *IMIS Beiträge 26: Sprache und Migration*, 89-133.

MAAS, U. & MEHLEM, U. (2005). *Schriftkulturelle Ausdrucksformen der Identitätsbildung bei marokkanischen Kindern und Jugendlichen in Marokko.* Osnabrück: Institut für Migrationsforschung und Interkulturelle Studien.

MAINELLA, M. (2012). *Pedagogical implications of cross-linguistic awareness-raising: An exploratory study* [mémoire de maîtrise inédit]. Université Concordia, Montréal, Canada.

MARCEL, J.F. (2023). Une « vraie place » dans la recherche-intervention. *Recherche En Education, 51.*

MARKO, J., ORTINO, S., PALERMO, V.L. & WOELK, J. (Eds.) (2005). *Die Verfassung der Südtiroler Autonomie. Die Sonderrechtsordnung der Autonomen Provinz Bozen/Südtirol.* Baden-Baden: Nomos.

MARTINEZ, D. C. (2017). Imagining a language of solidarity for Black and Latinx youth in English language arts classrooms. *English Education, 49*(2), 179-196.

MARY, L. & YOUNG, A. S. (2021). 'To make headway you have to go against the flow': Resisting dominant discourses and supporting emergent bilinguals in a multilingual pre-school in France. In L. Mary, A.-B. Krüger & A. Young (Eds.). *Migration,*

Multilingualism and Education: Critical Perspectives on Inclusion. Bristol, UK: Multilingual Matters.

MECHERIL, P. (2014). Über die Kritik interkultureller Ansätze zu uneindeutigen Zugehörigkeiten – kunstpädagogische Perspektiven. In B. Clausen (Ed.). *Teilhabe und Gerechtigkeit.* Münster/New York: Waxmann, 11-19.

MEIßNER, F.-J. (2004). Modelling plurilingual processing and language growth between intercomprehensive languages. In L.N. Zybatow (Ed.). *Translation in der globalen Welt und neue Wege in der Sprach- und Übersetzerausbildung. Innsbrucker Ringvorlesung zur Translationswissenschaft* II. Frankfurt am Main: Lang, 1-57.

MENKEN, K. & GARCÍA, O. (2010). *Negotiating Language Policy in Schools: Educators as Policy Makers.* New York: Lawrence Erlbaum/Taylor & Francis/Routledge.

MERLEAU-PONTY, M. (1945/2009). *Phénoménologie de la perception.* Paris: Gallimard.

MERLEAU-PONTY, M. (1962). *Phenomenology of Perception.* (Collin Smith, Trans.). London: Routledge & Kegan Paul.

MILEIDIS G. & HAMM-RODRÍGUEZ, M. (2022). Centering language and communicative purpose in writing instruction for bi/Multilingual learners. *The Reading Teacher, 75*(6), 693-706.

MINISTÈRE DE L'ÉDUCATION ET DE L'ENSEIGNEMENT SUPÉRIEUR (2019). *La collaboration entre le titulaire et l'enseignant d'anglais, langue seconde, dans un contexte d'enseignement intensif de l'anglais.* Paris : France.

MINISTÈRE DE L'ÉDUCATION ET DE L'ENSEIGNEMENT SUPÉRIEUR (2018). *Évaluation des effets de l'enseignement intensif de l'anglais, langue seconde, en 6e année du primaire.* Paris : France.

MINISTÈRE DE L'ÉDUCATION ET DE L'ENSEIGNEMENT SUPÉRIEUR (2017). *L'anglais intensif au troisième cycle du primaire. Guide à l'intention des enseignants d'anglais, langue seconde.* Paris : France.

MINISTÈRE DE L'ÉDUCATION NATIONALE (2019). *Modèle harmonisé d'enseignement bilingue au Sénégal* (avec révisions). Dakar : Sénégal.

MINISTÈRE DE L'ÉDUCATION NATIONALE (1981). *Les États-Généraux de l'Éducation et de la Formation (EGEF) de 1981*. Dakar : Senegal.

MOHANTY, A. K. (2018). *The multilingual reality: Living with languages*. Multilingual Matters.

MOHANTY, A. K. (2006). Multilingualism of the unequals and predicaments of education in India: Mother tongue or other tongue. In O. García (Ed.) *Imagining multilingual schools*, 262-283.

MOLL, L. (2019). Elaborating Funds of Knowledge: Community-Oriented Practices in International Contexts. *Literacy Research: Theory, Method, and Practice, 68*(1), 130-138.

MOLL, L., AMANTI, C., NEFF, D. & GONZALEZ, N. (1992). Funds of Knowledge for Teaching: Using a Qualitative Approach to Connect Homes and Classrooms. *Theory Into Practice, 31*(2), 7-141.

MOTTIER-LOPEZ, L. (2015). Au cœur du développement professionnel des enseignants, la conscientisation critique. Exemple d'une recherche collaborative sur l'évaluation formative à l'école primaire genevoise. *Carrefours de l'éducation, 39*, 119-135.

MWAI (2019). Report of the external evaluation of the support program for quality education in mother tongues for primary schools in Senegal. Prepared for Dubai Cares by C. Benson, S. Miske, E. Iwasaki, M. Diagne & M. Meagher. Shoreview MN: Miske Witt and Associates, International.

NATLAND, S. (2021). Dialogue skills and trust. Some lessons learned from co-writing with service users. In K. Driessens & V. Lyssens-Dannebom (Eds.). *Involving service users in social work education, research policy. A comparative European analysis*. Bristol University Press, 158-169.

NDIAYE, T. M. (2021, April 28). Communiqué du Conseil des ministres de ce mercredi 28 avril 2021. *SENEGO*.

NERBONNE, J. & HEERINGA, W. (2010). Measuring Dialect Differences. In J.E. Schmidt & P. Auer (Eds.). *Language and Space: Theories and Methods. An International Handbook of Linguistic*

Variation. (= Handbooks of Linguistics and Communication Science 30.1). Berlin: De Gruyter Mouton, 550-567.

OECD (2010). *PISA 2009 results: Learning to learn—Student engagement, strategies and practices (Volume III).* Paris.

ORTIZ, F. (1987) [1940]. *Contrapunteo cubano del tabaco y el azúcar. Prólogo y cronología de Julio Le Riverend. Reimpressión de la primera edición de 1940.* Caracas: Bibliotheca Ayacucho.

OTHEGUY, R., GARCÍA, O. & REID, W. (2019). A translanguaging view of the linguistic system of bilinguals. *Applied Linguistics Review, 10,* 625-651.

OTHEGUY, R., GARCÍA, O. & REID, W. (2015). Clarifying translanguaging and deconstructing named languages: A perspective from linguistics. *Applied Linguistics Review, 6(3),* 281-307.

PASSARELLA, M. (2011). Alfabetizzazione bilingue. In S. Cavagnoli & M. Passarella (Eds.). *Educare al plurilinguismo. Riflessioni didattiche, pedagogiche e linguistiche.* Milano: Franco Angeli, 67-84.

PATTANAYAK, D.P. (2003). Language issues in literacy and basic education: The case of India. In A. Ouane (Ed.). *Towards a multilingual culture of education.* UNESCO Institute for Education.

PATTANAYAK, D.P. (Ed.) (1990). *Multilingualism in India.* Multilingual Matters.

POZA, L.E. & STITES, A. (2022). 'They are going to forget about us': Translanguaging and student agency in a gentrifying neighborhood. In M. Sanchez & O. García (Eds.) *Sin miedo: Transformative translanguaging espacios.* Multilingual Matters, 71-94.

PRASAD, G. (2016). Beyond the mirror towards a plurilingual prism: Exploring the creation of plurilingual "identity texts" in English and French classrooms in Toronto and Montpellier. *Intercultural Education, 26*(6), 497-514. Special Issue ed. A. Gagné & C. Schmidt.

RENAUD, J. (2020). Évaluer l'utilisabilité, l'utilité et l'acceptabilité d'un outil didactique au cours du processus de conception continuée dans l'usage. *Éducation et didactique, 14*(2), 65-84.

PROMONET, A., & LEMOINE-BRESSON, V. (Eds.) (2025). Écrire ensemble ? *Revue Partages, 2.* PUG.

RISSE, S. (2020). «Zerschtl schaug ma olm af die Respirazione». Mehrsprachige Schreibroutinen von deutschsprachigen Studierenden in Südtirol. In M. Hepp & K. Salzmann (Eds.). *Sprachvergleich in der mehrsprachig orientierten DaF-Didaktik: Theorie und Praxis.* Rom: Istituto Italiano di Studi Germanici, 205-220.

RISSE, S. & FRANCESCHINI, R. (2016). Auftrieb durch parallele Alphabetisierung: Analysen aus dem dreisprachigen Schulsystem in Gröden und Gadertal (Südtirol). In C. Schroeder & P. Rosenberg (Eds.). *Mehrsprachigkeit als Ressource in der Schriftlichkeit.* Berlin: de Gruyter Mouton, 235-260.

RISSE, S. (2014). Deutsch als Zweitsprache im mehrsprachigen Kontext. Zum Erwerb von Konjunktionen als Indikator für Textqualität. In *Zeitschrift für Literaturwissenschaft und Linguistik LiLi, 174*, 86-95.

RONJAT, J. (2013). *Le développement du langage observé chez un enfant bilingue.* Berlin: Peter Lang.

ROSENBERG, P. (2023). Deutsch in Lateinamerika: Sprachinseln, Archipele, Atolle. In P. Wolf-Farré; L. Löff Machado; A. Prediger & S. Kürschner (Eds.). *Deutsche und weitere germanische Sprachminderheiten in Lateinamerika: Methoden, Grundlagen, Fallstudien.* Frankfurt am Main: Lang, 23-69.

ROSENBERG, P. (2018). Lateinamerika. In A. Plewnia & C.M. Riehl (Eds.). *Handbuch der deutschen Sprachminderheiten in Übersee.* Tübingen: Narr Francke Attempto, 193-264.

ROSENBERG, P. & SCHROEDER, C. (2016). Vorwort. In P. Rosenberg & C. Schroeder (2016). *Mehrsprachigkeit als Ressource in der Schriftlichkeit* (= DaZ-Forschung [DaZ-For], Band 10); De Gruyter Mouton, v-xiii.

ROUSSEL, S., & GAONAC'H, D. (2016). *L'apprentissage des langues.* Paris, Retz, coll. « Mythes et réalités ».

ROUSSEL, S., TRICOT, A., & SWELLER, J. (2016). *Is learning content and a second Language simultaneous a good idea?* Communication au 9th International Cognitive Load Theory Conference, Bochum, Allemagne.

SAILLOT, É. & MALMAISON, S. (2018). Analyse des ajustements réciproques dans une activité de co-enseignement : étude de cas dans le dispositif « Plus de maîtres que de classes ." *Éducation et socialisation. Les Cahiers du CERFEE, 47.*

SALZMANN, K. (2022). Der Einsatz von parallelen Bilderbüchern in der bilingualen Alphabetisierung. In N. Burneva; M. Hepp & A. Middeke (Eds.). *Kulturrealia in Paralleltexten als didaktischer Fokus trans- und interkultureller Germanistik.* Frankfurt u.a.: Peter Lang.

SÁNCHEZ, M., ESPINET, I., & HUNT, V. (2022). Student inquiry into the Language Practices de sus Comunidades: Rompiendo Fronteras in a Dual Language Bilingual School. In M. Sanchez & O. García (Eds.). *Sin miedo: Transformative translanguaging espacios.* Multilingual Matters, 134-155.

SASS (2016). *Der neue Sass. Plattdeutsches Wörterbuch. Plattdeutsch-Hochdeutsch. Hochdeutsch-Plattdeutsch. Plattdeutsche Rechtschreibung.* 8. Auflage. Kiel, Hamburg 2016: Wachholtz.

SAVOIE-ZAJC, L. (2010). Les dynamiques d'accompagnement dans la mise en place de communautés d'apprentissage de personnels scolaires. *Education & Formation, e(293),* 10-20.

SCHEUTZ, H. (2016). *Insre Sproch. Deutsche Dialekte in Südtirol.* Bozen: Athesia.

SCHNEIDER, A. (2019). *Dicionário Escolar Conciso: Português-Pomerano / Pomerisch-Portugijsisch.* Porto Alegre: Evangraf.

SCHULZE-ENGLER, F. (2006). Vom „Inter" zum „Trans": Gesellschaftliche, kulturelle und literarische Übergänge. In H. Antor (Ed.). *Inter- und transkulturelle Studien. Theoretische Grundlagen und interdisziplinäre Praxis.* Heidelberg: Winter, 41-53.

SELINKER, L. (1972). Interlanguage. *International Review of Applied Linguistics in Language Teaching, 10,* 209-241.

SELTZER, K. & GARCÍA, O. (2020). Broadening the view: Taking up a translanguaging pedagogy with all language-minoritized students. In T. Zhongfeng, L. Aghai, P. Sayer & J. Schissel (Eds.) *Envisioning TESOL through a Translanguaging Lens*. Switzerland: Springer, 23-42.

SELTZER, K., & DE LOS RÍOS, C. V. (2018). Translating theory to practice: Exploring teachers' raciolinguistic literacies in secondary English classrooms. *English Education, 51*(1), 49-79.

SENSEVY, G. (2022). Un instrument pour la recherche en éducation ? In R. Monod-Ansaldi, C. Loisy & B. Gruson (Eds.). *Le réseau des lieux d'éducation associés à l'institut français d'éducation*. PUR, 7-19.

SIL LEAD. (2021, June 21). *MOHEBS Video May 2021* [Video]. YouTube.

SIMS BISHOP, R. (1990). Mirrors, windows, and sliding doors. *Perspectives: Choosing and using books for the classroom, 6*(3).

SOMMER-FARIAS, B. (2020). *"This is helping me with writing in all languages": Developing genre knowledge across languages in a foreign language course* [Thèse de doctorat, University of Arizona, États-Unis]. Proquest.

STREB, R. (2022). Woraus besteht Sprachwissen? Zur Komplexität des mehrsprachigen Repertoires – von der Empirie zur Theorie. In J. Erfurt, M. Leroy & M. Stierwald (Eds.). *Mehrsprachigkeit und Transkulturalität in frankophonen Räumen: Modelle, Prozesse und Praktiken / Plurilinguisme et transculturalité dans les espaces francophones : des modèles théoriques à la négociation des pratiques*. Tübingen: Narr Francke Attempto, 87-109.

STREB, R. (2016). *Ausbau mehrsprachiger Repertoires im Two-Way-Immersion-Kontext. Eine ethnographisch-linguistische Langzeituntersuchung in einer deutsch-italienischen Grundschulklasse*. (Sprache, Mehrsprachigkeit und sozialer Wandel 28). Frankfurt/Main: Peter Lang.

STRIEB, L., CARINI, P., KANEVSKY, R. & WISE, B. (2011). *Prospect's Descriptive Processes: The Child, the Art of Teaching and The Classroom and School* (revised Edition). North Bennington, VT:

The Prospect Center: The Prospect Archives and Center for Education and Research.

TASDEMIR, H. & YILDIRIM, T. (2017). Collaborative Teaching from English Language Instructors' Perspectives. *Journal of Language and Linguistic Studies*, *13*(2), 632-642.

TEALE, W. & SULZBY, E. (1986). *Emergent literacy: writing and reading*. Norwood, N.J.: Ablex Pub. Corp.

THE WORLD BANK (2023): *Gini index*.

TORRES CACOULLOS, R. & TRAVIS, C. (2018). *Bilingualism in the community: Code switching and grammars in contact*. Cambridge University Press.

TREMBLAY, P. (2020). Le coenseignement : fondements et redéfinitions. *Éducation et francophonie*, *48*(2), 14-36.

TREMBLAY, P. (2013). Comparative outcomes of two instructional models for students with learning disabilities: inclusion with co-teaching and solo-taught special education. *Journal of Research in Special Education Needs*, *13*(4), 251-258.

TRESSMANN, I. (forthcoming). *Dicionário Enciclopédico Pomerano Multilíngue. Multilingual Pomerisch Encyklopedisch Wöörbauk*. 2ª edição. Santa Maria de Jetibá, ES.

TRESSMANN, I. (2006). *Dicionário Enciclopédico Pomerano-Português (Pomerisch-Portugijsisch Wöirbauk)*. Vitória, ES: Sodré.

UIS (2019). *Education and literacy – Senegal*. Montréal: UNESCO Institute for Statistics.

VELASCO, P. & FIALAIS, V. (2016). Moments of metalinguistic awareness in a Kindergarten class: Translanguaging for simultaneous biliterate development. *International Journal of Bilingual Education and Bilingualism, 21*(6), 760–774.

VERTOVEC, S. (2007). Super-diversity and its implications. *Ethnic and Racial Studies, 30*(6), 1024-1054.

VIDESOTT, R. (2021a). Kontrastive Grammatik im Sprachunterricht in ladinischen Schulen Südtirols. In P. Wolf-Farré et al. (Eds.). *Sprachkontrast und Mehrsprachigkeit.*

Linguistische Grundlagen, didaktische Implikationen und Desiderata Tübingen: Narr, 127-152.

VIDESOTT, R. (2021b). Plurilinguismo nell'area ladina dell'Alto Adige. Quando plurilinguismo istituzionale e individuale si intrecciano. In *DiDit – Didattica dell'italiano. Studi applicati di lingua e letteratura, 1*, 55-83.

VIDESOTT, P. (2018). Der Deutschunterricht in Ladinien im 19. Jahrhundert. In H. Glück (Ed.). *Die Sprache des Nachbarn. Die Fremdsprache Deutsch bei Italienern und Ladinern vom Mittelalter bis 1918*. Bamberg: University Press, 221-244.

VOGEL, S., HOADLEY, C., CASTILLO, A. R., & ASCENZI-MORENO, L. (2020). Languages, literacies, and literate programming: Can we use the latest theories on how bilingual people learn to help us teach computational literacies? *CUNY Academic Works, Publications and Research*. City University of New York.

VOGT, M.T. (2018). Interkulturalität als systemische Herausforderung für Europas Nationalstaaten. *EJM. Europäisches Journal für Minderheitenfragen, 11*(1-2), 180-204.

VYGOTSKY, L.S. (1978). *Mind in Society: the Development of Higher Psychological Processes*. Cambridge, MA: Harvard University Press.

WEIRICH, A.-C. (2018). *Sprachliche Verhältnisse und Restrukturierung sprachlicher Repertoires in der Republik Moldova, 30*. Berlin: Peter Lang.

WENGER, E. (1998). *Communities of Practice: Learning, Meaning and Identity*. Cambridge: University Press.

WOKUSH, S. (2008). Didactique intégrée des langues : la contribution de l'école au plurilinguisme des élèves. *Babylonia, 1*, 12-14.

About the Authors

Carol Benson, PhD, is the director of MLE International, an organization supporting the implementation of L1-based multilingual education in low-income contexts. Her career has combined academic teaching and research with technical assistance in teacher education, curriculum development, and policy implementation for multilingual programs in the Asia/Pacific, Africa, and Latin America regions. Her scholarly interests include assessing emergent multilinguals and creating a multilingual habitus in educational development.

Gabriele Budach is an Associate Professor of Teacher Education, Learning, and Diversity at the University of Luxembourg. Her work focuses on teaching, learning, and communicating in multilingual and multicultural contexts. She has been conducting research in the realm of multilingual literacies and multimodal pedagogies. More recently, she has explored arts-based approaches to teaching and learning, notably digital storytelling and stop-motion animation, to articulate pressing concerns of social and environmental justice through means of expression with and beyond language.

Brigitta Busch is an applied linguist at the University of Vienna and is also affiliated as a Professor Extraordinary with Stellenbosch University (South Africa). In 2012, she was granted a Berta-Karlik research professorship for excellent female scientists by the University of Vienna. She has also been working for many years as an expert for the Council of Europe's Confidence-Building Measures Programme and was a member of the Advisory Committee on the Council of Europe's Framework Convention for the Protection of National Minorities between 2009 and 2018. Her main interests focus on sociolinguistics, multilingualism, biographic approaches in linguistics, and language and trauma.

Damien Céné is a teacher at Jean Jaurès Elementary School in Nancy. After training in environmental education, which led him to work as a guide and educational trip coordinator, he turned to teaching in 2009. He left to teach in the United States (Salt Lake City, Utah) for a year. There, he discovered bilingual immersion teaching, which he later transposed to France at the Jean Jaurès school, where he still teaches. He has always given pride of place in his teaching to the classroom climate and the joy of learning, primarily through musical education.

Anne Choffat-Dürr, PhD, is a former teachers' trainer at the University of Lorraine, France. She is a member of the ATILF, UMR 7118 research center, Nancy, France, where she specializes in plurilingualism, teaching young learners, and autonomy in foreign language learning. Within the PRIMERA LéA IFé 2021-24 project, she guided teachers in questioning their practices in an 'English immersion' system to develop renewed practices that ensure better consideration of the diversity of students. She is now a member of the new Léa IFé project, which centers on the same central questions.

Jim Cummins is a Professor Emeritus at the Ontario Institute for Studies in Education of the University of Toronto, Canada. Over the past 50 years, his research and theoretical contributions have had a profound influence on the education of multilingual learners in various global contexts. These contributions include the distinction between conversational fluency and academic language proficiency, the common underlying proficiency (CUP) that enables the transfer of concepts and knowledge across languages, and instructional strategies to promote teaching for crosslinguistic transfer.

Anne-Marie de Mejía is a Professor of Linguistics in the area of Bilingual Education at Universidad de los Andes, Bogotá, Colombia. Her research interests include bilingual classroom interaction, intercultural communication, empowerment processes, and the development of bilingual teachers. She is the author and co-editor of several publications in the field of bilingual/multilingual education in Colombia. Her most recent edited book is *Language Education in Multilingual Colombia* with Norbella Miranda and Silvia Valencia Giraldo (Routledge, 2024).

Ulrike Dreher is an elementary school teacher in Frankfurt, Germany. She implemented the bilingual German-Italian project at her school and worked together with Gabriele Budach at the University of Frankfurt between 2004 and 2008. She has been teaching bilingual classes ever since.

Jürgen Erfurt is Professor Emeritus at the Goethe University Frankfurt am Main, Institute for Romance Languages and Literatures. He has published more than 30 books, 250 articles, and book chapters on many topics in Romance linguistics, sociolinguistics, multilingualism research, Francophone studies, and Transculturality. His empirical research has focused on aspects of multi- and plurilingualism, pluriliteracies, plurilingual learning, language policy, and language practices in Canada, Quebec, Ontario, Acadia, Germany, France, and the Republic of Moldova.

Cecilia M. Espinosa, Ph.D., is a Professor in Early Childhood/Childhood at Lehman College/CUNY. Her research focuses on bilingual children's writing, translanguaging, descriptive processes, and children's literature that affirms and nurtures multiple identities. Key roles: Cecilia was an Associate Investigator (AI) in the CUNY NYSIEB Project. She serves as AI of the CUNY IIE Project, co-led the NY Project on Practices for Multilingual Learners and the NGL Standards, and co-authored the book Rooted in Strength: Using Translanguaging to Grow Multilingual Readers and Writers (Scholastic, 2021).

Valérie Fialais is a researcher and teacher trainer at the Académie de Strasbourg and the University of Strasbourg, affiliated with LiLPa UR 1339. She is currently responsible for supporting the implementation of a pilot project in a bilingual school with team teaching. She has also established a training program for monolingual teachers interested in joining the French-German bilingual education system at the Strasbourg Academy. Her expertise focuses on pedagogical translanguaging, with an emphasis on building bridges between languages in bilingual classrooms, as well as metalinguistic awareness. She is also involved in collaborative research as part of the "Lieux d'éducation associés" network of the French Institute of Education with a bilingual school (English-French immersion) in Nancy.

Marie-Hélène Forget is a professor of French education at the secondary level in the Department of Education Sciences at the Université du Québec à Trois-Rivières. In school settings, her research focuses on the cultural approach in French classes, reading and writing as cultural practices, and the teaching and learning of justificatory genres. In university settings, she is interested in the development of cultural competencies in French education and the development of pedagogical mediation practices. Previously, she worked as a high school French teacher and a pedagogical advisor.

Ofelia García is Professor Emerita in the Ph.D. programs in Urban Education and Latin American, Iberian, and Latino Cultures at The Graduate Center, City University of New York. García has published extensively on language education, sociolinguistics, and translanguaging. She has received distinguished lifetime awards from the Literacy Research Association, the Modern Language Association, and the American Education Research Association. She has been inducted into the American Academy of Arts and Sciences and the National Academy of Education.

Cynthia Groff is a researcher at Kohnstamm Institute, University of Amsterdam. For her Ph.D. in Educational Linguistics at the University of Pennsylvania's Graduate School of Education, she conducted ethnographic research in North India, as described in the book *The Ecology of Language in Multilingual India: Voices of Women and Educators in the Himalayan Foothills*. She has since conducted research in Québec at Université Laval, in Mexico at Universidad Autónoma Metropolitana, and in the Netherlands at Universiteit Leiden. Her research interests include the adequacy of education for linguistic minorities and the experiences and discourses of minority youth around language and belonging.

Christine Hélot is an emerita professor of English at the University of Strasbourg, France. As a sociolinguist, her research focuses on language in education policies in France and Europe, as well as on bi-/multilingual education, critical language awareness, early childhood education, children's literature, and multiliteracy. In 1988, she obtained her PhD from Trinity College, Dublin, Ireland, for a thesis on bilingualism in the family. In 2005, she was awarded a Habilitation from the University of Strasbourg for her research on bi/plurilingualism in schools. She has published extensively in both French and English and co-edited several volumes on bilingual and multilingual education. Her research on critical language awareness was the subject of a documentary film entitled "Raconte-moi ta langue/Tell me how you talk." She is the president of the French NGO *DULALA* (D'une langue à l'autre), which aims to support multilingualism in family and educational contexts and to address social and linguistic discriminatory practices.

Aurore Isambert taught for ten years in priority education. Recognized for her innovative teaching practices and commitment to inclusion, she is now the principal and teacher at the bilingual public school Jean Jaurès in Nancy, France. She also serves as the education site coordinator for two collaborative research projects within the Lieu d'éducation associé network of the French Institute of Education. This commitment led her to resume her studies, and she is currently pursuing a PhD focused on integrating families' voices in a bilingual school setting, with the goal of co-constructing a more inclusive and equitable school environment.

Erina Iwasaki, PhD, is a Postdoctoral Research Fellow at the Pulte Institute for Global Development, University of Notre Dame. Her work focuses on language issues in international educational development, particularly on language-in-education policy and the efforts of non-dominant ethnolinguistic communities in implementing education in their languages. She has also consulted for various organizations, designing and implementing multi-year teacher training curriculum development, as well as conducting analyses and evaluations for multilingual education programs.

Dhir Jhingran is the Founder and Executive Director of Language and Learning Foundation, a non-profit focused on improving students' foundational learning at scale in early childhood and primary education. He has worked in the primary education sector for over 30 years within and outside the government. A key focus of his work has been the development and implementation of early-grade reading programs in Asia and Africa, as well as first language-based multilingual education (MLE) programs in India. He has researched and published on the theme of multilingual education.

Delphine Jeandel is a teacher at École Jean Jaurès in Nancy. After completing an LLCE in foreign language, literature, and civilization in English, she took the competitive examination to become a schoolteacher in 2008. She then moved to the USA to teach in Salt Lake City, Utah, where she learned about immersion teaching practices. Back in France, she teaches in immersion at the Jean Jaurès school. For several years, she has been involved with a LéA. She is taking part in a collaborative research project that focuses on supporting the multilingual well-being of her students.

Véronique Lemoine-Bresson is a senior lecturer (HDR) in language education and educational sciences at the University of Lorraine (ATILF CNRS). Her theoretical interests focus on interculturality in education and training, as well as collaborative research and writing. She coordinates collaborative research as part of the Lieux d'éducation associés network of the Institut français de l'éducation. In the field of education, she has published on intercultural skills and practices applicable to various levels of the school and university curriculum. She teaches at INSPÉ Lorraine in the Master's program in Pedagogical Design.

Latisha Mary is an associate professor at the Faculty of Education and Lifelong Learning at the University of Strasbourg, France. Her research focuses on teacher knowledge, attitudes, and beliefs regarding multilingualism, teacher education for supporting second language acquisition, and the development of language awareness in educational contexts. She has been involved in several funded national and international research projects focusing on language awareness, multilingualism, and intercultural education. She is co-editor of Migration, Multilingualism and Education: Critical Perspectives on Inclusion.

Marcela Ossa Parra is a Colombian teacher educator serving as an Assistant Professor in the Department of Elementary and Early Childhood Education at Queens College, CUNY. She teaches courses in bilingual education, literacy, and social foundations. Her research examines the relationship between identity, language, and literacy to inform the design of curriculum and instruction that centers and expands students' voices. She has published in TESOL Quarterly, Journal of Education, and Journal of Language and Literacy Education, among other notable publications.

Ricardo Otheguy is Professor Emeritus of Linguistics at the Graduate Center of the City University of New York. His work has appeared in top-tier international journals and respected publications. His theoretical interests include functional-cognitive and semiotic approaches to grammar, quantitative-variationist sociolinguistics, and communicative/conceptual perspectives on language continuity and change in contact situations. In applied linguistics, he has published extensively on Spanish for native speakers and on educational practices affecting Latino students in the United States.

Stephanie Risse is an Associate Professor of Germanic Philology at the Faculty of Education of the Free University of Bozen-Bolzano. She is co-editor-in-chief of the European Journal of Applied Linguistics and has gained experience in Russia, Ukraine, Central Asian States, and the Balkans. She also works as a policy advisor on multilingual education, conflict prevention, and settlement for governmental and supranational organizations. Her theoretical interests include pragmatics, language didactics, and language policies. She has published extensively on German as a first, second, and foreign language.

Peter Rosenberg is a Senior Scholar at Europa-Universitaet Viadrina Frankfurt (Oder). He was a visiting professor at UFF, Rio de Janeiro, and at Altai State Pedagogical University, Barnaul, Russia. He holds a PhD in Linguistics and Geography from Freie Universität Berlin (1985). His areas of work are dialectology (editor of the North German Language Atlas 2015/2022), research on German-speaking islands (numerous publications and conferences), and language in the context of migration (member of the German Society for Applied Linguistics, organizer of conferences on language work with refugees).

Mônica Savedra is a scholar focused on minority language rights, language revitalization, and bilingual education in Latin America. With interdisciplinary training in applied linguistics and anthropology, she has collaborated on research projects investigating Pomeranian-Portuguese communities and other multilingual groups in Brazil. Her publications, appearing in international academic forums, analyze the relationship between language, identity, and cultural continuity. She advocates for inclusive educational policies that recognize the rights and contributions of speakers of heritage languages.

Kate Seltzer is an Associate Professor of Bilingual and ESL Education at Rowan University, where she teaches pre- and in-service teachers of emergent bilingual students. Her research focuses on helping schools and teachers build on students' rich language practices while also disrupting their ideologies about these students and their ways of using language. She is the co-author of the book "The Translanguaging Classroom: Leveraging Student Bilingualism for Learning," as well as book chapters and articles in journals such as the Journal of Literacy Research, Research in the Teaching of English, and TESOL Quarterly.

Reseda Streb holds a Ph.D. from Goethe University Frankfurt, Germany, and conducts research on multilingualism, multilingual learning processes, and minority languages in schools. From 2017 to 2023, she served as a DAAD Lecturer at the Federal University of Ceará (UFC) in Fortaleza, Brazil. She also completed a postdoctoral fellowship in multilingual education at the Fluminense Federal University (UFF), Brazil. Since 2023, she has been working as an Advisor for the Promotion of the German Language at the DAAD Regional Office in Rio de Janeiro, Brazil.

Joël Thibeault is an associate professor of French education in the Faculty of Education at the University of Ottawa and an adjunct professor in the Faculty of Education at the University of Regina. His research focuses on the teaching of grammar and writing in plurilingual and minority contexts, the use of children's literature in the teaching of linguistic conventions, and plurilingual approaches in French education.

About TBR Books

TBR Books is a program of the Center for the Advancement of Languages, Education, and Communities. We publish researchers and practitioners who seek to engage diverse communities in education, languages, cultural history, and social initiatives. We translate our books into various languages to further expand our impact.

BOOKS IN ENGLISH

Bilingual Children: Families, Education, Development by E. Bialystok
Myths and Facts about Multilingualism by J. Franck, F. Faloppa, T. Marinis
Mosaic of Tongues: Multilingual Learning for the Arabic-speaking World by C. Allaf, F. Jaumont, and S. Tahla Jebril
Speaking the World: Multilingualism and Cultural Fluency in the Professional World. M. Lazar & F. Jaumont
Conversations on Bilingualism with *E. Bialystok, F. Grosjean, A. I. Ansaldo, O. García, C. Hélot, and M. Diagne* by F. Jaumont
A Bilingual Revolution for Africa by A.C. Hager M'Boua, F. Jaumont
The Heart of an Artichoke by L. Ashour and C. Lerognon
French All Around Us, Volume I and II by K. Stein-Smith and F. Jaumont
Salsa Dancing in Gym Shoes: Developing Cultural Competence to Foster Latino Student Success by T. Oberg de la Garza and A. Lavigne
Navigating Dual Immersion: A Teacher's Companion for the School Year and Beyond by V. Sun
The Hummingbird Project: Creating from Scratch by V. Frémont
One Good Question: How Countries Prepare Youth to Lead by R. Broussard

Can We Agree to Disagree? Exploring the differences at work between Americans and the French by S. Landolt and A. Laurent
The English Patchwork by P. Tozzi and G. de Lima
The Word of the Month by B. Lévy, J. Sheppard, A. Arnon
Two Centuries of French Education: The Role of Schools in Cultural Diplomacy in New York by J. Ross
The Bilingual Revolution by F. Jaumont

BOOKS FOR CHILDREN (available in several languages)

The Adventures of Zenzi and the Talking Bird by F. Gwaradzimba
Biscotte and The New Kid by K. Cohen-Dicker and A. Angeles
Lapin is Hungry; Lapin is Cold by T. & O. Czajka
Uniquely You!; Regards sans complexe by B. Tchoumi
Franglais Soup e by A. Mei
Morgan; Rainbows, Masks, and Ice Cream by D. Sobel Lederman
Korean Super New Years with Grandma by M. Kim, E. Feaster
Math for All by M. Hansen
Rose Alone by S. Decosse
Uncle Steve's Country Home; The Blue Dress; The Good, the Ugly, and the Great by T. Moja
Immunity Fun!; Respiratory Fun!; Digestive Fun! By D. Stewart-McMeel
Marimba by C. Hélot, P. Velasco, A. Kojton

Our books, such as paperbacks and e-books, are available on our website and in all major online bookstores. Some of our books have been translated into over twenty languages. For a listing of all books published by TBR Books, information on our series, or our submission guidelines for authors, visit our website at:

www.calec.org

About CALEC

The Center for the Advancement of Languages, Education, and Communities (CALEC) is a nonprofit organization that promotes multilingualism, empowers multilingual families, and fosters cross-cultural understanding. The Center's mission aligns with the United Nations' Sustainable Development Goals. Our mission is to establish language as a critical life skill by developing and implementing bilingual education programs, promoting diversity, reducing inequality, and providing quality education. Our programs aim to preserve world cultural heritage and support teachers, authors, and families by providing the knowledge and resources to foster vibrant, multilingual communities.

The specific objectives and purpose of our organization are:

- To develop and implement education programs that promote multilingualism and cross-cultural understanding and establish an inclusive and equitable quality education, including internship and leadership training. [SDG # 4, Quality Education]

- To publish and distribute resources, including research papers, books, and case studies that seek to empower and promote the social, economic, and political inclusion of all, focusing on language education and cultural diversity, equity, and inclusion. [SDG # 10, Reduced Inequalities]

- To help build sustainable cities and communities and support teachers, authors, researchers, and families in advancing multilingualism and cross-cultural understanding through collaborative tools for linguistic communities. [SDG # 11, Sustainable Cities and Communities]

- To foster solid global partnerships and cooperation, mobilize resources across borders, participate in events and activities that promote language education through knowledge sharing and coaching, empower parents and teachers, and build multilingual societies. [SDG # 17, Partnerships for the Goals]

SOME GOOD REASONS TO SUPPORT US

Your donation helps:

- Develop our publishing and translation activities to increase the representation of more languages.
- Provide access to our online book platform to daycare centers, schools, and cultural centers in underserved areas.
- Support local and sustainable initiatives that promote education and multilingualism.
- Implement projects that advance dual-language education.
- Organize workshops for parents, conferences with large audiences, meet-the-author chats, and talks with experts in multilingualism.

DONATE ONLINE

For all your questions, contact our team by email at contact@calec.org or donate online on our website:

www.calec.org

www.ingramcontent.com/pod-product-compliance
Lightning Source LLC
Chambersburg PA
CBHW030522230426
43665CB00010B/733